THE PERMANENT REVOLUTION

GEOFFREY BEST, on moving from the Sir Richard Lodge Chair of History at Edinburgh University to a chair in European Studies at Sussex, turned from Victorian studies to international humanitarian law. He will soon follow up his *Humanity in Warfare* and *Honour among Men and Nations* with a book on war and law since 1945.

NORMAN HAMPSON is Professor of History in the University of York and a Fellow of the British Academy. His lifetime's study of the French Revolution and the Enlightenment has produced, among other books, *The Social History of the French Revolution* and *The Life and Opinions of Maximilien Robespierre*.

DOUGLAS JOHNSON is Professor of French History in the University of London. His books include *Guizot* and *France and the Dreyfus Affair*, and *France, 1914 to the Present* (forthcoming), part of the Fontana History of Modern France of which he is the general editor.

EUGENE KAMENKA is Professor of the History of Ideas at the Australian National University (Research School of Social Sciences). He is the author of, among others, *The Ethical Foundations of Marxism* and editor of books on the Paris Commune, the revolution of 1848, and human rights.

CONOR CRUISE O'BRIEN's work as historian includes a landmark edition of Burke's *Reflections on the Revolution in France*. His earlier years as a diplomat produced *The United Nations: Sacred Drama*, and his latest book is *God Land: Reflections on Religion and Nationalism*.

GEORGE STEINER is Professor of Comparative Literature at the University of Geneva and Extraordinary Fellow of Churchill College, Cambridge. His books include *Language and Silence*, *On Difficulty* and *Antigones*.

HEW STRACHAN is a Fellow of Corpus Christi College, Cambridge, and before that was Senior Lecturer (War Studies) at the Royal Military Academy, Sandhurst. His best known book is *European Armies and the Conduct of War*.

EUGEN WEBER is Joan Palevsky Professor of Modern European History in the University of California, Los Angeles. His publications include *Action Française*, *Peasants into Frenchmen* and *France, Fin de Siècle*.

THE PERMANENT REVOLUTION

The French Revolution and its Legacy 1789–1989

Edited by
GEOFFREY BEST

FONTANA PRESS

First published in 1988 by Fontana Paperbacks
8 Grafton Street, London W1X 3LA

Fontana Press is an imprint of Fontana
Paperbacks, part of the Collins Publishing Group

Printed and bound in Great Britain by
William Collins Sons & Co. Ltd, Glasgow

Contents

Preface

Any honest author (or, as also in this case, editor) must be aware of a large indebtedness to all who, through the years, have helped him to attain such understanding of things as may be his and to produce whatever may be proximately of his doing. I feel this very powerfully; not least, towards the seven fellow-scholars who have genially collaborated in the production of this book. Specific acknowledgment however I will confine to three persons in particular: Maurice Hutt, valued colleague and friend from my years in the University of Sussex's School of European Studies, who has been more helpful and supportive than he can imagine; and the two editors at Collins who respectively supervised the book's conception and birth, Helen Fraser (no longer there) and Stuart Proffitt. Without their creative care and professional skills *The Permanent Revolution* could never have got off the ground.

GEOFFREY BEST

Editor's Introduction

Revolutions figure little in world history before 1789. Since then, it sometimes seems world history has consisted of little else; unless it be the wars revolutions often cause or are caused by. The word itself took on new breadths of meaning to meet the demands henceforth to be made of it. From the mid-seventeenth century it was indeed filtering into a variety of uses converging on its modern sense but Dr Johnson's Dictionary's first and second definitions in the mid-eighteenth were the same as those known to the ancient Greeks and Romans: 'the course of anything which returns to the point at which it began to move', and 'space measured by some revolution'. Only his third definition, 'change in the state of a government or country', picked up the new meaning the word had acquired following what the English had done to their kings and constitution in the previous century, but even that lacked the force of what was to flood in at the end of the 1780s. Its commonest English usage, 'the glorious revolution of 1688', described an event which looked backward as well as forward and a social context which stayed exactly the same.

The extraordinary events which began in France during the summer of 1789 changed all that. They were similarly ambiguous to begin with but their fundamentally disturbing and radical innovatory drive soon gave the word its modern and contemporary colouring as it became hitched indissolubly to the French chariot. We may wonder how much of that was actually understood by the courtier who, on the evening of the fourteenth of July, in response to Louis XVI's astonished comment on the storming of the Bastille, 'Why, this is a revolt,' seemingly said, 'No, Sire, it is a revolution.'[1] The Duke of La Rochefoucauld-Liancourt was surely on the right track in his search for a big enough word for what he knew was

[1] See page 86 for one of several possible interpretations of this remark.

going on, but he could not have sensed the half of what 'revolution' was soon going to mean, not just for France but for the whole world. So apt would it become for the proper description of giant transformations in any major area of human experience that a century or so later historians and social scientists would be regularly referring to the industrial revolution, the scientific revolution, the demographic revolution and so on. But the heart of its meaning remains where it was put between 1789 and 1795: violent transformation of the political and the supporting social arrangements of a country, replacing one species of ruler by another and giving itself and its people something of a new look. The French Revolution did much that went beyond politics, besides a good deal that was not as transforming as it claimed to be, and there was much in it that sprang from other than political causes: but it was above all as a political event that it exploded upon the Europe of its day and that it became the living presence it is in the world still.

Why does the French Revolution still matter so much? How can its importance be impressed upon those living millions with no inkling that they live as they do because of the French Revolution and because, in some senses, it is still going on? These questions, which of course have been exercising the minds of all of us essayists in this volume, are close kin to the questions which beset any scholar who seeks to reduce his past to its primary elements, distinguishing from the congealed mass of our whole historical inheritance the particular contribution of any one episode, even the biggest. And given that the French Revolution happened when and as it did, and accepting for the sake of the argument that the more 'developed' parts of the world were forever thereafter affected in their political behaviour by it, how can one distinguish what we citizens of the world (to borrow one of the early Revolutionary favourite phrases) owe to it from what we owe to the Russian Revolution, or the Chinese, or even the Cuban? No historian doubts but that these revolutions, like those subsequently experienced in France herself, owed something directly to the original French model, but so many layers of revolutionary theory may have intervened that our contemporary revolutionary may be going through the motions of a Danton, a Robespierre or a Dumouriez, a Saint-Just or a Fouquier-Tinville without ever having heard of them. Contemporary social science helps to sustain this state of innocence with books on 'revolution' and on the comparative study of revolutions which can be so richly supplied with examples from our own century that they can do without reference to anything further back. Political activists are not necessarily reluctant to acknowledge sources of inspiration but only the historically-minded among them will wish to know from whence their inspirers got *their* inspiration, and by what processes that inspiration may have got around. However many revolutionary roads now lead in the first instance to Hanoi, to Havana, to what we have recently learned to call Beijing and what from 1914 to 1924 was called Petrograd, all revolutionary roads before 1917 led to Paris; and, as was remarked at the outset, before 1789 there were no clearly marked revolutionary roads at all.

At this point the thoughtful reader is likely to be wondering, had not such a road recently been laid down to what would soon be called Washington DC, and did not an older and rougher but still passable track lead to London? There is more to these questions than can be accounted for by an over-elastic and anachronistic use of the word, revolution. The United States' Declaration of Independence, followed only seven years later by the establishment of a big and promising new state, was as astounding an event as the political world had ever witnessed or would witness again; its immediate effects were certainly more revolutionary than otherwise, and would have been more disturbing still had they not occurred so far away and in a milieu beyond most Europeans' imaginations. So successful an exhibition of how to harass and humiliate an unresponsive monarchy cheered 'liberals' and radicals in the old world who would have been glad to do likewise, at the same time as it offered a sort of model to the independent-minded among the elites of the Spanish and Portuguese empires occupying most of the rest of the continent. National liberators from Poland to Peru revered George Washington as the greatest of the great. Admirers and would-be emulators were further encouraged by the rhetoric of the Americans' declarations of independence and bills of rights, couched in the same universalist language of natural rights which many of the French revolutionaries too would adopt: for example, from the celebrated Virginia Bill of Rights of 12 June 1776,

> 1. That all men are by nature created free and independent and have certain inherent rights . . . namely the enjoyment of life, liberty, with the means of acquiring and possessing property, and pursuing and obtaining happiness and safety.
> 2. That all power is vested in, and consequently derived from, the people. . . .
> 3. That government is, or ought to be instituted for the common benefit, protection and security of the people, nation or community . . . and that, when any government shall be found inadequate or contrary to these purposes, a majority of the community hath an indubitable unalienable and indefeasible right to reform, alter or abolish it. . . .

Given that the first flush of French revolutionary rhetoric could go no further than this, and that the Americans' original political design stuck as the French one did not, one may well wonder why it is not the American Revolution (as that too began to be called once the French Revolution had popularized the word) which has generally been considered 'the decisive event of modern history'. A European seeking to give an honest answer soon realizes that such a flattering assessment has more than a little cultural complacency in it. However high France stood in the world before 1914, and however highly the French might even now believe in their country's cultural superiority (that *mission civilatrice* which has survived the passing of their territorial empire), it is clearly not France but the United States which is the state standing highest in the world of the twentieth century – it is the United States, not France, which provides the cultural lingua-franca of the later twentieth-century world – and it is from the United States above all that that world draws, in forms no matter how confused and self-serving, its ruling concerns with democracy and human rights. But all those matters are of relatively recent provenance. Not only were the United States' history and situation so singular as to keep it from being an example that could invite imitation, it was for long remote from the rest of the 'developed' world, and contentedly so. Only within the past eighty years or so has the United States acquired its lofty position in world politics and been able to indulge to the full its sense of ideological mission. Most of what there was of world-historical significance in the American Revolution – and there was at least as much in the matter of parliamentary development and human rights (if nothing else) as there would be in the French – was in effect restricted to the Americas for the first century of the great republic's existence; leaving the field of all the other 'developed' countries open for France, than which, it is important to remember, in the eighteenth and early nineteenth centuries, there was no greater military power in the world.

The field lay open also, it must be said, to the other greatest power, Britain, whose seventeenth-century revolution culminating in the enforced abdication of James II in 1688 and the Bill of Rights of 1689 gave that country too a prima facie title to consideration as dispenser to humankind at large of some of the same liberal benefits that are claimed to stem from 1789. This British claim (or, better, English claim, since all the important action took place south of the border) is real enough but limited. It rests, like the American, on its pre-eminent regard for political and civil rights, which were only a small part of the content of the French Revolution, and it was even more unpromising a model for emulation because of its apparent constitutional conservatism; the rights and freedoms secured by 'the glorious revolution' being conceived as treasures from a good past no less than as foundations for a better future. So insular were its circumstances that the British had no thought of inviting other peoples to follow suit. That didn't stop continental European admirers of British freedom from, as they thought, discovering that the secret of its success lay in the 'separation of powers'. Once that was grasped, Montesquieu and his school believed, the rest would follow. Insofar as the judiciary was concerned, they were right enough. The rule of law needs an independent judiciary to sustain it and cannot otherwise deliver the civil and political rights which are assumed to go with it. Concerning the legislature and executive, however, Montesquieu was famously misleading, as many constitution-makers and liberal optimists were to discover. There was no short cut to the English Bill of Rights, neither in the eighteenth century nor at any time since; nor has any country found a short cut to the whole common-law-cum-parliamentary political culture which historically produced it.

The English and American Revolutions (as the French one caused them retrospectively to be known) did not amount to more than piecemeal prefigurings of the much more turbulent, ambitious and experimental French event. The embattled and passionate French Revolutionaries did not, by 1793, need the English precedent for executing a monarch. The Americans' successful armed struggle for what we have come to know as national self-determination and their declarations of universal good-will, which much encouraged the French at the outset of their revolution, became more and more remote from French realities as these progressed through their hectic course of unprecedented innovations justified by appeals to reason and science, their drastic and often lethal expedients justified as necessary for the safety of the state and nation. Only after the passage of many decades would the British and American Revolutions clearly appear in their different styles as world-historical events also, with perhaps comparable effects. As the UK and USA in turn attained dominant imperial stature and took to promoting their ideals of parliamentary government and political and civil rights, so was attention drawn to the affinities between those prime concerns of their 'revolutions' and the appearance of the same in the richer and confused French mixture. And as democracy and human rights became fixations of the *soi-distant* free world after 1945, so the comparatively self-controlled British and American roads towards those good goals attracted admiration at the expense of the French road, now made out by its more severe and searching critics (Jacob Talmon and Hannah Arendt, their standard-bearers) to have led less to democracy than to dictatorship, not so much to the expansion of human rights as to their suppression. They were pleased to proclaim that the severest contemporary critic of the French Revolution, Edmund Burke, had been proved right yet again; the only safe road to secure change and improvement in the political and social fabric of a nation was the history-rooted, culture-conserving, property-preserving road, keeping one foot fondly in the past while advancing the other cautiously towards the future, keeping one hand firmly on the masses (which need not, however, prevent the other hand from manipulating them for approved political purposes), and above all eschewing visions and promises of Utopia.

Placed in such company, the French Revolution began to look less beneficent than it had generally been taken to be, and the English and American 'revolutions' looked more generally appealing and applicable than they perhaps actually were. But none of the waves of this tide of sceptical and even hostile reappraisal which, as George Steiner's essay especially shows, has found mounting expression as our century has gone on, could give any revolution before that of 1917 anything like the same explosive centrality as that of 1789. Nor could they rob it of its continuing appeal to the radicals and revolutionaries of the world, the men and women who could not rest content or confident in the measured, prudent changes commended by those of the line of Burke, and who anyway believed (who shall dare to say, incorrectly?) that a principal purpose and regular result of such changes was to keep a ruling class or elite in effective power; a point neatly put by the smart young radical-chic nobleman in Giuseppe di Lampedusa's great novel about the French Revolution's mid-century fall-out in Italy, when he puts it thus to his princely uncle: 'If we want things to stay as they are, things will have to change.' And however just and merited that critical reappraisal might be, sensitive conservatives might note with a shudder that although the counter-revolutionary movement had Talmon and Arendt at one end of its spectrum, it had Hitler, Franco and Mussolini at the other, as it has General Pinochet still.

And yet Hitler, Mussolini and Franco were themselves heirs of the French Revolution, for all that they and their fascist kind talked explicitly of their mission to undo the work of the Revolution, to take their people back to the values they imagined to have prevailed in Europe before the Revolution inaugurated their destruction. There may be room for argument as to how far the twentieth-century phenomenon of plebiscitary dictatorship (Talmon's 'totalitarian democracy') has its roots in Rousseau's political ideas and in what the Jacobins made of them. (Europeans, who have come closest to the results of dictatorship, may well find some difficulty in sharing the Latin American jest, that 'the general will is the will of the general'.) But there is little room for argument about the Revolution's share in the launch of nationalism as our modern world has known and continues to know it. Fascism was, fascism is, a version or, better, perversion of the nationalism which has been the most far-reaching and passion-rousing political creed of the past two centuries; and its many faces display better than any other item of the revolutionary legacy its inherent ambiguities and contradictory tendencies. Nationalism has shown itself to be a creed adaptable equally to the needs and likings of conservatives, liberals, radicals and socialists. It has appeared to be as indispensable to new-nation-building as it is familiar in the continuing story of empire-demolishing. It has proved to be a stronger bond of brotherhood among men than religion (the strongest known from the past) or class (pronounced by Marx to be the strongest for the future). It has become itself a sort of religion, besides bringing religions and churches into easy consonance with it; and its giant protean force is matched by the stretch of its meanings, for despite most copious and heavy theorizing on the subject, no free inquirer has ever been able to be sure what a nation practically is, and how far it may actually match the entities which it is usually tied to, or used as a synonym for: people, state, and race.

From the outset of the planning of this book, nationalism stood in the centre of our sights as a subject demanding priority treatment. Essays on 'Nationalism' *tout court* and on its military appendage, 'The Nation in Arms', seemed appropriate and, we supposed, sufficient. It says something about the status of the subject that all the other contributors (who wrote their pieces as seemed best to them, once the themes and minimal main lines were determined) have had to say something about it too. This degree of prominence is likely to surprise people who associate the French Revolution primarily with this one or that among its many proclaimed attributes (*la souveraineté du peuple*, for example, or *égalité*), and is unlikely to please French and Francophile readers. But the fact is that the French have lost their near-monopoly of Revolution scholarship (see the later pages of Norman Hampson's chapter), and having moreover become willing to consider the whole affair with a certain detachment (see the later pages of Douglas Johnson's and George Steiner's) more of them must be willing than they once were to give a fair hearing to the contention that, from the point of view of the world at large and for that world's weal or woe, the Revolution's most permanent big legacy – to the French themselves no less than to the other peoples of the planet – has been the apotheosis of the nation-state within the modern theory and practice of nationalism.

Discussion of this contentious word nationalism is easily confused by differences of definitions and misunderstandings about meanings. About chauvinism, the word for extreme xenophobic nationalism, no more need be said than that its etymology begins and ends with the revolutionary and Napoleonic soldier Nicolas Chauvin. French dictionaries properly distinguish between *nationalisme* and *patriotisme*, noting the collective egoism and aggressive inclinations which mark the former. But the two are easily – and conveniently – confused. I must say that I was struck, when reviewing for *The Times Literary Supplement* a heavyweight French scholarly anthology of de Gaulle's ideas as expressed in his writing and speeches, how consistently *patrie* and its derivatives were used when *nation* and its derivatives would have been more apt. De Gaulle certainly was very much of a nationalist as well as a patriot. (It is of course impossible to be a nationalist without being some sort of patriot beneath.) The ease with which all French political parties from far left to far right concur in a prickly Gaullist defence policy unafraid to give offence to everyone else from the South-West Pacific to NATO, suggests that its description as simply patriotic might not be quite enough. One might also note the unabashed, though no doubt unconscious, culturally nationalistic notions being aired as appropriate for the bicentenary; as if, while consensus about the rest of the Revolution's legacy to the nation has dissolved, *that* part of it at any rate is alive and well.

Conor Cruise O'Brien, to whom our centrepiece on this gigantic theme was entrusted, has used the limited space at his disposal to focus more on what the French Revolution made of nationalism than on what nationalism has made of us. Prime promoter, with imperialism its blood-brother, of wars between nations, and principal obstructor of those international and *supra*national constructions which many people deem indispensable to peace in the world, nationalism and its accompanying cult of national sovereignty is too rampant and prosperous a performer on the stage of our destinies to require demonstration; besides which, there is a plethora of literature about it, which all who run may read. But where and how did it begin, and what exactly was the French Revolution's role in forming it? Such questions open up a field of inquiry scarcely smaller than that about the workings of nationalism now. George Steiner joins Dr O'Brien in remarking how German historicism and idealism, commonly considered the other main source of modern nationalism, sometimes even as its principal source, only fully found itself when aroused to protect its peoples from the aggressive pressures of a French nationalism already fully formed. So many political progressives and intellectuals who subsequently became chorus-masters of German nationalism began as fans of the Revolution – some staying so for a surprisingly long time – that it is difficult to doubt but that the incubation of the German variety of the virus would at least have taken a lot longer had the French Revolution not breathed so fiercely upon it. There is of course no possibility of denying that the nationalisms which developed in Germany and the whole half of Europe beyond it (from the French viewpoint) soon evolved their own peculiarities; especially that 'organic', biological and ultimately racist bent which never fitted all supposed nationalities as closely as it might seem to fit some, and which fed the fascisms when they duly appeared. The political power-house of nationalism remained for all takers precisely where the French Revolution put it: in the divinized nation-state and the compulsions to national uniformity of thought and feeling which the French revolutionary regimes so smartly envisaged and enforced. That they were able to do this so quickly – something which must surprise anyone with exaggerated ideas of the liberal cosmopolitanism of the pre-revolutionary Europcan world – is, by Dr O'Brien's account of it, because suitable materials lay ready to hand. The nationalist fire was in fact already aglow. The French Revolution's nationalism was not a product of some sudden and gargantuan parturition but the enthusiastic exploitation of ideas long circulated in a cultural and political atmosphere by then eagerly receptive.

To that sounding of the central theme, Hew Strachan's analysis of nationalism's military wing, the nation-in-arms, is a natural accompaniment; and again significance may be found in the fact that two others of us, as we wrote our essays on aspects without anything explicitly 'national' in the title, found ourselves obliged to comment on it. The Revolution's goodwill towards humankind blew from the barrels of its guns as well as from the mouths of its orators and propagandists and agitators. Our world has become plentifully familiar with the phenomenon of forcible liberation since the French Revolution, and with particular force and frequency since 1945, but history shows nothing quite like it before 1792 unless it be in religious wars and crusades, so often homicidal and acquisitive beneath the best of professed intentions. Dr Strachan's remit was not the political uses of revolutionary militarism but its doctrine and machinery, the latter at least of which was fearsomely original when the revolutionaries set it up in 1792–3. To begin with, indeed, its *raison d'être* was simply defensive and protective – defensive against enemies aboard, protective against enemies at home – but extraordinarily quickly this new-model mass army was turned to expansionist purposes, and became a fixture in both revolutionary and nationalist/patriotic ideologies; as, for many countries and creeds, it still is.

To Eugene Kamenka and myself fell consideration of the Revolution's other major political legacies. Some readers may be surprised to miss in our headings old favourites like 'democracy' and 'egalitarianism'. They need not be disappointed. Those classic items are here, within the larger scopes and contexts which the facts of the case seemed to require. The revolutionary watchword of equality, for example, is more accurately, not to say more economically handled in relation to revolutionary ideology on the one hand, human rights on the other. Its intellectual and historical roots are not in the French Revolution alone; and the same goes for popular sovereignty. But the French Revolution did for equality and for democracy in their many mixed senses the unique service of broadcasting worldwide the visions of the theme as being of interest, not simply as scraps of history from the past or figments of Utopia for the future but as realizable here and now for any people that could follow the French model or improve on it.

It mattered little to enthusiasts that the Revolution's achievements came to rather less in practice than in proclamation and propaganda. They came nearest to the mark in respect of equality. There was indeed a remarkable social breakthrough in the new atmosphere of equal opportunity for men of ability and education – and wealth! – though next to nothing of the more radical equalities soon to be coveted by utopian and 'scientific' socialists. Democracy was a different matter. For the young William Wordsworth, as for the young in heart everywhere, it was the 'sum and crown of all' to 'see the People having a strong hand/In making their own laws, whence better days/To all mankind'. It is true to say that in the early phases of the Revolution, the adult males of a great nation for a short while came closer to a say in managing their collective affairs than had ever happened before; it would be stretching truth too far to say that this transient achievement had more momentous an impact on the global development of democracy in the long run than the American and British models which, by the time representative government was really catching on in the world, were at least as influential as the French one. The vital difference, however, lay not in substance but in style. The French Revolution could not be contemplated with the same calculation as those others. Neither of them spread anything like the same effervescent and inflammatory excitement – that *Fire in the Mind* so vividly described by James H. Billington – which the French Revolution stimulated among the political stirrers and ideological enthusiasts of the developed and developing parts of the world, and neither had such power to arouse, in the less developed, the hopes of the wretched of the earth; it was the French Revolution and the rich mythology radiating from it which dominated their scene until the Russian and Chinese Revolutions much later made available more up-to-date models (not to mention contracts for servicing). When it came to lasting achievements and solid improvements in social and political arrangements, the French examples, sheared of myth and make-believe, are seen to be not more remarkable than the others, and in some respects are more ambiguous; not least, as I have sought to explain in my own contribution, in respect of human rights.

From the three essays on the Revolution's reception and legacy within its own nation's walls (I include among them Norman Hampson's, for reasons which he himself makes very plain), a clear picture emerges of a considerable cultural consensus lasting into the early years of our century. Of course, there were dissident interpretations and differences of emphasis. Republicanism, which by any test had to be at the core of the revolutionary legacy, did not seat itself securely in the national saddle until the 1870s. Christians in general might well recall the campaign to 'de-Christianize' their country. Roman Catholics in particular could not comfortably forget the martyrdoms and exilings of so many of their priests in the Revolution's early years, the humiliations later visited on the Pope by the Emperor. And yet there was so much pride and glory to be found in the military heroics and patriotic facts and fictions of the Revolution and its successor regimes (which in that connection were at their least separable from it) that even aristocratic monarchists, Catholics by definition, could scarce withhold the tribute of a patriotic sigh. However much the interpretation of it and of its most vital parts continued to set partisan teeth on edge, there was something in the revolutionary legacy for virtually everyone, even if, as Eugen Weber shows, it tended to serve no less as a script for social and family disputes than as a reservoir of social and national solidarity. Underpinning it, ever more stoutly as the nineteenth century wore on, was that 'great tradition' of French national history-writing, analysed here by Norman Hampson; a succession of skilful historians and (one must find means to distinguish a Tocqueville from a Michelet) historical writers who fashioned and re-fashioned 'the Revolution' to meet the needs and interests of each successive generation, fortifying the French people in the conviction psychologically attractive to them, in any case – that it had been a marvellous and beneficial event for their country and, by natural extension, for everyone else's too.

That 'great tradition' and that majority cultural consensus lasted a long while, but they have at last dissolved. It has become possible even for French writers in their own land to tot up the Revolution's losses and gains and to conclude that, so far as one can calculate these things, the Revolution did France a lot more harm than good. That plenty of ardent contemporary revolutionaries and nationalists would indignantly denounce the application of profit-and-loss tests to an event they believed to be pregnant with celestial fire for the regeneration of humankind only serves to prove the point made by counter-revolutionaries from early days, and with increasing urgency since the 1930s – the point that it is precisely the ardent revolutionary's belief in the total and exclusive value and *virtue* of his cause that leads him to contemplate relatively calmly what seem to non-believers mere frightfulnesses: massacres, anguishes, tortures, destructions and devastations, impoverishments and so on. Such sado-masochistic moral severity is by no means merely modern or only European; capabilities of it appear in several world religions, not least the Christian; but not until the French Revolution did such believers secure, for a year or so, direction of the government of a great nation and witness the translation of their virtuous principles into terror-enforced practice. Since then, our world has experienced not a few ventures to emulate them and to do, it is supposed, better; ventures launched equally from positions which are conventionally thought of as being respectively the far left and the far right of the parliamentary seating-plan, but which with only a modest adjustment of it may be seen to be standing side-by-side. There is chilling affinity of sentiment between the words of the Committee of Public Safety's enforcer on the lower Loire, Jean-Baptiste Carrier, 'We shall turn France into a cemetery rather than fail in her regeneration,' and the chorus of the Nazi soldiers' song: 'What does it matter if we destroy the world? When it is ours, we'll build it up again.'

The revolutionary potential, then, has been for evil as well as good. Human beings capable of understanding this inherent ambivalence (not to mention the sheer unpredictabilities of revolutions which are as many as those of war) are bound to mix it in with their other thoughts when wondering, as good people as well as bad have to in many countries from time to time, first, whether a revolution in given circumstances can be reckoned worthwhile, and second, whether revolution in itself can ever be judged justifiable. This second question is the deeper and more disturbing one, not to be answered without reference to religion and philosophy. George Steiner's essay appears at the centre of the book to emphasize the fact that from as early as 1790 there has existed alongside '1789' and its cult a profound counter-revolutionary critique which must equally be considered part of the legacy, logically inseparable from it. That it has not until relatively recently received that degree of respect and attention may be because the optimistic aura of the revolutionary cult inevitably prevailed during decades dedicated to scientific and democratic progress – because not until our own century could counter-revolutionary critics call upon really spectacular examples of revolutionary horror – and because it has to be admitted that some such critics have often had rebarbative characteristics, prickly, cheerless, unsentimental, careful to eschew the heart-warming revolutionary vocabulary of generosity, fraternity, progress etc. Such attributes tend to make them less engaging reading than those they have written against. The truths they have persisted in proclaiming seem, however, not to have been robbed of any part of their weight by continuing experience of revolutions, whether of 'the left' or 'the right'. Revolutions often (one can hardly say, always) devour not only their own children but others' children too. The French Revolution was the primary instance of that sombre truth for the modern world it in many respects inaugurated. We hope that this book about its nature, influence and continuing presence will help understanding of how to think about drastic political change, and of how many of the concepts and conditions of that thinking belong to that revolutionary legacy which holds us, willy-nilly, in its grasp.

Nationalism and the French Revolution

CONOR CRUISE O'BRIEN

'The nation exists before all, it is the origin of everything. Its will is always legal, it is the law itself.'

Abbé Sieyès, *What is the Third Estate?*, 1789.

'The image of the *Patrie* is the sole divinity which it is permissible to worship.'

Petition of the Agitators to the Legislative Assembly, 20 June 1792.

'It is from you that I shall ask for help, my noble country: you must take the place of the God who escapes us (*le Dieu qui nous échappe*), that you may fill within us the immeasurable abyss which extinct Christianity has left there.'

Jules Michelet, *Journal*, 7 August 1831.

I

The subject 'nationalism and the French Revolution' is usually discussed in terms of the rise of nationalism *after* the French Revolution. But I did not consider I could deal with the subject adequately without appraising the role of nationalism also *before* and *within* the French Revolution. So my treatment falls into three parts: first, nationalism as a factor among the processes that appear to have led to the French Revolution; second, the workings of nationalism within the Revolution itself, and in its expansion; and third, the role of both French revolutionary ideas and counter-revolutionary ideas in the later development of nationalism.

Some consider the term 'nationalism' as inapplicable to anything in pre-revolutionary France; perhaps even inapplicable to revolutionary France itself. The French word *nationalisme* appears to have been coined as late as 1798 by the Abbé Barruel, an anti-revolutionary writer (and correspondent of Edmund Burke's), who used the word in a pejorative sense. In this essay I am not using the word 'nationalism' either pejoratively or eulogistically. I am using it to mean: 'strong national emotion, combined with a strong tendency to exalt the idea of the nation above all other ideas'. I hope to show both that nationalism in that sense did exist, and was growing, in pre-revolutionary France, and that it played a major role in the Revolution itself.

Late-twentieth-century Westerners who read books are likely to regard the Enlightenment with approval, and nationalism with suspicion. So the idea of nationalism as possibly a product of the Enlightenment may appear a paradox, and a rather repulsive paradox at that.

Those who dislike the idea of nationalism deriving from the Enlightenment will be likely to point to the cosmopolitan, or universalist, character of the mainstream Enlightenment, and also to its benign, rational and tolerant temper, intrinsically opposed to the fanatical passion which has animated all the intense phases of modern nationalism. One who looks at the matter in that light may well see nationalism, like the Terror, as a revolutionary distortion: not merely a deviation from the true standards of the Enlightenment, but an actual usurpation by essentially the same forces that Voltaire and his friends had fought. On this view, the nationalist fanaticism of the nineteenth and twentieth centuries is the descendant, not of the Enlightenment, but of the religious fanaticism of the seventeenth century. The Enlightenment is the enemy of both, and of *all* forms of fanaticism.

Not only do I sympathize with that view, but I agree with it, to a considerable extent. Yet it seems, all the same, that the Enlightenment does play a significant and somewhat disconcerting part, as a kind of catalyst in the great metamorphosis from older to newer forms of fanaticism.

The *philosophes* hoped to rid the world of fanaticism, but what they actually seem to have done is to have provided fanaticism with a new deity. (At this point I am putting the thing in a simplified manner, subject to making it a bit more complicated again later.) The Christian religion became incredible, even ridiculous, but the God which the Enlightenment offered in place of the Christian God was emotionally inert. The monarchy was delegitimized, lacking its Christian sanction. For many of the French – and many other Europeans too – by the second half of the eighteenth century, there was a yawning emotional void, left by the discredited notions of God and king. And the idea of the nation, *la patrie,* was beginning to fill this void.

Nationalism, as a collective emotion (as distinct from a body of doctrine, or ideology), is far older than the Enlightenment. French nationalism is already passionately articulate in Joan of Arc. But Joan's nationalism is still inseparable from religion and monarchy: 'He who makes war on the Holy Kingdom of France makes war on King Jesus.' With the Enlightenment what emerges is a distilled form of the old nationalism. Purified of supernatural religion and monarchist ideology, the new nationalism becomes self-sufficient, acknowledging and needing nothing superior to the nation. Sieyès, at the beginning of the French Revolution, speaks for the new nationalism: 'the nation before all'. For later, yet more thoroughgoing revolutionaries, like the 'agitators' of 1792, no other cult than that of *la patrie* is any longer even 'permissible'. And Michelet, heir and historian of the Revolution, gives thanks to his country for having filled 'the immeasurable abyss' which the Enlightenment had left within him.

Those Enlightenment figures whom we think of as most 'typical' – Voltaire and Diderot among them – appear as *inter*nationalists, rather than nationalists: more at home in 'enlightened' foreign courts than in the dominions of His Most Christian Majesty. Yet there may have been something misleading, even then, about this internationalism on the French side. When Voltaire went to Berlin, and Diderot to St Petersburg, they did not have to learn a foreign language or adapt themselves to a foreign culture. The language of both courts was French. French culture – or a reputation for possessing French culture – was what the Prussian and Russian monarchs and their courts most wanted. Far from being 'uprooted cosmopolitans', the great *philosophes* were most resplendently at home when they travelled. To France, in their persons, the crowned barbarians paid tribute. The itinerant apostles of Enlightenment were also the cultural ambassadors of what the revolutionary generation would call *la grande nation*.

Too much should not be made of that, either. Voltaire and Diderot were certainly not chauvinists, as were so many of those who would later strut the European stage in the name of that same *grande nation*. These *philosophes*, especially Voltaire, had set themselves to learn from the English, and had popularized English ideas, both in science and in politics. They may have learned even more – without being nearly so candid about what they learned – from an excommunicated Sephardic Jew, resident in Holland, Baruch (or Benedict) Spinoza. The Enlightenment was a genuinely international phenomenon, even if one of its fruits was a secular and exacerbated form of nationalism.

Spinoza seems to have a better claim than anyone else to the title of Father of the Enlightenment. The seminal work is Spinoza's *Tractatus Theologico-Politicus*, published anonymously in Amsterdam in 1670. Smuggled into France and distributed clandestinely, the *Tractatus* was in great demand in the closing decades of the seventeenth century, and the early part of the eighteenth. From Bossuet down, the leading churchmen of the age of Louis XIV read the *Tractatus* with mounting anguish. First they decided that it was not to be refuted, because refuting it would only draw wider attention to it (and, implicitly, because what was to be refuted was likely to remain more impressive than any conceivable refutation). Then, as the clandestine readership and subterranean fame of the *Tractatus* grew and grew, even without the advertisement of attempted refutation, the French Church decided that refutation would have to be attempted after all. So the refutations followed, with exactly the results originally foreseen.

The part played by Spinoza's *Tractatus* in undermining the *ancien régime* can hardly be overestimated. His analysis of the Old Testament undermined the structures which generations of Christian theologians had built on Jewish foundations. All that is part of the *general* prehistory of the French Revolution. But Spinoza's thought is also profoundly significant in relation to the specific question of the rise of nationalism, in its relation to the Enlightenment in the period before the French Revolution.

More clearly than any other Enlightenment thinker – with the partial exception of Rousseau – Spinoza saw a close connection, almost an identity, between religion and politics. Indeed, this is proclaimed in the very title of what was to be his most influential work, in the spheres both of religion and politics: the *Tractatus Theologico-Politicus*. The Bible – the Hebrew Bible, the Old Testament – was for Spinoza essentially a collection of rules, exemplary stories and rituals, designed for the governance of a state. As these rules etc. were in accordance with the laws of nature, the Jews were nature's Chosen People, as long as they kept the rules, and preserved their state: 'Their election and vocation consisted solely in the temporal prosperity and advantages of their State.' Once the Jews broke the rules, and lost their state, they ceased to be the Chosen People. And in the third chapter of the *Tractatus*, 'De Vocatione Judaeorum', Spinoza argues that if the Jews once again get their land back and rebuild their state, they will again be the Chosen People.

The nationalist tendency of Spinoza's teaching, in relation to the Jews, is sufficiently obvious. But Spinoza also formulates the basic concept of nationalism in *general* terms: 'There is no doubt that devotion to country is the highest form of piety a man can show; for once the State is destroyed nothing good can survive.'

Here already we have 'deified nation' doctrine: 'devotion to country is the highest form of piety a man can show'. The supremacy of nationalism may appear as an anomaly within the French Revolution, if we think of the Revolution as among the consequences of the Enlightenment, and if we think of the Enlightenment as essentially internationalist in character. Yet the supremacy of nationalism is already central to the teaching of the most original thinker of the Enlightenment, at the very beginning of the Enlightenment process, and in the very work that did most to disarm the *corps d'élite* of the spiritual and intellectual defenders of the regime.

Not that Spinoza's specifically nationalist teachings appear to have had any significant influence among the *philosophes*. Spinoza had frightened the theologians almost out of their wits, but the *philosophes* who popularized the French Enlightenment discounted Spinoza, at least in public, quite systematically. Spinoza was more radical, and probably also more Jewish, than was convenient to those engaged in a great propaganda enterprise. Both his originality and his profundity are consistently underestimated in the writings of the *philosophes*, beginning with Bayle. Curiously, his personal character becomes more important – in appearance – than his work. As 'the virtuous atheist', Spinoza becomes a kind of saint in the calendar of the Enlightenment, from Bayle on. What happens here is that his very extremism is made to serve a propagandist purpose. The virtue of the celebrated atheist proves that Christianity is not necessary to morality. The Enlightenment deists present Spinoza as a man who was *wrong*, but good. Wrongness, in this way, becomes part as it were of Spinoza's signature tune.

In the retrospect of the mainstream Enlightenment, Spinoza stands out, rather absurdly, as nothing more than a lovable eccentric. So his teachings on nationalism can carry no particular weight, within the mainstream Enlightenment tradition. In that sense, there is no 'influence of Spinoza' factor helping to account for the development of nationalism in the pre-revolutionary process. The interest of the *Tractatus*, in relation to that matter, lies less in Spinoza's influence than in the lucidity of his insight. Spinoza saw that, if belief in a personal God is excluded, there is nothing left for people to worship, except the state. So Spinoza anticipates both Michelet's desolation and his consolation, of more than one hundred and fifty years later.

'State' or 'nation'? It is often not easy to distinguish between the two. Spinoza said 'State': the French Revolutionaries said *la nation* or *la patrie*. I think that Spinoza and the Revolutionaries had essentially the same concept in mind – a system of government of a people – and that the difference in terminology reflected a difference in situation.

For Spinoza, as for many Diaspora Jews, the term 'nation' was inherently a difficult one. Do the Jews constitute a separate nation, which though scattered remains one, or are they members of the separate, overwhelmingly Gentile, nations among which they live, being distinguished from other members of those nations only by religion? It does not seem that Spinoza could have been comfortable with either alternative.

But he did have a passionate devotion to the political insitutions under which he had grown up: those of the Dutch Republic. So it is hardly surprising that Spinoza chose the abstract and functional expression 'state', rather than the ancestral and cultural expression 'nation,' to refer to the ultimate object of human loyalty and devotion.[1]

When, nearly one hundred and twenty years after the *Tractatus*, the French revolutionary process entered its decisive phase, the term 'state' was not a serviceable one, from a revolutionary point of view. The Revolutionaries were indeed deeply concerned with the state, and bent on making a new kind of state. But they had first to get rid of the old one: that archaic complex formed around three discredited institutions:the church, the 'absolute' monarchy and the privileged nobility. That complex was the state, as it actually existed. As against that state, the revolutionaries evoked the much less precise and much more emotive concept of *la nation* (or *la patrie*, interchangeable with *la nation*).

The most decisive step in the whole Revolution was taken when the States-General were replaced by something wholly new: the National Assembly.

The term 'national' was to become so diluted and trivialized in endless subsequent combinations over succeeding generations that we may find it hard to take in the full force of the word, in the context of 1789. The words 'National Assembly' are in fact a mandate for revolutionary change, with no limit set to that process.

[1] It may be held of course that, if belief in a personal God is gone, the logical object of human loyalty and devotion should be humanity at large, not a particular nation or state. Unfortunately, humanity at large does not seem capable of evoking such emotions, in most humans. The nation/state does evoke them, more dynamically, and also more destructively, than anything else has yet done.

Sieyès, the chief spokesman for that change, had defined the nation (see the epigraph, above) in terms which left no room for any opposition to the will of a body of men constituted in its name. The assertion and acceptance of the name 'National' for the Assembly stripped, by implication, the church, the monarchy and the nobility of all legitimate authority or privilege, save what might be delegated or accorded to them by the representatives of the all-powerful nation.

It is not easy to see by what steps the word *nation* had attained the huge prestige and power which clearly belonged to it already by 1789. We can indeed form a general idea of at least some of the forces at work. Most obvious of these was what might be called 'the Spinoza factor': the vacuum created by the disappearance of belief in a personal God, and the need to fill that vacuum. I believe that was basic; but the thing didn't work as simply and mechanically as the 'vacuum' metaphor might imply.

Take first the role of the *philosophes*. This role was not quite as decisive, in relation to the pre-revolutionary process, as some post-revolutionary writers were to suggest, but all the same it was very siginificant. I shall use the term *philosophes* here in a slightly more restricted way than that in which it is normally used. I shall use it to refer to the anti-religious, and specifically anti-Catholic, writers of the earlier phases of the French (or Francophone) Enlightenment: to Bayle and Voltaire and their followers, and the writers most closely associated with the *Encyclopédie*. I shall leave Rousseau for separate treatment; his role, though even more important in the pre-revolutionary process, was quite distinct from that of the *philosophes* (with whom of course he is often, if dubiously, classed).

The formidable assault mounted by the *philosophes* on the Catholic Church necessarily delegitimized the monarchy also and with it the whole social and political edifice suspended from it. The whole system of the *ancien régime* was one – to a greater extent than the *philosophes* perhaps realized – and when its ideological base in Catholic belief began to crumble, the system as a whole could not stand for long.

It was not only the intellectual assault on Catholicism that made the Enlightenment so corrosive to the political structures of the *ancien régime.* It was above all the *method* chosen to discredit the church that made that discredit so contagious to institutions and individuals in any way associated with the church, and so to the whole political Establishment of the time. The method, highly appropriate to the culture within which it was applied, was *le ridicule.* Educated Frenchmen, whether noble or bourgeois, had long been almost morbidly susceptible to the shame of *le ridicule.* The Catholic Church in France was peculiarly vulnerable to ridicule. Even in France's *Grand Siècle*, before the dawn of the Enlightenment proper, the most French and best loved of French writers had delighted French audiences with his satire on the ultra-pious, *les dévots*, in *Tartuffe.*

Voltaire set himself to do for the pious in general what Molière had done for the sub-class of *les dévots*. Voltaire's success was such that by around the middle of the eighteenth century, the Catholic Church itself had become ridiculous in the eyes of those with whose formal education it had taken the greatest pains – as the Jesuits had done with Voltaire. The main political effect of all this was to prepare French people to be ashamed of their own political institutions, bound up as these were with the Roman Catholic Church. French national pride, once fiercely attached to the monarchy, began to look for new forms of expression; the idea that *la France* and *le ridicule* should be closely associated was intolerable. The concept of *la nation* – quite distinct from its existing institutions – untainted by superstition, above even the possibility of ridicule – met a growing need, after Voltaire had done his work.

The Marquis D'Argenson, writing in 1754, noted – apparently with some alarm – that the expression *la nation* was coming to the fore. It had never, he said, been heard of under Louis XIV. The marquis was wrong, literally, but right to be alarmed. *La nation* had been in earlier use, but without subversive overtones, as one way of referring to the Eldest Daughter of the Church, led by the Most Christian King. Now it was beginning to mean something very different. And the term, with its new and ominous resonance, was being heard increasingly. Professor Boyd Shafer notes in his book *Nationalism: Myth and Reality* that the expressions *la nation* and *la patrie* are significantly more frequent in the second half of the century – even before the Revolution – than they had been in the first half. The *Encyclopédie* in its entry under 'Autorité Politique' (vol. XIII) emphasizes the rights of *la nation*.

Somewhat similar processes, associated with declining belief in a personal God, were at work in other countries, but there were reasons why the challenge of nationalism to a religion-associated regime should be more explosive in France than in any of the other major powers of the period. In Britain, Prussia and Russia, the prevailing religion was a national one, and a source of national pride. In France, the prevailing and established religion was the *inter*national one of Catholicism and – in proportion as it was becoming discredited on other grounds – the religion was increasingly seen as foreign. It is true that the Austro-Hungarian Empire resembled France in that its official allegiance also was to that same international religion, the Catholic Church. But then the Empire was itself an international institution. Nationalism – stimulated by the French Revolution – would eventually rend the Empire apart, but in the eighteenth century, the potential nationalisms of the subject-nations of the Empire did not yet pose a very serious political threat. It was in France alone that an aroused and irritated nationalism faced the established authority of an international church.

With a certain amount of luck, used with a certain amount of shrewdness, the monarchy might still have survived. A king with a series of military victories to his credit could have enlisted French national pride on his side, revived the glorious memories of Henri IV, and successfully distanced himself from the discredited Church of Rome. Instead, the Seven Years War brought national humiliation for France – and what appeared as a specifically *Catholic* form of humiliation at that. The line-up of the powers in that war was – quite coincidentally – unfortunate for the regime in France, given the internal situation in that country. France's ally was the ostentatiously Catholic Austro-Hungarian regime of Maria Theresa. The Austrian alliance was unpopular at the time and came to be regarded in retrospect as equivalent to foreign occupation; Michelet writes of 'le règne de Marie Thérèse à Versailles'.[2] On the other

[2] Jules Michelet, *Histoire de la Révolution Française* (3rd edition, Paris, 1876), I, v.

side were the two modernizing Enlightened post-Reformation regimes of Britain and Prussia. The outcome of the conflict made an association in the public mind between Roman Catholicism and national failure hard to escape.

In the prolonged internal crisis of the regime which followed immediately on the military defeat, the leading part, culturally speaking, was played, not by the *philosophes*, but by a group of people who appeared ideologically impervious to the Enlightenment, but were nonetheless allied to it, to the extent of a common hostility to the power of Rome in France. These were the Jansenists, delighted now to get their revenge for their formal suppression by the Jesuit-influenced Louis XIV half a century or so before.

When that suppression closed the church to Jansenists as a career, many of them entered the legal profession, in which they prospered exceedingly. By the second half of the eighteenth century, Jansenists exercised predominant influence in the *parlements*, the powerful legal institutions of the *ancien régime* in France. The king could not impose new taxes, unless these were registered by the *parlements*. As a result of the cost of the Seven Years War, he needed new taxes. The *parlements* were therefore able to squeeze the king, and the Jansenists, using their 'clout' within the *parlements*, and also exploiting certain legal misfortunes and imprudences of the Jesuit Order, were able to induce the king, in 1764, to expel the Jesuits from France.[3] Other courts followed suit, whether under pressure from France or for reasons of their own. Finally, the Pope, persuaded by the French Court, and other courts, declared the Jesuit Order dissolved, through the brief *Dominus ac Redemptor* of 1773.

The expulsion and suppression of the Jesuits constituted (in one of its aspects) a major victory of nationalism over internationalism, and one which was pleasing to more *philosophes* than not. The Jesuits had been among the strongest pillars of the Catholic Church in France and the shattering of the Jesuit pillar put the whole edifice in imminent danger of collapse. Voltaire, who disliked

[3] This brief account is necessarily simplified. For the full story see Dale Van Kley's fascinating work, *The Jansenists and the Expulsion of the Jesuits from France, 1757–1765* (New York, 1975).

Jansenists more than Jesuits, genuinely detested all forms of fanaticism; d'Alembert and other *philosophes* did not object to fanaticism when it hurt the church, as in the case of the Jansenists.

The 'whole edifice', in the context of the 1760s, was not just the Catholic Church; it was the whole of the *ancien régime*. Yet *in other circumstances* that need not have been the case. Had a king, victorious in war, suppressed the Jesuits, he could have made a successful appeal to French national feeling. But the same act of suppression, carried out by a defeated king and in a time of national humiliation, could have no such favourable repercussion. Both king and Pope were seen as having yielded to pressure, and looked like weak-kneed cynics prepared to sacrifice people who – whatever their faults – had genuinely served a cause which was supposed to be sacred to both king and Pope. In those circumstances, the fall of the Jesuits appeared as a further demonstration of the rottenness both of the Papacy and of the French *ancien régime*, in collusion; a collusion which no longer even bore the appearance of being based on a genuinely shared religious conviction.

II

By the 1760s then, a void existed in many hearts, where once God and the King of France had been. But Jean-Jacques Rousseau, enchanting almost all the French, was showing how the void could be filled. Human goodness – *la vertu* – took the place of the old God of the churches; the nation (the general will) took the place of the king. Virtue was in accordance with nature, man being naturally good. And where man was free from deforming institutions, he would be good. Virtue, nature and a free nation were all in harmony. Thus the ideas of virtue, nature and the nation became so closely associated as to be almost synonymous. Rousseau's most sincere and dedicated disciple, Maximilien de Robespierre, defined *la vertu* as 'the love of the Good of *la patrie* and of Liberty'. (Note *la patrie* coming before Liberty.)

The curious thing is that Rousseau himself doesn't have all that much to say about *la patrie*. He doesn't even have any real *patrie* of his own. He defined himself for a time as *citoyen de Genève*. But that was an abstract Gencva, a cerebral Utopia. When the mature Rousseau got to know the real Geneva, he disliked it, and it him. But to have defined himself, even for a time, as citizen of a country other than France, would seem to disqualify Rousseau as a prophet of French nationalism. And yet that is what Rousseau became, posthumously.

The paradox increases if we consider the popularity of Rousseau's different writings, in the period *before* the Revolution, and then *during* the Revolution. Before the Revolution, the Rousseau that everybody read was mainly non-political Rousseau. What people liked, in those days, was the weepy Rousseau, the Rousseau who made you feel so good you had to cry – the Rousseau, especially, of *La Nouvelle Héloise*. There was very little demand, before the Revolution, for that arid little political treatise, *Du contrat social*. Yet from 1789 on, and especially from 1792, it is the *Social Contract* that becomes the Bible of the Revolutionaries. Not only for Robespierre, but also for Robespierre's enemies, at least as far as public professions were concerned. It was the Thermidorians, after they had guillotined Robespierre, who ordered (14 September 1784) that Rousseau's remains be placed in the Pantheon. In that ceremony, the *Social Contract* had a place of honour:

> The ceremony of pantheonization took place on October 11. There was a special service in the Convention and then a procession to the Pantheon. The *Contrat social*, the 'beacon of legislators', was carried on a velvet cushion and a statue of its author in a cart pulled by twelve horses.[4]

The *Social Contract* was published thirteen times between 1792 and 1795. One edition, as McNeil tells us, was published 'in pocket-Bible size for the use of the soldiers defending *la patrie*'. So we know, at least, that the reading of Rousseau, and specifically of the *Social Contract*, was regarded as highly conducive to national fervour, during the revolutionary period.

[4] Gordon H. McNeil, 'The Cult of Rousseau and the French Revolution', *Journal of the History of Ideas*, 6 (1945), 197–212.

To a modern reader of the *Social Contract*, this may seen strange. This is a theoretical work, making no direct appeal to national or other feelings. Indeed, it hardly refers to the nation at all. What it exalts is what it calls 'the general will'. But the general will in question can only be that of the nation. Sieyès in 1789, in making his absolutist claims for the nation – 'The nation exists before all', etc. – is strictly following Rousseau (stylistically as well as in substance) but making explicit what in Rousseau is implicit: for 'the general will' read 'the nation'.

In the early phases of the Revolution, up to the flight and capture of the king (June 1791), the consequences of the exaltation of the nation remain largely latent. This is a nation which, like other nations – contemporary England, for example – still *includes* the king; a nation like other nations, only more benign and more pacific. This was the nation of the *Déclaration de paix au monde* (22 May 1790) by which the poets Wordsworth and Klopstock were so greatly moved. The declaration stands out in retrospect as the high-water mark of pacific revolutionary internationalism: the happy flowering of Enlightenment cosmopolitanism.

In this period it was understood – as it was also understood later, but with drastic qualifications – that the interests of nations could not collide with one another. Rousseau's influence is also apparent here: one form of Rousseau's influence, not specifically that of the *Social Contract*. People were naturally good, when not corrupted by institutions. 'The Revolution' – which most people in 1790, with the exception of Edmund Burke, assumed to be *over* – had put the people (or nation) in control of the institutions, so all would be well. Wars had been caused by the ambitions and rivalries of dynasties. A nation which had brought its dynasts under control would automatically have freed itself from warlike inclinations.

The flight and capture of the king did not entirely discredit these assumptions, but it brought about dramatic changes in the perspective from which they were viewed. The French nation was indeed peace-loving, but it had to live in a hostile world. Its king had tried to take refuge with other kings, no doubt in order to make war upon the nation. *Emigré* nobles, at foreign courts, were still bent on levying such a war, though no one had declared it.

In April 1792, the National Assembly drew what it regarded as the logical consequences of that by declaring war on 'the King of Hungary and Bohemia'; that is, on the Austro-Hungarian Empire. In taking this step, the National Assembly was clearly embarrassed by the earlier *Déclaration de paix au monde*, the terms of which were by now part of the French Constitution (of 1791). In a 'solemn declaration of the French nation' preliminary to the actual declaration of war, the National Assembly boldly resolved the apparent contradiction:

> The French nation renounces the undertaking of any war with a view to making conquests, and will never employ its forces against the liberty of any people. Such is the text of the Constitution, such is the sacred wish by which we have bound our happiness to that of all peoples, and we will be faithful thereto.
>
> But who could still regard as a friendly nation one in which an army awaits only the hope of success before attacking! And is not the voluntary lending of one's offices, not only to enemies who have declared war against us but to conspirators who have long since begun it, equivalent to a declaration of war? Everything, then, imposes upon the powers established by the Constitution for the maintenance of peace and security the imperative necessity for using force against the rebels who, from a foreign land, threaten to rend their *patrie*.

The actual Declaration of War (20 April 1792) further declared: 'That the war which (the French nation) is forced to undergo is not a war of nation against nation, but the just defence of a free people against the unjust aggression of a king.' The Declaration of War also contained the assurance: 'That it adopts in advance all foreigners who, abjuring the cause of its enemies, range themselves under its banners. . . .

These declarations, at the beginning of the war, stopped short of declaring a general revolutionary war of nations against kings: France itself, at this time, still had a king. But after the French deposed their own king – 10 August 1792 – they soon began to call for national insurrection in other countries. In what is called the First Propagandist Decree (19 November 1792):

> The National Convention declares, in the name of the French nation, that it will grant fraternity and aid to all peoples who wish to recover their liberty; and it charges the executive power with giving the generals the orders necessary for bringing aid to such peoples and for defending citizens who have been, or who might be, harassed for the cause of liberty.

A remarkable document annexed to the Second Propagandist Decree (15 December 1792) is headed simply: *The French People to the —— People.*

This document was sent off to all the revolutionary generals, who were to fill the blank space with the name of any country they might conquer and/or liberate. The document included the words:

> Henceforth the French nation proclaims the sovereignty of the people of. . . . You are henceforth, brothers and friends, all equal in rights, and all equally summoned to govern, to serve and to defend your *Patrie.*[5]

It is necessary here to distinguish between two different – or at least ostensibly different – revolutionary approaches to the revolutionary expansionism reflected in the documents just cited. The Girondins were the revolutionary war-party. The original Declaration of War was mainly their work, and the documents cited (with the partial exception of the Second Propagandist Decree) are essentially Girondin documents. Robespierre's Jacobins opposed the declaration of war and the Girondin conduct of the war. After the fall of the Girondins – early June 1793 – Robespierre, in power, publicly declared 'the abandonment of any policy of conquest and liberation of peoples'[6] (17 November 1793).

[5] J. H. Stewart, ed., *Documentary Survey of the French Revolution* (New York, 1965), 384.

[6] Jacques Godechot, *La Grande nation: l'expansion révolutionnaire de la France dans le monde, 1789–1799* (Paris, 1956), I, 85.

The expansionist policies formally renounced by Robespierre were resumed after his fall by Robespierre's victorious enemies, the Thermidorians: or – in Ernest Hamel's apt designation – the Thermido-Girondins.

From these contrasts, one might infer that Robespierre was 'less nationalistic' than his rivals and enemies, the Girondins and Thermido-Girondins. But such an inference would be unwarranted. Even the fiery nationalist historian, Michelet, who disliked Robespierre, and was an enthusiastic admirer of Girondin expansionism, writes of Robespierre's 'real patriotism'. Michelet is also impressed by the '*patriotisme fanatique*' of the Revolutionary Tribunal of 1793–4 – a tribunal which he rightly describes as being, through its composition, 'a portrait of Robespierre'.[7]

Essentially, the difference between Robespierre's nationalism and that of his rivals is that his expressed itself with gloomy intensity, concentrated on the life of the nation itself; theirs was more diffuse and optimistic and concerned with the real and/or assumed appeal of France to the spirit of nationality in other lands.

Robespierre, at the head of the Jacobins, was concerned, above all, with the struggle, within France, between *la nation* and its internal enemies, who relied on foreign support. The great test-case here was that of the king: his indictment, trial and death. And Robespierre drew a terrifyingly clear line between the king on one side and *la nation* on the other. If you were *for* the king, you put yourself outside *la nation*. If, like the Girondins – then in control of a shaky government – you tried to hedge on the question of the death of the king, your national credentials began to look dubious.

The indictment of the king (11 December 1792) is essentially for crimes against *la nation*:

> Count one: '. . . You attacked the sovereignty of the people' . . . Count two: 'you wished to dictate laws to the nation' . . . Count four: 'You persisted in your designs against national liberty . . . In orgies held before your very eyes you permitted

[7] Michelet, *Histoire*, *op. cit.*, V, iii and 24.

the national cockade to be trampled under foot, the white cockade to be raised, and the nation blasphemed. . . .'[8]

'The nation blasphemed. . . .' The monarch, who had regarded himself as the representative of God on earth, is put under notice that he has been worshipping a false God, and is to be condemned in the name of the true one.

Being outside and against the nation, the king was also outside nature itself: *hors nature*. So argued Robespierre's ally Saint-Just, calling for death without trial. (The Rousseau-inspired juxtaposition – perhaps ultimately derived from Spinoza – between 'nature' and 'nation', is quite frequent at this time.) Since the king was *hors nature*, a monster, to kill him was not homicide. Robespierre, in the name of *la nation*, concurred. On 11 December 1792, he said: 'No trial, but a measure of public safety, an act of *providence nationale* to be carried out. Louis must die, because *la patrie* must live.'[9]

On 20 January, the Convention decreed the condemnation of the king. 'On the following day, amidst the roll of drums and shouts of '*Vive la nation*' Louis expiated his "crimes" under the revolutionary blade of steel'.[10] *Le roi est mort! Vive la nation!*[11]

It was through being accepted as spokesman for *la nation* that Robespierre established his fearsome moral, and consequently political, ascendancy, from shortly before the execution of the king to shortly before his own execution, eighteen months later. Rousseau, in the *Contrat social*, had spoken of 'guides', whose function it is not merely to interpret the General Will ('of the nation') to the

[8] Stewart, ed., *op. cit.* 386–7.

[9] Michelet, *Histoire, op. cit*, IV, 272. Michelet himself was a devoted worshipper of the deity to which Louis was sacrificed. 'This is my blood, drink,' Michelet represents the French nation as saying at the time of the victory of Jemappes: '*Ceci est mon sang, buvez!*' (*Histoire*, III, 469.) And much else to similar effect. See epigraph.

[10] Stewart, ed., *op. cit.*, 385.

[11] The execution of Louis as an act of ritual sacrifice is the theme of a very interesting work (unfinished as I write this) by Professor Susan Dunn, of Williams College, Mass. I am indebted to Professor Dunn for the Michelet reference quoted in the epigraph.

populace, but even to explain it to itself.[12] Robespierre was such a guide, and sole and undisputed guide from June 1793 to July 1794. The *Social Contract*, Book II (chapter III) also speaks of a 'censor' whose function is to pronounce on the virtue, or lack of virtue, of individual citizens. Robespierre was censor, as well as guide, during this same period. As authority on *la vertu* – which included, as noted earlier, *l'amour de la patrie* – Robespierre was in a position to measure by his personal moral authority, against which there was no appeal, the patriotism, or lack of it, of any prominent citizen. In that period, a negative opinion, in a speech by Robespierre, meant certain death for the citizen stigmatized. Such a person was outside the nation, even *hors nature*, like the king according to Saint-Just: a monster to be struck down on sight.

It was the sheer panic and terror which that situation inspired in surviving members of the repeatedly purged Convention that brought about the fall and death of the great Guide and Censor on 9 Thermidor, 1794.

From early 1792 to early 1793, the Girondins had been the most enthusiastic spokesmen for French nationalism, in relation to other countries. But Robespierre, within the same period, had succeeded in making himself arbiter of what the will of the nation meant, in relation to the most important national issue: the fate of Louis Capet, calling himself Louis XVI. Like a good chess-player, Robespierre had concentrated on the position of the king.

After the king had been executed, against the wishes of most Girondins, the Girondins looked suspect of disloyalty towards the entity to which the king had been sacrificed: *la nation*. Had the Girondins been lucky, French victories abroad might have banished that suspicion. But they were not lucky. Instead the Grand Coalition – after the Girondin Government had declared war on England (February 1793) – made headway against the French armies, which had to abandon their earlier conquests. Dumouriez, the general appointed by the Girondins, defected to the enemy. After the defeats and the defection, Robespierre's assumption of a

[12] *Du contrat social*, Book II Chs. VI and VII.

correlation between mercy to the king and treachery to the nation appeared as borne out by events. The Girondins fell and a vindicated Robespierre emerged as incarnating the spirit of the besieged nation, defying its external enemies and unmasking and chastising its internal ones.

III

I should now like to look at French national policies towards countries and territories conquered (or expected to be conquered) by French revolutionary armies; and at some of the implications of these policies for the development of nationalism in Europe. We are here necessarily looking mainly at the 'Girondin' and 'Thermido-Girondin' periods, which were those in which these matters were part of practical politics. The 'Girondin' period, for these purposes, extends from the first Declaration of War in April 1792 to the fall of the Girondins in June 1793. The 'Thermido-Girondin' period extends from the victory of Fleurus and the fall of Robespierre (June–July 1794) to that somewhat indeterminate date in the late 1790s when revolutionary policy becomes submerged in the personal and proto-dynastic policies of Napoleon Bonaparte.

The national policies of the French Revolution in these periods of expansion might be summarized as follows, using the key terms of the revolutionary vocabulary itself:

> *La grande nation* must first establish itself within its restored *frontières naturelles*. In liberating the areas rightly belonging within the *frontières naturelles*, but formerly separated from the rest of France, *la grande nation* will count on the aid of *les patriotes* living within, or coming from, the areas in question. Established within its *frontières naturelles*, the *grande nation* will encourage other nations to establish their own *républiques soeurs*, dedicated to the same principles as *la grande nation* and in alliance with it. Within all such nations, the local *patriotes*

will strive to establish such *républiques soeurs* under the general guidance of *la grande nation*[13]

Of the expressions *grande nation*, *frontières naturelles*, *républiques soeurs*, and *les patriotes*, the first three are terms of art; the last belongs among the 'complex words' in William Empson's sense: words exceptionally rich in ambiguities. The expression *les patriotes*, being both complex and particularly important in relation to our subject matter, needs special attention. But first a brief note on the three terms of art:

The expression *une grande nation* was in early use in the National Assembly, but it seems to have been through the enthusiasm of foreign admirers that this turned into *la* Grande Nation. 'We observe with joy the spectacle of your *grande nation* giving liberty to Europe,' ran a message to the Convention from a gathering of Irish *patriotes* in 1792. The exaltation of a *grande nation* was useful to the French Revolutionaries in legitimizing both their claim to *les frontières naturelles* and – later – their hegemony over *les républiques soeurs*. Also in asserting the primary claim of revolutionary France to the allegiance of *les patriotes* everywhere. The whole system is remarkably cohesive.

Frontières naturelles: Unknown under Louis XIV, according to Godechot: 'The idea of a *frontière naturelle* appears only in the eighteenth century, with the general craze (*engoûment*) for *la nature*.'[14]

Rousseau again. In the 1780s, even before the Revolution, the idea was pushed by some Francophile Germans hoping to see the Rhineland incorporated in France. Carnot's definition – of February 1793 – was generally accepted and became a kind of article of faith in revolutionary and Imperial France: 'The ancient and natural limits of France are the Rhine, the Alps and the Pyrenees.' In practical terms, *les frontières naturelles* meant mainly the permanent incorporation of Belgium and the Rhineland. These *frontières*,

[13] For the detailed workings of this system see Godechot, *op. cit.*, *passim*. Godechot might be labelled 'school of Michelet', in a broad sense – nationalist and pro-revolutionary – but he is much more candid than Michelet about how the system actually works.

[14] Godechot *op. cit.*, I, 78.

being *naturelles* and thus non-negotiable, were the main reason why the wars were so protracted.

Républiques soeurs: This idea seems to have originated, early in the Revolutionary period, among Dutch *patriotes*. It was originally discouraged by the National Assembly – in 1791 – but was adopted as official policy after the declaration of war, and especially following the First and Second Propagandist Decrees of November and December 1792 (quoted above). The first *république soeur*, the Batavian Republic (Netherlands), had a certain autonomy and a degree of solidity. The others, especially those which multiplied in Italy, were a little, but not much, more than French satrapies. Godechot, who has studied the workings of the system in great detail, defines it thus: 'The system of *républiques soeurs* had the advantage, not only of satisfying the national pride of the French by spreading the influence of the new France with the support of the patriotes of all countries, but it also undoubtedly secured (*sic*) strategic benefits by covering the recent frontiers, and economic benefits.'[15]

And that brings us straight, but already stumbling over difficulties, to the critical question of *les patriotes*. The French Revolutionaries, in setting the French nation above the king and the church, saw themselves as exemplary *patriotes*, and they were so seen by people of similar views and dispositions in other countries. The French Revolutionaries saw the pro-French-Revolution people in other countries as the *patriotes* of those countries, and the people in question came to describe themselves as *patriotes*, at least in their dealings with the representatives of *la grande nation*.

But it is sufficiently clear that to be a *patriote* of *la grande nation* was something different in kind from being a *patriote* of [ ][16] A French *patriote* was a full-blown nationalist, setting his own nation above all other nations, and contemplating it with feelings bordering on adoration. For a *patriote* of a blank-space '*patrie*' things were by no means so simple. Such a *patriote* might love two nations: *la grande nation* and his own. He might originally

[15] Godechot, *op. cit.*, I, 83. My translation is literal. Godechot is not a graceful writer, but he gets a lot into a sentence.

[16] See above, page 32; form annexed to Second Propagandist Decree.

believe that there was no contradiction; by following the example and the guidance of *la grande nation* he was serving the best interests of his own nation: a patriot in the ordinary sense, as well as a *patriote* in the new, technical sense.

Others among the non-French *patriotes* were full-fledged internationalists, with little interest in their own nation, or in any, other than *la grande nation*: focus for a general transformation of humanity, and fusion of nations. The term *patriote universel* was in vogue for a time. The best-known of these was a German, Anacharsis Cloots, the famous 'orator of the human race'. Cloots had been one of the first propagandists – as early as 1785 – of *frontières naturelles*. He hailed revolutionary Paris as 'the Vatican of Reason'. To the Vatican in question Cloots even summoned that noted unbeliever, Edmund Burke: 'Quittez votre Ile, mon cher Burke. Venez en France.'

Another universal patriot was John Oswald, of Edinburgh, subject of a recent and illuminating monograph by David V. Erdman.[17] Oswald called himself neither English nor British nor Scottish but an *Anglo-Franc: Franc* was an ingenious coinage, meaning both 'free' and 'Frankish', alias 'French', also equated to 'free'. Oswald was among a 'set of Gentlemen, British by birth' who prepared, in May 1790, to publish a newspaper in Paris, London and Calais, called *The Universal Patriot*. As Professor Erdman says: '*The Universal Patriot* by title and language ... offered itself as a cross-Channel companion to Brissot's *Le patriote français*.'[18] 'Universal' as a companion to 'French' hits the whole phenomenon off very nicely, and all the better for being without ironic intent. Later, in a manifesto of March 1792, Oswald wrote: 'I can no longer doubt it. The nations are awaking. They are uniting.'[19] Later still in a discourse of early February 1793 – just after the death of the king – Oswald applied this principle to Anglo-French relations. He proposed 'a friendly descent of 600,000 *sans-culottes* who will march straight to London to aid their

[17] David V. Erdman, *Commerce des Lumières: John Oswald and the British in Paris, 1790–1793* (University of Missouri Press/Columbia, 1986).
[18] Ibid., 114.
[19] Ibid., 171.

brothers, the *sans-culottes* of England.' Through the action of the combined forces 'George the sanguinary will soon suffer the fate of Louis the traitor' and then – after many further executions: 'France and England shall then form a single republic and the Anglo-French people (*le peuple Anglo-franc*) will lose all corporate spirit and all local prejudice in the sublime title of Free, Fraternal People (*Peuple Libre-Frère*).'[20] Oswald was killed fighting for the French Republic in La Vendée later in the same year.

Not all *patriotes* were universal to the same degree as Cloots and Oswald. Theobald Wolfe Tone, for example, was undoubtedly an Irish patriot, in the ordinary sense, as well as a *patriote* in the French revolutionary sense. But if Wolfe Tone's French-backed revolutionary enterprise in Ireland had succeeded, in 1796, or 1798, then Wolfe Tone would have found himself a citizen of a *république soeur*. And in that case, he would have had to behave as a *patriote*, strictly according to the exigent expectations of *la grande nation*, or cease to be of any account in his own country.

The lot of *les patriotes* was exceedingly disconcerting, and increasingly difficult, from the first French expansion, in 1792, to the winding up of the *patriote* business by Bonaparte, towards the end of the century.

The first to be disappointed were among the first to be occupied, the Belgians. The Belgian *patriotes* – themselves a minority of the Belgian population – originally welcomed the French as liberators. These *patriotes* expected – and were originally encouraged to expect – a status of *république soeur*. But then *frontières naturelles* doctrine prevailed in Paris, and Belgium was simply annexed, piecemeal, by fifteen decrees of the Convention in March 1793. In the same month, in the Rhineland, 'a *convention rhénane* met at Mainz, composed only of *patriotes*, elected by a tiny minority of inhabitants. It voted, on 21 March 1793, Union with France.'[21]

The *républiques soeurs* were treated with a little more ceremony, but not much, and less and less as the years went on. The Batavian Republic, the sturdiest of the *soeurs*, was told it must pay reparations

[20] Ibid., 260. Winston Churchill probably did not have this precedent in mind when, in 1940, he proposed an Anglo-French Union.
[21] Godechot, *op. cit.*, I, 99.

for the misdeeds of its *ancien régime* predecessor, for whose sins it remained responsible. The Committee of Public Safety told the Batavians, in 1795, why they would have to pay up: 'The coalition into which your nation (*sic*) entered wanted to dismember France; if it had succeeded, you would have shared our spoils among you.'

The French nation was the antithesis of the old *régime* and acknowledged no financial or other responsibility for the misdeeds of its predecessor. But this privilege was not conceded to the kinds of nations whose names were to be filled in by French Generals on forms provided for the purpose. Other *républiques soeurs* – like the multiplicity of *ad hoc* creations of that name in Italy – were treated with even less consideration. Italian *patriotes* who thought that Italy itself was the proper *république soeur* were ignored or suppressed.

Things got even worse for the exterior *patriotes* as a result of changes in France itself. The Girondins had been favourably disposed to external *patriotes*, at least in principle. After the Girondins fell, in June 1793, things were never quite the same for these *patriotes*. The immediate successor, Robespierre, did not believe in foreign *patriotes*. To those beyond France's frontiers, he gave no encouragement. The foreign *patriotes* whom he found in France he regarded as enemies: pro-Girondins and probably spies as well, and in both capacities participants in *le complot des étrangers*. So he guillotined a number of them. Among these was Anacharsis Cloots.

When Robespierre himself fell, the foreign *patriotes* hoped that they might regain the status they had held under the Girondins. But they never really did. True, the Thermido-Girondins were *grande nation* people, committed to expansion, *frontières naturelles*, and *républiques soeurs*. But they were suspicious of foreign *patriotes*, partly because these, not being attuned to the new Paris fashions, still sounded like Jacobins. So the *patriotes*, always lagging behind, suffered under Robespierre for being Girondins, and then under the Thermido-Girondins for being Jacobins. Finally, a succession of factional coups in post-Thermidorian Paris brought terminal discredit on the idea of *les patriotes*. Each coup was followed by a purge, not only in France, but among the foreign *patriotes*. By about 1797, in territory under French control, to be a *patriote* meant no more than to be known as a person who would automatically toe the line, and make the right noises, at the behest of whatever faction happened to be holding the reins of power in Paris.

So few tears could have been shed when Bonaparte – who had no more time for foreign *patriotes* than Robespierre did – scrapped a disguised hegemonic rhetoric which had become both archaic and repulsive. The old *patriotes* were replaced by courtiers waiting on hereditary princes of the Bonaparte blood, appointed by the Emperor of the French. In some cases, the new courtiers had been *patriotes* too, in their day.

The French Revolution, like the twentieth-century Russian one, killed off or shed its international supporters stage by stage, until in the end each Revolution was left only with a diminished and uninfluential band of unconditional servants of the masters of the revolutionary capital. And in both cases, this development saw the growth of a concomitant band of disillusioned and embittered *former* supporters (ex-*patriotes*, ex-communists).

Let us consider briefly the cases of two disillusioned German *patriotes*: Klopstock and Fichte. On 14 July 1790, on the heady first anniversary of the fall of the Bastille, and in the halcyon period immediately following the National Assembly's *Déclaration de paix au monde* Klopstock had read an ode at Hamburg, celebrating 'the Divine Liberty of the Gauls', which had chained up 'the most treacherous of monsters, War'. After revolutionary France, less than two years later, had itself declared war, Klopstock wrote another ode, 'The War of Conquest'.

> Alas! Woe unto us! Those who once tamed
> The monstrous beast, themselves have destroyed
> The holiest of laws, their own; in their battles
> They have become conquerors!
>
> If you know words for cursing, curse them!
> No other law was ever like that law:[22]
> More terrible than any other let the curse be also
> On the transgressors of the holy law
> On the traitors to Humanity!

[22] That law: the *Déclaration de paix au monde*.

Fichte remained a *patriote*, long after Klopstock had ceased to be one, but his revulsion, when it came, was no less violent than Klopstock's, and of much more moment. Fichte's *Addresses to the German Nation* (1807) – delivered in French-occupied Berlin after Napoleon's crushing defeat of Prussia – form the manifesto of a new German nationalism. Fichte is telling the Germans to realize their destiny as the *true* Great Nation.

Within ten years of the beginning of the Revolution, revolutionary internationalism seemed to have turned to ashes. The French Revolution had made a mockery of *les républiques soeurs* and had insisted that *patriotes* be puppets. What stood out, in contrast with those international shams, was the huge exalted and long-triumphant national reality: *la grande nation* itself. It is hardly surprising if succeeding generations were less inclined to emulate what now looked like shams than to emulate a triumphant reality, with the glory that it seemed to trail.

The expansion of French political hegemony under the Revolution and the Empire did much to destroy France's former *cultural* hegemony. The symbolic figure in that respect may appear as Count Rostopchin, Governor of Moscow, starting to learn *Russian* in 1812, while the French armies were approaching his city. He and his kind were being taught by the French themselves that they were Russians and must learn 'their own language'. The international culture of Europe's Francophone aristocracy was breaking down, more or less as the international religious system of the Counter-Reformation had broken down, and as the effort to create revolutionary and post-revolutionary international systems around the French example had broken down. Multiple forms of nationalism were to be the main heirs of the failed internationals. New forms of *inter*nationalism were to be attempted also, by Marx and others in the later nineteenth century, and to be replaced in their turn, in the twentieth century, by new nationalist entities in international dress: Soviet Union, China, Vietnam, Cambodia, Yugoslavia, Romania, Albania etc., all theoretically part of 'international communism'.

Nationalism should not be – as it sometimes is – seen as 'caused' by the French Revolution. Rather, as argued above, the growth of nationalism is among the causes of the French Revolution and of its expansion. And a part of what we see as 'reactions to the French Revolution' is rooted in reaction against French international cultural hegemony *before* the French Revolution. 'Spit out that green slime of the Seine' – meaning the French language – cried Herder in Germany in the 1770s; two generations before Rostopchin, in beleaguered Moscow, brought himself to spit it out.

The most that can be said is that the French Revolution accelerated the growth of nationalism, secularized it and thereby helped to set it above all other values. That tendency seems to have been at work, in different and sometimes contradictory ways, from Waterloo on, throughout the nineteenth and into the twentieth century.

Nationalism – the nationalisms of the English, the Russians, the Prussians and the Spaniards – was probably the main force that defeated Napoleon; just as French nationalism was the main force that sustained him. But the victorious powers – meaning the ruling classes of post-Waterloo Europe – were in general highly suspicious of nationalism. They disliked enthusiasm of all kinds, and nationalism is one of the most disquieting forms of enthusiasm. Some of the victors – the Austrian and Russian Empires in particular – had practical reasons to fear the rise of nationalism among their subject peoples. In general, the restored dynasts and aristocrats suspected both liberalism and nationalism as twin manifestations of a possibly renascent Jacobinism: bourgeois power. And all of them were watchful for warning signs of a revival of the most alarming of all possible forms of nationalism: that of the now suppressed *grande nation* itself.

The main focus of resurgent nationalism in nineteenth-century Europe was the Franco-German interaction. The crucial year was 1848. This was, of course, a year of multiple, national revolutions, mostly unsuccessful, led by bourgeois, with some backing from workers and peasants, and conducted under both liberal and nationalist slogans, with a nostalgic symbolism of French Revolutionary type (tricolours etc.).

The seminal events of that year, the events that were to shape the course of modern history, occurred in Paris and in Frankfurt.

The events of Paris were relatively simple and appeared – at least at first – as the major success of the Year of Revolutions. The cautious and uncharismatic House of Orleans fell, never to return. What replaced it, after a short interval, was Louis-Napoleon Bonaparte, first as Prince-President, and then as Napoleon III, Emperor of the French. Europe was put under notice that *la grande nation*, under the inherited name of its most illustrious champion, was once more in quest of *la gloire*: other nationalisms were stimulated, as before.

What happened in Frankfurt was more complex, and also more ominous. The Frankfurt Parliament offered the Imperial Crown of Germany to the King of Prussia, Friedrich Wilheim IV, who refused to accept the Crown, from the Parliament. The offer signalized the desire of German nationalists, including liberals, to place themselves under the leadership of Prussia. The refusal of that particular offer, at that particular time, signified that if German unity was to be achieved it would have to be on Prussia's terms, and at Prussia's chosen time.

Prussia's relation to German nationalism had been ambiguous. It was from the Prussian capital that Fichte's seminal *Addresses to the German Nation* had gone forth. And it was to Prussia that German nationalists necessarily looked for leadership. It was Prussia, alone in Germany, that had played a heroic role against Napoleon, and had helped to bring about his downfall, through the battles of Leipzig and Waterloo. So Prussia was the Germanic heir of the Napoleonic charisma. But the Hohenzollerns distrusted the noisy nationalism of the *Burschenschaften* and *Turnvereine* (gymnastic societies and students' associations). That was South-German stuff, bourgeois, civilian, tainted with neo-Jacobin hankerings after liberalism and democracy. The nationalists might be useful, in opening the imperial way for Prussia, but they would have to dance to Prussia's tune, not Prussia to theirs. And that tune would have nothing in common with the *Marseillaise*.

Ironically, the Hohenzollern attitude towards German nationalists outside Prussia paralleled that of Robespierre towards foreign *patriotes*. And this is logical enough. For was not Prussia the core of the *new* Grand Nation?

1870 marks – along with much else – a change in the meaning and associations of nationalism. With the debacle of the last Bonaparte, the French and revolutionary aspects of the nationalist heritage became devalued; the *counter*-revolutionary aspects, long present, are enhanced. With the triumph of Prussianized Germany, nationalism takes on an increasingly Germanic tone, not only in Germany itself, but on *both* sides of the Rhine, and consequently throughout Europe. Nationalism becomes more and more an affair of the right, and more and more charged with racism. The French revolutionary heritage, now understood in an *inter*nationalist sense, becomes the heritage of the left, almost exclusively.

Nationalism in Imperial Germany was right-wing *ex-officio*: supreme authority always remained in the hands of an aristocratic military elite, which German nationalists supported to the bitter end. The only aspect of the French revolutionary tradition which Imperial Germany made its own to a significant extent was glorification and quasi-divinization of the state (Rousseau–Sieyès, Germanized through Hegel). But it was a somewhat watered down, semi-Christianized version. The state itself was not the supreme value; it was only the walk of God on earth: *Der Gang Gottes an der Erde*. In all other respects, the nationalism of Imperial Germany is in sharp contrast to French revolutionary nationalism. But German nationalism – even before the triumph of the Prussian elite – was also distinct from the French revolutionary kind in another important aspect (besides the aristocratic one). This was the special German emphasis on the purity of the *Volk*: an emphasis which, after 1870, became more and more explicitly racist.

The theory was that the German *Volk*, never having been conquered by the Romans, remained pure, both linguistically and racially, unlike the French and the English. This theory is already present in the 1770s in Herder, though mildly expressed as is usually his way. After the Napoleonic impact, *Völkisch* nationalism became strident in Fichte and his following. This was quite congenial to the authorities of the new Germany, after 1870. The idea of a hereditary elite is itself a racist idea, so that the rising influence of racism within German nationalism bolstered the authority of Germany's Prussian ruling class.

In France, the collapse and disintegration of Bonapartism after Sedan led to the emergence of a right-wing nationalism, rejecting not merely Bonapartism but the entire heritage both of the French Revolution and of the Enlightenment itself. French nationalism, while virulently Germanophobe in form and intent, in fact imitated its victorious adversary. The compliment which German nationalism had paid to the French kind, after Jena, was returned by the French nationalists, after Sedan.

The German cult of the purity of the *Volk* – a cult which persists today among the Afrikaner *volk* – took root, to a more limited but still significant extent, among the French right also. Anti-semitism became the most conspicuous common feature of the nationalist right on both sides of the Rhine. And the fact that anti-semitism was now *à la mode* in the most civilized countries of the Continent probably helped the rulers of Russia to return to old-fashioned persecuting anti-semitism from 1881 on. Among the Jews themselves, those who were most clearly conscious of the way the wind was blowing were the Zionists. The rediscovery of Jewish nationalism, in the late nineteenth century, was a response to the discovery that the European nationalisms had turned racist.

Nationalism had been a force in pre-revolutionary France, and had played its part, along with Enlightenment, in the pre-revolutionary process. Nationalism had become dominant in the Revolution itself, in the expansion of the Revolution, and in the Empire of the Emperor of the French. French revolutionary universalism had been mainly a matter of rhetoric, and the cynicism of its manipulators had led to the bitter disillusionment of the international sympathizers. Yet through the authority of the rhetoric, some of the Enlightenment tradition was preserved and transmitted within nationalism up to 1870 (and thereafter also, to some extent, on the margins of Europe). Though there are traces of racism in some Enlightenment writers – Voltaire's anti-semitic gibes, for example – the Enlightenment tradition as a whole, being both tolerant and universalist, worked against active racism. It was only after nationalism, under German leadership, had liberated itself from almost all French revolutionary influence, and then from the whole Enlightenment, that mainstream nationalism turned racist and anti-semitic.

In the triumphal period of Wilhelmine Germany, the racism of German nationalism remained largely intellectual and social. But defeat in the First World War activated the manically destructive forces latent in the new nationalism. The only major common feature between the nationalism of the French Revolution and the nationalism of the National Socialists was the concept of the nation-state as the supreme value. In that respect, the National Socialists were closer to the French Revolutionaries than they were to Wilhelmine Germany, since the Nazis, like the French Revolutionaries, were radically deChristianized, and so able to go the full length, in deifying the nation-state. But the nature of the nation-state so deified had radically changed, through the introduction of the Germanic concept of the need to defend the purity of the *Volk*. The deification of a racist nation-state, biologically inimical to certain other races, produced a modern Moloch, and the Holocaust.

The Nation in Arms

HEW STRACHAN

I

The French Revolution also inaugurated a revolution in warfare. That is the conventional textbook generalization, and – for all its begging of the question as to what constitutes a revolution – it is probably accurate. Yet the changes which 1789 marks are not the customary points of reference by which military historians carve up their subject-matter. France underwent no industrial revolution at the end of the eighteenth century. No great technological innovation, comparable with the adoption of the spur or the introduction of gunpowder, occurred in 1789. Indeed the weaponry with which the revolutionary armies were equipped would have been recognizable to the soldiers of Louis XIV a hundred years earlier. The smooth-bore musket with which the French infantrymen fought right through to 1815 was of a pattern adopted in 1777; the French even spurned the greater sophistication and accuracy of rifled barrels adopted by light infantry units in most European armies in the last decades of the eighteenth century.

The revolution in warfare which 1789 triggered did affect tactics just as directly as would have the adoption of new technology. But the change was not technical; it was intellectual and, above all, political. It established definitively a link between political rights and civic responsibilities. The citizen, in return for the legal freedom which the state now guaranteed him, came under an obligation to shoulder a musket in defence of the nation. Thus the moral power of the state reached its greatest possible extent: in exchange for guaranteeing the natural rights of man, the state could demand the willingness to accept discipline, danger and ultimately death in its defence. What transformed warfare was therefore a revolution in the power of the state, acting in the name of the general will. Military service, from having been the lot of a small section of society, could now in theory be truly universal. Armies might fight with the same weapons, but their reserves of available manpower could be dramatically increased, and their reasons for waging war identified individual self-interest with the interests of the state.

The *philosophes* of the eighteenth century had sketched out the theory of such a change in warfare, seeing it as a necessary corollary of constitutional development. Jean-Jacques Rousseau recognized both the principle of universal military service, and the justification on which it might rest. In a 'new people', where the common interest flourished, 'The life which [the individual] devotes to the State', he wrote in *The Social Contract* (1762), 'is, by the State continually protected, and, when he offers it in the State's defence, what else is he doing than giving back the very boon which he has received at its hands?'[1]

However, although the theory of the nation in arms had been made explicit before 1789, the National Assembly did not in that year rush to put principle into practice. That the French Revolution marked the introduction of a dramatically new form of army organization was entirely the product of expedience. The comte de Guibert, the military theorist most clearly influenced by the ideas of the Enlightenment, spoke warmly of citizen soldiers in his *Essai génèral de la tactique* (1772). But his model was the Roman republic: he saw citizen soldiers as qualitively better than the vagabonds whom he characterized as the staple recruits of his own day. Citizen armies, he was able to argue in a later book of 1779, were no substitute for regular forces, and his search for a better class of soldier did not constitute a case for a quantitative increase in military manpower. The Assembly, when it debated the issue at the end of 1789, reflected Guibert's view. Although it affirmed the principle of military service as a civic obligation, it resisted a

[1] J. J. Rousseau, *The Social Contract*, Book II, ch. IV.

proposal for a national citizen army. The Assembly needed a strong army to carry through a moderate revolution, to check radicalism on the one hand and counter-revolution on the other. To give effect to the former aim, it avoided the arming of the masses, it rejected conscription and it endorsed the professional army. The term of service was fixed in March 1791 as eight years. But, to guard against the possibility of counter-revolutionary influences being transmitted by noble officers, the Assembly took steps to make the army directly answerable to itself. In July 1791 it sent the first *commissaires* to serve with the army to ensure the latter's loyalty to the constitution. By improving conditions of service, rendering the military disciplinary code comparable with civilian law, increasing pay, and opening the ranks to all, the Assembly wooed the soldier. Furthermore, the particularisms of individual regiments were ousted in favour of a more truly national spirit – numbers replaced regimental titles, and foreign units were removed from French service. But none of this was planned. The Assembly responded to circumstances, and what it did was essentially reforming rather than revolutionary.[2]

Two successive pressures, both outwith the immediate control of the Assembly, determined the reshaping of the French army. The first was domestic: the army did not remain immune from the effect of the Revolution on French society as a whole, and under its impact the old royal army disintegrated. Secondly, the external threat, the creation of a coalition against revolutionary France, had the result of fusing the army with the Revolution and the nation and of justifying desperate measures in the defence of both.

The royal army of 1789 was not a balanced representation of the population of France. Of its 10,000 officers, 90 per cent were noble, the majority of them poorer, provincial nobles who had traditional links with the army. Like their civilian equivalents, these officers found themselves excluded from the higher ranks of their

[2] The most important recent works on the impact of the French Revolution on the army are Jean-Paul Bertaud, *La Révolution armée: les soldats-citoyens et la révolution française* (Paris, 1979); John A. Lynn, *The Bayonets of the Republic: Motivation and Tactics in the Army of Revolutionary France, 1791–94* (Urbana, Illinois, 1984); Samuel F. Scott, *The Response of the Royal Army to the French Revolution: the Role and Development of the Line Army 1787–1793* (Oxford, 1978).

calling by the richer and grander nobility of the court. They also feared the challenge of newly ennobled wealth, but measures in the 1780s to shore up their own professionalism had successfully restricted this particular threat. Furthermore, only about a thousand officers were commoners, and many of them were to be found in the technical arms to which the now better educated nobles also gravitated. More surprising than the composition of the officer corps was that of the ranks. Urban backgrounds accounted for 19 per cent of the French population but for 34 per cent of infantry soldiers and over half of the sergeants. Peasants constituted 80 per cent of the French people but under a quarter of the French army. Half the army was aged under twenty-five. Because the army was disproportionately young, urban and artisan, and particularly so among its NCOs, it was potentially more revolutionary in composition than if it had been genuinely representative of society as a whole.

The bond that held the royal army together, a sense of professional pride, fell victim to the circumstances of 1789. Troops brought into Paris to keep order were inadequately fed and poorly accommodated. Serving in detachments, they were removed from the influence of their officers, and frequented the cafés and political clubs, listening to the debates of the day and learning to cloak professional grievances in the rhetoric of revolution. The incidence of insubordination in the line army increased almost sevenfold between 1788 and 1789. In 1790 the rate of desertion was almost 5 per cent (compared with below 2 per cent in 1788); discharges were running at four or five times their pre-revolutionary figures, and enlistments were down by between a half and a third. The officers, frustrated by the ambivalence of the National Assembly towards them, and increasingly undermined by Jacobin influence, found their authority challenged. Any lingering professionalism and sense of loyalty to the king were ended by Louis' abortive flight to Varennes, and from June 1791 officers emigrated at an increasing rate. By the end of 1791 6,000 had gone. In the space of two years, the royal army of 1789 had to all intents and purposes been dissolved.

Parallel with the decline of the line army, and indeed a major contribution to it, was the emergence of a new force, the National Guard. A key factor in thc pcasantry's hatred of the pre-1789 army had been the auxiliary force, the militia, whose numbers were conscripted by ballot, and which had acted as a reserve for the regular army. The Assembly, reflecting the grievances presented to the Estates General, decided at the end of 1789 to abolish the ballot and to replace the militia with volunteers. As with its management of the line army, the Assembly hoped to raise a force which would be a counterweight to aristocratic and monarchical influence on the one hand, and would protect property and curb radical excess on the other. By 1790 2.5 million men had joined the National Guard. Its bourgeois nature was confirmed in April 1791 when it was organized into battalions, and enrolment was limited to those who paid annual taxes equivalent to three days' labour or more. In June the Assembly, anxious to have its own force free from royal influence, voted to call for volunteers to serve for one campaign. The role of the National Guard was no longer purely domestic, but the Assembly still saw the volunteers as a supplement to the regular army, not a substitute. However, the conditions of service in the two bodies were very different: not only was the pay of the National Guard better and its period of service less, but also it elected its own officers. For the ambitious NCO of the regular army, it provided an opportunity for promotion. In the main the volunteers of 1791 were young (79 per cent were under twenty-five); the officers came from professional backgrounds and contained a good leavening of military competence; and the social composition of the ranks, including shopkeepers, clerks, and construction workers, bore comparison with the high quality of that of the line.

In 1792 the Assembly continued its dual policy of fostering the line and the National Guard. Its response to the outbreak of war in April, the declaration *la patrie est en danger* of 12 July, set a target of 50,000 recruits for the regulars and forty-two more volunteer battalions. The Assembly's faith in the line did not go unrewarded: the combination of hunger and popular enthusiasm boosted enlistments to the point where the regulars' strength topped 180,000 early in 1793. Furthermore, the social and political profile of the line army was very different from that of 1789. Peasants now constituted 38 per cent of the total, and artisans and shopkeepers only 48 per cent: both socially and geographically the army was more representative of French society. Furthermore, most of the army had enlisted since 1789, was young, and was fired with revolutionary and patriotic sentiment. The vacancies in the officer corps had been filled, in the highest ranks, by the impoverished but professionally minded nobility and in the battalions by former NCOs. In 1793 70 per cent of regimental officers had had experience in the ranks, and 85 per cent of lieutenants had been sergeants four years previously. The line had changed its composition and its *mentalité*, but had not forfeited its professionalism.

However, it was the behaviour and attributes of the volunteers of 1792 that were far more striking. Rather than forty-two battalions, two hundred and seventy-five were raised. Enrolments outstripped expectation: Paris had been set a target of two battalions but raised thirty-one. The 1792 volunteers have been characterized as the army of the *sans-culottes*: physically and financially they represented a poorer slice of society than had the volunteers of 1791. The level of military experience was less than in 1791, and, although many officers were bourgeois, none was noble and more were peasants. The instruction and discipline of the 1792 volunteers did not match those of 1791, even if as a body they were more truly representative of equality and fraternity. Nor were they all enthusiastic soldiers. In November 1792 France had 450,000 men under arms; by February less than 300,000 remained, and most of those were regulars. Desertion in 1793 ran at 8 per cent: peasants returned to their land, volunteers regarded their commitment as met after one year. With the battle of Jemappes in November 1792, the immediate danger to the French frontiers had been removed, and in the winter the army dispersed to feed, so undermining cohesion and control yet further. The decision in February 1793 to declare war on Britain and the Dutch Netherlands, and to invade the latter, was accompanied by a levy of 300,000 men. Although all single men aged eighteen to forty were permanently requisitioned, and thus the principle of conscription adopted, replacements were allowed and voluntary enlistments were to be tried first. Departments, left to their own devices, administered the call for men in different ways. In the south and west of France, and also among peasants anxious about the spring sowing, reluctance to enlist was particularly marked: the Pyrénées fell 79 per cent below its target. At best 150,000 men were raised.

The French army was in a mess. In the field, it suffered defeats at Neerwinden in March 1793 and at Valenciennes in May. Dumouriez, the commander of the Armée du Nord, fled to the allies. Structurally, the varying conditions of service and patterns of organization stood in the way of rational management. From late 1792, demands for the unification of the National Guard and the line grew. The crisis reached by the summer of 1793 swept away any resistance to such proposals. The amalgamation of one regular battalion with two volunteer battalions in *demi-brigades*, begun informally in 1792, was approved in June 1793 and was extended to include the fusion of volunteers and regulars in the same companies. Thus the former could impart their revolutionary *élan* to the latter, and the latter could share their standards of military competence. Although the bulk of the restructuring was complete by the end of 1794, the process was not finished until 1796. By mixing localities and backgrounds, the *amalgame* created an army united by a sense of nationality and patriotism.

The transformation of the French army was therefore a slow process, a succession of *ad hoc* decisions, not the imposition of a theoretical blueprint. Even now, although more genuinely a citizen army than it had been in 1789, it did not incorporate truly universal conscription. The coping-stone, the declaration of the *levée en masse* on 23 August 1793, was the product of both ideology and pragmatism. The Committee of Public Safety, finding the Revolution assailed from within and without, responded with the Terror. Counter-revolution in the Vendée and elsewhere, prompted not least by resistance to conscription, was accompanied by defeat on the frontiers. Dumouriez's treason was symptomatic of the political unreliability of France's generals: of 1,378 generals in service between 1792 and 1799, 994 were to be relieved of their duties or even guillotined, 67 being executed in 1794 alone. Jacobin pressure for a *levée en masse* was in part a doctrinaire wish to swamp the generals in a truly democratic and revolutionary army; it was also a response to dwindling manpower and the failure of the February levy. The Convention's declaration of 23 August, in itself a stirring piece of propaganda, has become the classic statement of the nation in arms:

> From this moment until that when the enemy is driven from the territory of the republic, every Frenchman is permanently requisitioned for the needs of the armies. The young men will go to the front: the married men will forge arms, and carry food: the women will make tents and clothing and work hospitals: the children will turn old linen into bandages: the old men will be carried into the squares to rouse the courage of the combatants, and to teach hatred of kings, and the unity of the republic.

The levy was rapidly implemented. In practice some minor departures from the ideal of universality occurred, but in principle all men aged eighteen to twenty-five were called up. Where revolutionary enthusiasm was strong, in Paris, the towns and the traditional recruiting areas on the frontiers, the measure was welcomed. Peasant resistance, in the abstract to centralized government, and in reality to leaving their land, was greater and spilled into counter-revolution. Nonetheless peasants, who constituted the bulk of the population, formed also the bulk of the levy. Only 16 per cent of the men requisitioned came from the towns – a dramatic turn-round from the profile of the recruits in 1789. The total size of the French army in the winter of 1793–4 is hard to compute: the flow of deserters, sick, and prisoners, and the inaccuracy of returns all combined to give a fluctuating figure. But the effective strength was in the region of 750,000 men, and one estimate, albeit high, is that France had a million men under arms in August 1794.

How different was the French army of 1794 from that of the eighteenth century? How truly revolutionary was the nation in arms? The simple statistical answers, that only 5 per cent of the army had enrolled before 1789, and that 77 per cent of the army was aged under twenty-five, are in danger of obscuring more fundamental continuities. Half the officers were professional soldiers, and this was more true the higher the rank. Thus 87.3 per cent of generals had been serving in 1789, 73.1 per cent of battalion commanders, and 59.6 per cent of captains. What these men owed to the Revolution was not their calling as soldiers but their rank: of the captains 54.8 per cent had been corporals, and even of the generals 22.9 per cent had been NCOs. The links with the old line army were not completely ruptured.

Furthermore, the principle of conscription, the creation of large armies, and their link to the increasing power of the state all had their eighteenth-century precursors. The received wisdom on eighteenth-century armies, that they were recruited from mercenaries or from a narrow and underprivileged section of the population, that they were small, and that they fought limited wars, is not the whole truth. Conscription, in a restricted form, was practised. The canton system, which gave a regiment a locality in which to recruit, and which called up the peasant for a period of training every year, was developed in Sweden in the seventeenth century, and was applied in Prussia in the early 1730s and in Austria in 1770–81. In France itself, Louis XIV adopted conscription for the part-time militia, and increasingly the French militia was used as a reserve for the regular army. Although all these systems were hedged about with numerous exemptions and allowed the principle of substitution, and although none of them equated civic rights with civic duties, they did enable large armies to be formed and make military service a widespread experience. Probably one in six Frenchmen had been called to arms by the end of Louis XIV's reign: about 2.5 per cent of the total population had served in the War of Spanish Succession, and the army's field strength in war rose from 150,000 to 400,000. Prussia, with a smaller population, enrolled 25 per cent of its eligible male population at one stage of the Seven Years War, and in general recruited 4.2 per cent of its total population. For comparison, France had about 2.5 per cent of its population under arms in 1794, and 1.2 per cent in 1800.

The strength on paper of the French army at the end of the eighteenth century was greater than it had been at the beginning more because the population had grown than because the burden of military service on the individual was increased. Furthermore the chief factor keeping armies small, the constraints on their command and supply in the field, was little different. Eighteenth-century commanders had reckoned that about 50,000 men was the maximum that an individual could direct in battle. At Fleurus on 26 June 1794, Jourdan had over 70,000 troops under his command, but most battles fought in the revolutionary and Napoleonic wars until Wagram in 1809 (where Napoleon's army was 160,000 strong) involved smaller armies, whose sizes were no greater than those of the eighteenth century. The manpower mobilized by the Revolution gave France an advantage of a rather different nature. The close-order formation of eighteenth-century warfare meant that once armies were engaged in combat they suffered losses at a much higher level over a shorter period than was true even in the First World War: 30 per cent casualties in a single day were not uncommon, and armies therefore engaged in battle infrequently. The individual battles in which revolutionary France engaged were less intense (judged by their casualty rates) but they were much more frequent. Conscription permitted France to engage in successive battles, to sustain losses over a longer period, and thus to apply the manpower superiority which conscription gave her.

It was of course victory in battle that hallowed the nation in arms. If France's armies had not won, then there might have been no long-term challenge to regular and professional armies. Furthermore, those victories cannot be accounted for by many of the conventional explanations. Manpower alone did not give the revolutionary armies their successes. Tactically, the army did stand at the climax of a long process of gestation and debate in French military thought, albeit one whose origins and main conclusions were apparent before 1789. The infantry ordinance of 1791 finally achieved a solution to the debate between the advocates of the shock and mobility of the column and those of the concentrated fire of the line. The 1791 ordinance established regulations whereby infantry could approach the battle in column, deploy into line to fire, and then reform column without a great loss of time and momentum. The authors of the ordinance had seen the column as a means of movement not of attack. The popular cult of the bayonet, and even of the pike, in revolutionary France found expression in the use of the column for assault. The loss of firepower inherent in the use of attack columns was compensated for in three ways. The first was the adoption of horse artillery in the winter of 1791–2. Secondly, infantry battalions had their own integral artillery. Finally, the refusal to adopt the rifle reflected the view that light infantry was not a specialist arm but a role for all infantry. The rifle was slower to load than the musket, and by retaining the latter French infantry achieved a higher rate of fire – even if it was more inaccurate. In 1793 the whole army might – as it did at the battle of Hondschoote – disperse and fire. Between 1794 and 1796 the French developed their tactical hallmark, the use of light infantry to screen and support attack columns.

It is the more extensive use of light infantry that is the key to understanding the difference between the French nation in arms and its unreformed rivals. For most of the eighteenth century, the duties of light troops lay not on the battlefield but in petty war, patrolling, raiding and so on. Furthermore their numbers were restricted because in dispersed formations the soldier needed to be self-reliant, intelligent and loyal. Given the opportunity to operate independently, many pressed men would display insufficient initiative or would desert. Discipline for skirmishers needed to be enlightened, not repressive, to stimulate the skills of the individual. Embedded in the more extensive use of light infantry, and the application of their techniques to the main battle itself, was the elevation of the soldier to citizenship.

The French could therefore skirmish and disperse on a larger scale than their opponents because their soldiers could be trusted. The fundamental difference between the French armies and those of their enemies lay not in the externals of manpower or tactics (important though both these were), but in motivation. The will to win stamped itself on the armies of revolutionary France. Without it, they could never have absorbed so many men over such a short period and yet mastered through assiduous training the drills of battlefield tactics. For the abilities to deploy speedily from line to column and to skirmish effectively were the qualities of well-trained and competent troops. Furthermore, the training complete, the general doctrine enunciated for the revolutionary armies, that of the offensive *à l'outrance*, demanded that technical proficiency be combined with high morale.

Students of morale in the Second World War have emphasized the importance of the small group, the rifle section: soldiers, they contend, fight for their mates, not for their regiments or their countries. The French army was divided into *ordinaires*, fourteen to sixteen men who would mess together and who were commanded by a corporal. Furthermore, although the Revolution had crushed regimental particularisms, it had actively promoted fraternity. Thus the *élan* of the French soldier is in part accounted for by the primary group. In addition the rapidity of promotion, the possibility of elevation from the ranks, stimulated and rewarded ambition.

These, however, are purely military determinants of morale. What is also striking is how intensely political the soldiers of 1794 were. The suspicion of generals and their victimization by the Committee of Public Safety reflected the permeation of the army by the Jacobins. The Committee's Representatives on Mission had almost unlimited powers to ensure political orthodoxy. The *sans-culottes*, introduced into the army by the successive levies, also brought in the means of purveying popular culture, disseminated in the press, in songs such as 'Le Chant du départ', and to a lesser extent in political clubs. Above all the soldier, unlike his white-coated predecessor in the royal army, had not cast off his status as a citizen when he donned the blue coat of the Revolution. The army was genuinely popular: soldiers were present at festivals and marriages, their presence gave authority to the proceedings, they became symbols of the new order. Society came to reflect the army as much as the army reflected society. Fashion aped military uniform. Thus was the soldier's calling validated: he was no longer engaged in a trade, but fighting for a cause. If he died, he was venerated and he had fallen for *la patrie*. Patriotism may not be a major factor in the morale of twentieth-century Western armies, but the evidence for France in the 1790s suggests it would be unwise to generalize from this experience. It breathed ferocity into France's soldiers. The *sans-culottes* applied the Terror to war. In the eighteenth century codes of honour operated between soldiers. By 1794 such attitudes were symptoms of an outmoded restraint. The war was one of rival political systems, to be fought without limit, the enemy – the Committee of Public Safety instructed – was to be pursued 'until he is utterly destroyed'.

But the Terror was a response to a crisis. The *levée en masse* was still not seen as a form of permanent military organization: it was a temporary solution, a once-and-for-all effort to rid the Revolution of its enemies, both external and internal. Furthermore, once the immediate danger had been ended, and France's soldiers had progressed beyond the frontiers, the justification for the nation in arms was less apparent. Twenty to thirty thousand troops were requisitioned each year between 1794 and 1797. Deserters, having fallen to 4 per cent in 1794, had reached 8 per cent again in 1796, and in August 1797 the strength of the army was 381,909. Experience and campaigning reasserted military values over Jacobinism. The suppression of the *commissaires aux armées* in December 1796 removed any direct political control over the generals, and the army – now fusing its republicanism with professionalism – was free to be an independent political actor. Increasingly it saw itself as an ideal version of what France should be, not the representative of what France actually was. When conscription was institutionalized, with the *loi* Jourdan in 1798, only 74,000 of 143,000 passed fit for service actually reached the army. In 1799 the principle of truly universal service was undermined with provision for volunteers and replacements. Married men and, after 1801, seminarists were exempted. Increasingly the burden of soldiering fell on the poorer sector of the eligible male population. Thus did the nation in arms pass from actuality to rhetoric; thus also could the army's conviction that it possessed qualities lacking in civil society remain unchallenged.

Napoleon's rise to power confirmed the trend. Between 1800 and 1812, 4,340,000 men reached military age in France, but only 1,437,000 were drafted. By 1806 official replacements made up 4.5 per cent of those taken, and this figure excludes any private arrangements. The *Grande Armée* grew to sizes comparable with the total of 1794: in 1812 Napoleon had 630,000 men in Russia and a further 250,000 in Spain, but two-thirds of the former were foreigners. The army was no longer national; it was no longer representative of society as a whole; and it was no longer the avenue for advancement. Despite its expansion, the current of promotion slowed. Napoleon favoured the wealthy, the bourgeois and even the old nobles as his officers. Furthermore, in the Empire's own nobility, it was the army that dominated. With its glorification of military achievement, Napoleon's France tried to reconstitute the nation in the army's image, not vice versa. After all, the Revolution had embraced the nation in arms through force of circumstances; its underlying lack of enthusiasm for the concept in practice (as opposed to theory) ensured that the principle was not long sustained. The justification for the nation in arms was the defence of France; once France's armies were clearly committed to the offensive, to conquest, and to protracted campaigning, the political legitimacy of the nation in arms had gone.

II

The original nation in arms may have been short-lived, but its influence has been continuous. The growth of state-power, the increasing legitimacy of the state's authority over its subjects, and the emergence of nationalism were not transient phenomena. The power they have given states to create mass armies has been hard to resist. The tendency of war, as Clausewitz observed after the experience of the revolutionary and Napoleonic campaigns, is to reach towards absolutes. However, political sense may determine that a nation will employ economy of force, that it will use no greater effort than the circumstances require. The tension between these two pressures is weighted in favour of the former: the risk of defeat, the difficulty of sustained political control during war itself, and – on campaign – the commander's need to concentrate masses on the decisive point have all constituted arguments against self-imposed limitations.

However, what is striking in the short term, over the period from 1794, through the restoration of 1815 and up until the revolutions of 1848, is the reluctance with which the dynastic monarchs of Europe departed from traditional forms of military organization. In the nation in arms revolutionary France had created a powerful military instrument both in motivation and in manpower. But the implications of its adoption were themselves revolutionary. Soldiers needed to have legal rights and political privileges to fight as free citizens; if their talent was to be tapped and their ambition to be fostered the officer corps had to be opened to all comers. Thus, even when Napoleon showed that there were no limits to his ambition, when he had crushed the Austrians and Russians at Austerlitz in 1805 and the Prussians at Jena in 1806, and when he had overthrown the compromise with Russia which the treaty of Tilsit in 1807 offered, the powers of Europe preferred to adopt the trappings of the nation in arms rather than its essence. Tactical proficiency, the more extensive use of light infantry, better training and improved military education were the favoured responses. A preponderance in manpower, as at Leipzig in 1813, was achieved by the coalition of three allies more than by the *levée en masse*. Russia, it is true, did evoke a sense of nationalism in the 1812 campaign, and Austria dithered with a popular national militia in 1807. Prussia alone declared a nation in arms, but only after a prolonged internal debate and against the wishes of the king. The smashing of the Frederician army at Jena had ousted the more ancient and incompetent of the noble officers, and gave the advocates of change their head. The reform of Prussian education and the emancipation (albeit with limitations) of her serfs began the process of turning subjects into citizens, and of creating opportunities for the talented and educated. In 1813, with Napoleon's retreat from Russia, a popular militia was formed to carry through a national revolt against France. The king was forced to introduce conscription, without exemption, for the duration of the war.

In 1813 Prussia put 6 per cent of her total population into the field. However, although the price of victory over Napoleon therefore implied an elevation of nationalism over dynasticism, the effects did not survive the peace. Peacetime contraction restored the aristocratic dominance of the officer corps, and in 1819 in

Prussia the reactionaries succeeded in subordinating the *Landwehr*, the popular auxiliary force designed to counterbalance the regular army, to the latter. The reformers in Prussia had hoped that military innovations would inaugurate constitutional change. But the European monarchs saw their armies in very different terms. They were to be long-service (except in Prussia where at least the principle of short-service was retained) and professional, a bulwark against revolution and not an agent of reform. Small and drawn once again from a narrow sector of society, divided from the civil population by seven (in France from 1832) or more years of service, armies were the forces of counter-revolution in 1848. Protracted service outside their own homelands was the lot of many nineteenth-century soldiers, the French in North Africa and the British in India, or the Austrians in Italy and the Russians in the Caucasus, and thus was the divorce between the nation and the army made real.

Since 1815 the ideas associated with the nation in arms have fallen into three principal strands. Revolution was the first and most immediate link, and the major source of monarchical abhorrence. The *sans-culottes* had fought for France because the nation and the Revolution were mutually dependent, and their war had been one against kings. Secondly France had, by the *levée en masse*, created a true citizen army with which to defend herself. Frenchmen, animated by patriotism, had temporarily put aside their usual callings to form a mass amateur army. And thirdly, in France the state had arrogated to itself the power to conscript without formally renouncing the line army: thus professionalism and compulsory military service had not been at loggerheads. The ethos of the conscripted army had become professional and regular. Although each of these three strands has not remained entirely distinct in practice, in analytical terms the division is helpful. Furthermore, each of the three can be linked to a particular style of fighting. Revolutionary war has looked to guerrilla tactics; the *levée en masse* justifies its call to arms by the needs of defence; the conscript army is by virtue of its training and greater competence capable of the offensive.

In practice the link between the French nation in arms and either revolutionary or guerrilla war is tenuous. The strength of the Revolution lay in the towns and cities; the bases of guerrilla support are rural. In 1792 the Revolutionaries already controlled France (or most of it). The threat was external, and the efforts to overthrow the domestic government from within were associated with counter-revolution. Indeed the same point could be made about the nationalist uprisings directed against Napoleon elsewhere in Europe. Nor were the tactics of the French in the 1790s – for all their use of skirmishers – those of guerrillas. The most successful guerrilla operations of the Napoleonic wars, those in Spain, were conducted in conjunction with regular armies and had as their object the expulsion of the French not the overthrow of the Spanish monarchy. It is not therefore the fact of revolution which links the French nation in arms to the twentieth-century leaders of guerrilla movements. Guerrillas avoid battle, prey on lines of communication, retreat rather than fight, precisely because they do not embody the power of the state and therefore cannot organize and equip armies. Guerrillas are committed to protracted war, to a war of attrition not the war of annihilation favoured by revolutionary and Napoleonic France. But the theory of guerrilla war, both in its revolutionary objectives and in its means, links the guerrillas themselves to the civilian population. The guerrilla fights on his own ground; he wears no uniform and is indistinguishable from a non-belligerent; he is fed and supplied by the local population. Thus, when the regulars advance against him, he can disappear – figuratively into the rest of the community or actually into the rural fastnesses that are his home. The pre-eminent theorist of rural guerrilla war, Mao Tse-tung, likened the people to water and the guerrillas to the fish who inhabit it. In their purest form, he argued, guerrilla units are organized directly from the people themselves. He would have noted with approval the description of the Chouans in the Vendée, 'in battle as at the doors of their churches on Sunday, they were surrounded by their acquaintances, their kinfolk and their friends.'[3] It is the link between people and armies that

[3] Joseph Clemenceau, quoted in Walter Laqueur, *Guerrilla: a Historical and Critical Study* (London, 1977), 26.

constitutes the link between modern guerrilla war and the nation in arms. Furthermore, the guerrillas claim that their aims are identical with those of the people themselves. Vo Nguyen Giap, the North Vietnamese general, wrote in 1959 of the expulsion of France from Indochina, 'Our resistance war was a people's war, because its political aims were to smash the imperialist yoke in order to win back national independence, to overthrow the feudal landlord class in order to bring land to the peasants.'[4]

If successful, the guerrilla pedigrees of the revolutionary forces have shaped the armed forces of the subsequent governments. In power both Mao and Giap stressed the continuing link between the army and the people. The Vietnam People's Army, Giap stated, 'is the true army of the people, of toilers, the army of workers and peasants, led by the Party of the working class'.[5] Despite wars in Korea, India and Vietnam, the Chinese People's Liberation Army has probably put greater weight on its domestic roles, particularly agriculture, than on its military functions. The army is not only subordinate to the political party, it is also its agent for the accomplishment of the aims of the revolution. Military service is therefore a form of political education, but in reciprocal fashion that political education is also the basis for morale in time of war. As in France in the 1790s, the demands of professionalism, the development of a self-contained military ethos, have challenged the revolutionary foundations of peoples' armies. Purity of political doctrine and competence in military performance can stand in opposition to each other. High manpower levels are incompatible with the cost of sophisticated equipment or training in its use, particularly in relatively underdeveloped countries. In 1983 the strength of the Chinese army was over four million men: its reduction in strength since then is indicative of a shift from political to military priorities, of the creation of a counter-attack capability, and in consequence of a less rigorous emphasis on the political and popular nature of the army.

The second strand of the legacy of the nation in arms, the *levée*

[4] Russell Stetler, ed., *The Military Art of People's War: Selected Writings of General Vo Nguyen Giap* (New York, 1970), 101.
[5] Ibid., 110.

en masse, the citizen army, can obviously be an outgrowth from a people's army. But the links of the citizen army with the armies of revolutionary France are much clearer and more direct. The principal theorist of the citizen army, the French socialist Jean Jaurès – although he also drew inspiration from the Swiss model – devoted much of his book, *L'Armée nouvelle* (written in 1910), to a study of the French revolutionary tradition. Jaurès, worried that a professional army posed an ongoing threat to the political stability of the Third Republic, harked back to the *levée en masse* of 1793 as unifying the nation and the army. To have an army that was subordinate to political authority, and that was truly democratic, military service must be a genuine obligation of citizenship. The period of training should be short, and the army in peacetime would of necessity be small and concerned above all with training. But its strength would be its capacity for rapid expansion: in peace it could constitute no latent threat to its neighbours but in war it would provide a true defence, founded on patriotism and the manpower of the entire nation.

For Jaurès and his contemporaries, and indeed for Marx and Engels, the most immediate application of the citizen army had been that of France in 1870–1. The defeat of the French regular army by the Prussians at Sedan in 1870 and the surrender of Napoleon III had not extinguished French resistance. Léon Gambetta, citing the example of 1792, endeavoured to organize a national rising, based in the provinces and employing guerrilla tactics. All males aged twenty-one to forty were mobolized, and the nation in arms was interpreted to include industrial mobilization. The Prussians won: in the test of citizen militia against standing army the latter was vindicated. The local response was frequently feeble; the partisans were few, elicited little peasant support, and were ruthlessly suppressed by the Prussians.

The French defeat provided ample material to support professional military criticisms of popular militias, and developments in warfare since – with their increasingly sophisticated technical demands on the soldier – have done little to mitigate their validity. Nonetheless, citizen armies are to be found in the contemporary world, although each has developed independently through national circumstances rather than through the imposition of a Jaurèsian blueprint. A small population in Israel has meant that only a citizen army can create a force of sufficient size; mountainous terrain in Switzerland, Sweden and Yugoslavia has favoured the development of guerrilla styles of fighting. Sweden and Yugoslavia have embraced strategies of territorial defence, the latter building on the heritage of guerrilla operations in the Second World War. Territorial defence exploits the civic attributes of a nation's soldiers: they serve in their own localities, they disperse to fight, and so render the whole country a hedgehog, possessed of the capacity for all-round resistance.

However, it has been the example of Israel, with its succession of lightning victories over superior forces, that has most convincingly answered the professional critics. Increasingly, however, the penalty of military efficiency has been the doubts of liberals. Israel has a mobilizable strength of over a million men and women, out of a population of 4.5 million. The result of war is therefore economic dislocation, and Israel's operational strategy has not been that of other citizen armies, defence, with its commitment to long and potentially indecisive war (something for which it is in any case geographically ill-designed), but of pre-emptive attack and a short war. Pre-emption can look like unwarranted aggression, particularly and most recently in the case of the Lebanon. The training demands of modern weapons have been met by a high level of specialization in terms of military skills. They have also involved, since 1967, a period of service of three years for male other ranks. Nineteenth-century socialists, such as Jaurès, regarded such a time span as too long: rather than civilianize the military, compulsory service on these terms would militarize society. There is some evidence that they were right, that creeping militarism is a problem in Israel's society. 'Every civilian', said Yigal Yadin, who as chief of staff helped establish the Israeli defence forces, 'is a soldier on eleven months' annual leave.'[6] Built on such diverse linguistic and cultural backgrounds, Israel has of necessity used the army as a vehicle for the creation of a national identity. But the army has also

[6] Edward Luttwak and Dan Horowitz, *The Israeli Army* (London, 1975), 79.

become a ladder to political success, and in 1982 an independent actor in politics, aping the worst attributes of regular and professional forces.

These last arguments were familiar ones in nineteenth-century Europe where it was the third legacy of the nation in arms that dominated. Conscription operated selectively, the well-off paying for substitutes if they had the misfortune to be balloted for service. Those who served were less likely, not more likely, to enjoy the privileges of citizenship. Until after 1870 long periods of enlistment meant that even conscript armies developed the esprit de corps of professionals. The bourgeois might revile the regular army as an agent of monarchical power but they had no wish to serve themselves: in the 1848 revolution France rejected universal military service. However, the Prussians stuck to short service (two years with the regulars) and so were able to create a large reserve of trained but still relatively youthful men. Their victories over Austria in 1866 and France in 1870 advertised the virtues of short service and large reserves: if France had created a trained reserve, as had been advocated before 1870, it would not have had to resort to the *levée en masse.* German victory hallowed the principles of short service, and during the 1870s and 1880s her neighbours moved towards conscripting a larger proportion of their populations for a more limited period, and then transferring them to a reserve. France in 1914 mobilized 82 per cent of her eligible male population. Behind the standing armies of Europe in 1914, conscription had created the reserves for four and more years of total war.

Compulsory military service in this form was not the agent of democracy but of militarism. Owing to their geographical positions, neither of the leading democracies of the day, Great Britain and the United States, had had recourse to conscription: indeed, there may have been a link between the absence of conscription and the health of liberalism. In 1868, after a long struggle in the Assembly, service with the colours in Prussia was formally increased to three years. Wilhelm I had triumphed over the liberal opposition, and ensured that the soldier be removed from his civilian background, that, if the army was to be the people's, the people themselves should be loyal to the army and to the monarchy. Increasing the annual intake of recruits gave the opportunity for the army to be the school of the nation, or rather of nationalism. In Tsarist Russia, after the introduction of shorter service, the educational role of the army was instruction in reading and writing. But elsewhere it became a focus for bellicose nationalism. Through conscription European society was profoundly marked by military values. In France, where the struggle between citizen armies and professional forces formed a continuing debate (and threat to military efficiency) in the Third Republic, Jaurès and the socialists lost their case, three-year service was enacted in 1913, and in 1914 virtually all France (only 1.5 per cent of recruits failed to report) rallied to fight the Germans.

Much of the argument for longer periods of service rested on the needs of the offensive. Ill-trained citizen armies, the conventional wisdom ran, were good only for defence. The fire-swept battlefield of 1914 required troops to disperse to survive: without the self-reliance and tactical proficiency born of training, soldiers would not attack. The motivation fostered by patriotic *élan* would be insufficient. And, if troops did not attack, wars would become protracted, industry – its manpower conscripted into the army – would languish, and economic chaos and even revolution would follow. The argument may at bottom have rested on the self-interest of professional soldiers but it had logic.

And so in 1914 vast armies, almost all of them conscripted (Britain's was not until 1916), launched a series of tactical and operational offensives which resulted in enormous casualties but ended in stalemate. The pattern of the French revolutionary wars was amplified: what was striking was not the intensity of individual battles, but the continuousness of combat, the capacity to sustain successive battles and to suffer losses at a steady rate. Furthermore, the fact that the war did indeed prove to be long reactivated an aspect of nation-in-arms thought which had been neglected in the Napoleonic emphasis on quick and decisive victory. The declaration of August 1793 had laid the basis for state control of war industries and for the mobilization of technicians and scientists for weapons production. Even more did the First World War demand that the state orientate its entire economic effort to the needs of battle. The crucial issue relating to manpower was not conscription for armed forces but the sensible division of men between the competing but complementary demands of combat and war industry. 'In this war', one of its foremost commanders, Erich Ludendorff, wrote in his memoirs, 'it was impossible to distinguish where the sphere of the Army and Navy began, and that of the people ended. Army and people were one.'[7] British appeasement of Germany in the 1930s was underwritten by a realization that rearmament for European war was incompatible with peacetime capitalistic growth. It was France herself who in the inter-war period took the implications of the First World War for the nation in arms most to heart. Victory had been secured by a short-term reserve army, and therefore in 1928 the period of universal service was set at one year. The Maginot Line would defend France while the army mobilized and war production was put into gear: in 1939 France's nation in arms was preparing for a long war of attrition.

However, military theory elsewhere in the inter-war period reacted against the pattern of the Western Front. The mass army had crushed mobility; short-term enlistments on a large scale had been achieved at the expense of training and tactical efficiency; mechanization, particularly the advent of the tank and the aircraft, promised to restore movement to the battlefield and to re-emphasize the value in training of long-service, regular and smaller armies. If a single machine-gun could do the work of 200 riflemen, then technology might be a substitute for the mass army. Such were the arguments of de Gaulle in France and Liddell Hart and Fuller in Britain. In Germany, restricted to an army of 100,000 men in 1919, such theory came nearer to practical application.

Technology had indeed been used as a substitute for manpower in the latter stages of the Great War. But governments did not then conclude that the mass army no longer had a role. The push to Clausewitz's ideal of absolute war operated: armies would employ both new technology and mass armies, and so multiply their firepower many times over. Furthermore, France's flirtations with

[7] Erich Ludendorff, *My War Memories 1914–1918*, 2 vols. (London, 1920), I, 2.

a Jaurèsian model were not to find much favour elsewhere. The skills required in the maintenance and battlefield drills of the tank and of the aircraft meant that standards of professional competence would be required of conscript forces. The Napoleonic and pre-1914 fusion of a professional ethos with the principle of compulsory service became the twentieth-century norm. Even in revolutionary Russia the arguments for military efficiency outweighed those for ideological purity. Trotsky, the Soviet Union's first Commissar for War, advocated a defensive territorial force. But Frunze, in 1925 his successor as Commissar for War, argued that the revolution must be offensive, and the contributions of Tsarist officers, retained after 1917 for the sake of military efficiency, ensured that by the 1930s the tone of the Red Army was regular and professional.

At least for those who possess them, the advent of nuclear weapons since 1945 ought to have constituted an end to the nation in arms. Beginning in 1953–4 with the doctrine of the American Secretary of State, John Foster Dulles, that of massive retaliation with nuclear weapons in the event of aggression, hydrogen bombs were seen as a substitute for manpower. The new technology, it was argued in Britain in 1957, did replace the mass army: conscription was ended and the economic burden of defence controlled. Even in the Soviet Union, Khrushchev – reflecting some of the Western ideas on the deterrent value of nuclear weapons – in 1960 set a manpower target for the armed forces which was less than half that of 1955. In practice, however, once again new technology was added to the concept of the mass army, but did not replace it. In 1960 Khrushchev still posited active forces of 2.4 million men, and the Soviet Union's 1987 total exceeded 5 million. In resisting conscription Britain and, more recently, the United States, have been exceptional.

The causes of the survival of the nation in arms, the military legacy of the French Revolution, differ according to the nuclear status of a nation. Those countries possessed of nuclear weapons or indirectly protected by them have since the 1960s argued for conventional forces to create a more flexible range of military options. The actual employment of nuclear weapons is seen as incredible and their value is therefore purely political. The doctrinal impetus to rebuilding armies has been reinforced in the 1980s by the arguments of unilateralism: the awfulness of European war fought by mass armies is regarded as preferable to a possible nuclear exchange. Both a fall in the manpower available to Western nations and the need to strike a defensive posture have given fresh life to arguments about citizen armies and territorial defence. The Jaurèsian ideal of the army of the French Revolution still finds its applications. For those states that have not acquired nuclear weapons, wars – like that between Iran and Iraq – can still involve mass armies engaged in attritional battles, resting their hopes for victory on manpower and motivation. In peace, many countries still find value in this last aspect of the nation in arms. For newly formed states, the army is an agent in the process of national integration. It renders the Bedouin tribesman a Jordanian, the Serb or the Croat a Yugoslav. Furthermore, in a preindustrial or even industrializing society, the army is by virtue of its sophisticated weaponry the means by which the peasant is trained in the use of modern technology, in which mechanical skills are disseminated. And, if war does come, then the fact that the army is the school of the nation may mean that patriotic fervour will carry its soldiers into battle as it did those of France in 1793.

Revolutionary Ideology and 'The Great French Revolution of 1789–?'

EUGENE KAMENKA

I

The French Revolution, Alexis de Tocqueville wrote in a famous passage of his *L'Ancien régime et la révolution*,

> seemed to lead to the renewal of mankind and not merely to the reform of France. It inflamed a passion such as even the most violent political revolutions had hitherto not been able to produce. It inspired conversion and gave rise to propaganda. In this way, it eventually assumed that appearance of religious revolution which so appalled contemporaries; even more, it became itself a kind of new religion . . . which . . . has flooded the world with its fighters, its apostles and its martyrs.[1]

The Great French Revolution, as many Marxists now call it, was able to do so, Tocqueville and Hegel and Marx all confirm, because it was a 'world-historical' event. It was a local and particular uprising that contained a universal soul. For that reason, it shook Europe and the world. It inaugurated a political and intellectual crisis, carried further in the Napoleonic wars, that dominated the history of Europe till 1920 and that of Asia to the 1940s and 1950s.

No one was better aware than Tocqueville that the Revolution

[1] Alexis de Tocqueville, *L'Ancien régime et la révolution* (Paris, 1856) Book I, ch.3.

was a complex phenomenon with a multiplicity of causes. There were long-standing and general causes, and specific and recent causes, causes that were part of the special and often accidental history of France and causes that were part of wider European and 'Atlantic' developments. No one knew better than Tocqueville of the *continuities* that can and do underlie revolutionary transformation. For him, the French Revolution created neither a new people nor a new France. It was the culmination, rather, of long-term trends in the society of the *ancien régime* – some of them radical (trends toward democracy), some of them bureaucratic-administrative (trends toward the centralization of power that emerged from the victory of absolutist monarchs over the true feudal aristocracy). Implicit in Tocqueville's analysis of the passion displayed in and engendered by the Revolution, however, and implicit in the position the French Revolution occupied and occupies in the consciousness of the world around it, is the recognition that it constitutes not only the culmination of past histories, but the dawn of a new ideological age.

History may truly belong to the past, or it may not. The study of the French Revolution, as François Furet reminds us in a brilliant work,[2] continues to arouse in the historian and his public a capacity for identifying with the political and religious passions of the Revolution in a way which shows that they continue to express the issues of each historian's own times, his values and his choices. It is this recognition that gives the French Revolution its special status in history and ideology as an unfinished, unconsummated revolution whose values and problems continue to live, and whose very dates are uncertain: did it end in 1794, 1799, 1804 or even 1814? That is not true, in anything like the same way, of the Roman Republic or the Merovingian kings.

The eighteenth century, Leonard Krieger[3] and others have argued, saw a shift from the authority of origins to a teleological authority of ends in which governments began to derive their

[2] François Furet, *Interpreting the French Revolution* (trans., Cambridge and Paris, 1981), 1–2.

[3] Leonard Krieger, *An Essay on the Theory of Enlightened Despotism* (Chicago, 1975), 52–6.

legitimacy from their claim to promote human happiness. In the earlier part of the century, Furet reminds us, 'the theme of Clovis and the Frankish invasions was of burning interest ... because historians of that era saw it as the key to the social structure of their time. They thought that the Frankish invasions were the origin of the division between nobility and commoners, the conquerors being the progenitors of the nobility and the conquered those of the commoners.' In the conquest itself lay the legitimizing foundation of aristocratic society. In France, by 1789, 'the obsession with origins, the underlying thread of all national history, came to be centred precisely on the revolutionary break ... 1789 became the birth date, the year zero of a new world founded on equality.'[4] This the Abbé Sieyès had proclaimed already a few months before the Revolution in his great and influential pamphlet *Qu'est-ce-que le Tiers état*? Of course, to proclaim the dawn of a new age, the French Revolutionaries had to invent terms and definitions, had to redescribe the bad old age. They popularized the terms *féodalité* and *ancien régime* to dramatize the magnitude of their break with the past. The new age substituted the concept of the citizen for that of the subject, of the people for the monarch, of the nation for the dynasty. In place of 'liberties' and privileges attached to estates, corporate bodies and regional associations, it put liberty and rights of human beings as such; in place of authority, humility and obedience, it put equality, self-determination and fraternity; in place of religion as a social public institution, the voice of reason and the common good, the *volonté générale*. In these slogans and aspirations, and not in the aping of past Republican virtues, lies the basic ideological significance of the French Revolution for its own time and for subsequent times. It goes, in this respect, beyond both the English and the American Revolutions. Whatever the motives and beliefs of those involved, whatever the contingent accidents that radicalized the initial course of events and led to the deposition and execution of the king, there was no way, by 1791, of escaping the momentous implications of a new democratic order and no way, by 1793, of failing to see the lengths to which egalitarianism

[4] Furet, *op. cit.*, 2–3

can be pressed – against stability, against property, against social distinctions in fact as well as in law. In relation to the surrounding dynastic empires, the Revolution – like the American, but much more obviously so – is subversive from the start; in relation to the concept of a democratic *order*, the Revolution quickly reveals itself as having potentialities for further radicalization, for a revolution *en permanence*, in a way the American did not. Hegel, perceptive as ever, saw it as introducing a new age of rapid change and increasing instability, an age that would stand under the category of 'becoming'.

For Marxists, later, especially for those of the Second International, the driving force of this instability was an economic process, not a political event. But the French Revolution appeared to them to exemplify to a startling extent the second great motive power of history, the class struggle, brought about by those economic events. At one level, the French Revolution, for them, was the great bourgeois revolution that expressed in more coherent and developed form the necessary assumptions, the conditions of existence of the new bourgeois economic order shaking itself free of the constraints of feudalism. But it also exemplified the divergence of interests, among those opposing feudalism, between the property-owner and the propertyless, between the rich and the poor, between the bourgoisie and the *menu peuple*, soon to become proletarians. The political force that stiffened 'the will of the bourgeoisie', that assured its success and constantly drove it further than it wanted to go, Marxists could stress, was the pressure from below, violence and the threat of violence by 'the people' themselves. Not the 'Oath of the Tennis Court' but the riots in Paris and the fall of the Bastille inaugurated the Revolution, the National Guard and the *tricoleur*; not the National Constituent Assembly but the march of the women on Versailles transferred the capital of France and subjected the king to the power of the populace; not a constitution but the storming of the Tuileries brought about the end of the monarchy. Behind the radicalization of the Revolution between 1791 and 1793 stood not only the Cordelier and the Jacobin Clubs, but the people of Paris, the Paris of the forty-eight sections and 'imperative mandates', of bread riots, of the *journées*. Was it not the *sans-culotte* and *enragé* leader, Jacques Roux, who told the National Convention in June 1793: 'Liberty is a hollow sham if one class can deprive another of food with impunity. Liberty is meaningless where the rich may exercise the power of life and death over their fellows with impunity.'[5] And did it not signal the end of the Revolution, the establishment of a bourgeois order and not of 'Liberty, Equality, Fraternity', when the Thermidorian moderate, François-Antoine de Boissy d'Anglas, presented to the Convention on 23 June 1795 a new constitution? Its purpose was, he said, 'finally to guarantee the property of the rich and the existence of the poor; to guarantee to the industrious man the fruits of his labour and to assure liberty and security for all'. Property, Boissy d'Anglas assured the Convention, was the foundation of the social order; the man without property must strive endlessly to achieve the virtue required to concern himself with a political order in which he has no stake. His chances, in Boissy d'Anglas's view, were not high and the Convention 'must resist with courage the fallacious maxims of absolute democracy and unlimited equality. Civil equality offers all that the reasonable man could wish for. Total equality is an illusion.' For 'a country ruled by property owners exists in a social state; one ruled by the propertyless is in a state of nature.'[6]

Exciting as such reflections in and about the French Revolution may have been at the end of the eighteenth and in the first half of the nineteenth century, they have become commonplace now. The seemingly obvious commonplace arouses in the subtle and scholarly a desire to delve more deeply, to reveal greater complexity and ambiguity. Who would say of late that the French Revolution was 'made by the bourgeoisie'? Not even Albert Soboul, who began his summary of a life's work on the French Revolution with the sentence: 'The bourgeoisie did not make the French Revolution. The French Revolution made the bourgeoisie.' In the contrasuggestible, of course, the commonplace arouses an even greater desire

[5] Cited by G. F. E. Rudé, 'The French Revolution and "Participation"', in Eugene Kamenka, ed., *A World in Revolution?* (Canberra, 1970), 20.

[6] Cited in Albert Soboul, *A Short History of the French Revolution 1789–1799* (trans., Berkeley and Los Angeles, 1977), 127–9.

to qualify, to discredit excessive simplicity, to urge the merits of contrary interpretations. Nor do historians ever have difficulty in exposing the myth of discontinuity, in showing that the radical new departure has in fact numerous antecedents and precursors – a whole prehistory that makes its novelty less striking. Nevertheless, it is patently true that Europe and Latin America by the end of the nineteenth century, and Asia, Africa and the Pacific by the last quarter of the twentieth century, have come to stand in the shadow of the French Revolution, to live in the world history and in the new age inaugurated by that Revolution and symbolized by it. The appeal to reason, the elevation of the people as sovereign and of their welfare as constituting the point of government, the doctrine of progress, the acceptance of revolutionary ideologies and revolutionary transformations are a basic part of the modern world. For two hundred years, it has been impossible to speak of nationalism – a frightening new concept in the 1790s, e.g. to Augustin Barruel who denounced it under the name of 'patriotism' as a form of egoism – of socialism and democracy, of self-determination for peoples and nations, of government by law and of the belief in human rights, of socialism or 'the people's' demands, of revolutionary tactics and revolutionary ideologies, of 'secular' education, political propaganda and the state's role in promoting 'enlightenment', of popular participation, factional struggles and class conflicts, without thinking of or unconsciously echoing themes introduced by the French Revolution. In France the struggle between revolution and restoration has been seen by many as continuing right to the beginning of the Third Republic, passing through various episodes in 1815, 1830, 1848, 1851, 1870, the Paris Commune and 16 May 1877. The legitimacy of the Republic, indeed, as Furet has stressed, ceased being a point at issue in France only with the fall of Pétain and the defeat of Hitler. In Europe generally, the nineteenth century, or at least the first half of it, became the age of revolutions, consciously drawing inspiration from the revolutionary tradition in France. In Africa and Asia, in the Americas and the Pacific, in Moscow and Peking, the Revolution lives or has lived. French academics have or had it right when they divided the history syllabus into 'modern' history up to 1789 and 'contemporary' history from 1814 to the present, with the revolutionary and Napoleonic era forming a separate transitional and inaugural chapter.[7] If we must draw a line, that is where we would draw it. Neither the 'English Revolution' (i.e. the Civil War and the Protectorate) nor even the American speak to the world at large with the directness and comprehensiveness, with the urgency and apparent universality, that the thoughts and deeds of 1789–99, and even the Napoleonic Wars, carry with them. The French Revolution continues to legitimize or to undermine many of its most cherished hopes and beliefs, representing as it does the intersection of the Enlightenment, utopianism and revolutionary will. Whatever the French Revolution may have been as a historical event, or as a congeries of events, it has had an equally important continued existence as an ideological construct. It is a model for, and a warning against, action, not only in France, but in the world. Its relevance has simply not faded.

II

What is a political revolution?[8] When Aristotle spoke of revolutions, he used the term *metabole*, change, and where appropriate, *metabole kai stasis*, change and uprising. But what sort of change, and how important is the element of uprising or violence? Aristotle and the historian Polybius thought in terms of a cycle of government in which the change was a change from one to another of the four types of political organization that they regarded as fundamental, e.g. from monarchy to aristocracy, from aristocracy to oligarchy, from oligarchy to democracy. Today, we are much more aware of the logical and empirical difficulties associated with the attempt to distinguish 'fundamental' features of a social order from more ordinary, 'inessential' features; we know that definitions come at the end and not the beginning of a specific enquiry, and that

[7] See Furet, *op. cit.*, 3.

[8] I draw here on my 'The Concept of a Political Revolution' in Carl J. Friedrich, ed., *Nomos VIII – Revolution* (New York, 1966), 122–35, and my 'Revolution – the History of an Idea' in Kamenka, ed., *op. cit.*, 1–14.

different contexts and intellectual purposes require different definitions. We also tend, largely as a result of the French Revolution and its elevation of ideology into human history, to pay greater attention than Aristotle did to the ideology, the beliefs and habits, involved in the existence of a social order. As a preliminary approach to the problem of isolating and describing the meaning of the term 'revolution', let us say that revolution is a sharp, sudden change in the social location of political power, expressing itself in the radical transformation of the process of government, of the official foundations of sovereignty or legitimacy and of the conception of the social order. (This definition, too, bears the unmistakable imprint of the French Revolution and its impact on the modern mind.) Such transformations, it has usually been believed, could not normally occur without violence; if they did they would still be revolutions. The concept of a sharp, sudden change is no doubt a relative concept; what appears to the participants as the slow, gradual evolution of a new style of life may, to later generations, seem a sudden and revolutionary change. At the same time, acknowledged revolutions are rarely sharp and sudden enough to take place at a clearly defined point in time, or to reveal themselves unequivocally as revolutions at the very moment of the formal transfer of power. The violent outburst that heralds the beginning of the revolution for the chronicler may be understandable only as the product of important, if less spectacular, social changes that preceded it; the task of distinguishing a revolutionary outbreak from a coup d'état or a rebellion may be impossible until we see how the new masters use their new-won power. But unless we confine the term 'revolution' to the field of convulsive changes we shall find revolution everywhere, all the time.

There is, nevertheless, a real and important difficulty about defining the concept of revolution, which our preliminary definition only obscures. The definition of the concept requires a *theory* of revolution, a conception of what is important and unimportant in the study of violent social change and radical political upheaval. There is, after all, a whole cluster of concepts – rebellion, civil war, coup d'état, national uprising – whose relation to the concept of revolution is complicated and not at all the subject of general agreement. The existence of different *types* of revolution makes this relationship even more complex. Let me illustrate some of the difficulty by setting out the *typology* of revolutions that Chalmers Johnson develops in his book *Revolution and the Social System.*[9] Johnson identifies six *types* of revolution – using as criteria with which to distinguish them the targets selected for attack, the class or group that is the carrier of revolutionary activity and the goals and ideologies of the revolution. Different types of 'revolutions' may be aimed at government personnel, the political regime, or the community as a social unit; the makers of the revolution may, according to Johnson, be a mass or an elite, and their goal may be reformist, eschatological, nostalgic, nation-forming, elitist, or nationalist. We thus have his six types.

The first type, the *jacquerie*, is a spontaneous mass peasant uprising usually carried out in the name of the traditional authorities, of church and king, with the very limited aim of purging the local or national elites (as e.g. in the Peasant Revolt of 1381, the German Peasant Rebellion of 1525, Kett's Rebellion of 1549, and the Pugachev rebellion in Russia in 1773–1775).

The second type, the *millenarian rebellion*, is like the first but has the added feature of a utopian dream inspired by a living messiah (e.g. the Florentine revolution led by Savonarola in 1494, the Anabaptist Rebellion in Münster led by John Mathijs and John Beukels in 1533–1535, and the Sioux Ghost-Dance Rebellion inspired by the Paiute prophet Wovoka in 1890).

The third type, the *anarchistic rebellion*, is nostalgic reaction to progressive change, involving a romantic idealization of the old order (e.g. The Pilgrimage of Grace and the Vendée).

The fourth type, the *Jacobin Communist revolution*, though many would think it the real subject of revolutionary hopes from 1789 onward, is in fact a very rare phenomenon. It has been defined as

[9] Chalmers Johnson, *Revolution and the Social System* (Hoover Institute Studies No. 3, Stanford, 1964). Cf. Lawrence Stone, 'Theories of Revolution', *World Politics*, XVIII (1965–6), 159–76. I have drawn on Stone's summary extensively, and in part *verbatim*. Johnson's typology, it should be noted, is an open empirical collection rather than a theoretical construct and consequently capable of dating. The Iranian Revolution of the Ayatollahs combines features of the millenarian rebellion with the Jacobin model and has specificities of its own. Does it constitute a new type?

'a sweeping fundamental change in political organization, social structure, economic property control and the predominant myth of a social order, thus indicating a major break in the continuity of development'. It can occur only in a highly centralized state with good communications and a large capital city, and its target is government, regime, and society – the lot. The result is likely to be the creation of a new national consciousness under centralized, military authority, and the erection of a more rational, and hence more efficient, social and bureaucratic order on the ruins of the old ramshackle structure of privilege, nepotism, and corruption. The centrality of this conception of revolution in revolutionary ideology in the last 190 years is the direct legacy of the French Revolution.

The fifth type, the *conspiratorial coup d'état*, is the planned work of a tiny elite fired by an oligarchic, sectarian ideology. It qualifies as a revolutionary type if it in fact anticipates a mass movement and inaugurates social change (e.g. the Nasser revolution in Egypt or the Castro revolution in Cuba); it is thus clearly distinguished by Johnson from the palace revolt, assassination, dynastic succession-conflict, strike, banditry, and other forms of violence, which are internal wars but not revolutions. It too stems, in its hope to set off a wider revolution, from the revolutionary ideology born in France between 1789 and 1793.

Finally, we have the *militarized mass insurrection*, a deliberately planned mass revolutionary war, guided by a dedicated elite. The outcome of guerrilla warfare is determined by political attitudes, not by military strategy or matériel, for the rebels are wholly dependent on broad popular support. In all cases on record, the ideology that attracts the mass following has been a combination of xenophobic nationalism and Marxism, with much the greater stress on the former. This type of struggle has occurred in Yugoslavia, China, Algeria, and Vietnam. It draws, again, on the revolutionary motifs set off by 1789.

Why do we, nevertheless, tend to call these types, or at least most of them, revolutions and to distinguish them from 'internal' wars? Let me try to approach this problem through the history of the term 'revolution' and its role in thinking about society. Thomas

Babington Macaulay, in his famous speech supporting the 1832 Reform Bill,[10] said:

> All history is full of revolutions, produced by causes similar to those which are now operating in England. A portion of the community which had been of no account expands and becomes strong. It demands a place in the system, suited, not to its former weakness, but to its present power. If this is granted, all is well. If this is refused, then comes the struggle between the young energy of one class and the ancient privileges of another. Such was the struggle between the Plebeians and the Patricians of Rome. Such was the struggle of the Italian allies for admission to the full rights of Roman citizens. Such was the struggle of our North American colonies against the mother country. Such was the struggle which the Third Estate of France maintained against the aristocracy of birth. Such was the struggle which the Roman Catholics of Ireland maintained against the aristocracy of creed. Such is the struggle which the free people of colour in Jamaica are now maintaining against the aristocracy of skin. Such, finally, is the struggle which the middle classes in England are maintaining against an aristocracy of mere locality, against an aristocracy the principle of which is to invest a hundred drunken pot-wallopers in one place, or the owner of a ruined hovel in another, with powers which are withheld from cities renowned to the furthest ends of the earth for the marvels of their wealth and of their industry.

Until recently, this was – in one form or another – probably the most common view of revolutions among modern thinkers. And it is impossible not to perceive the role of the French Revolution and its conception of itself in shaping that idea. Nevertheless, people have seen revolutions in very different ways, and have set them in the context of quite different theories of revolution. To the men of the Italian Renaissance, as the German-American sociologist

[10] In the House of Commons on 2 March 1831, as printed in T. B. Macaulay, *Miscellaneous Writings and Speeches* (London, 1889), 483f.

Eugen Rosenstock-Huessy reminded us in his *Revolution als politischer Begriff in der Neuzeit* (Breslau, 1931), their term for 'revolution', *rivoluzioni*, described the motion of the planets under the iron laws of the celestial spheres. In transposing the term into the field of politics, they – like the Greeks before them – meant to recognize in the rise and fall of princes a superhuman, astral force, the revolving wheel of fortune that raised up one prince or government and threw down another. This concept of a revolution as a total, fundamental and objective transformation, as a natural catastrophe, Rosenstock-Huessy calls the naturalistic concept. It persisted, according to him, right up to the French Revolution. When the Duc de Liancourt informed Louis XVI of the storming of the Bastille, the King cxclaimed, 'But good God! That is a revolt!' 'No, Sire,' replied the Duc, '*c'est la révolution*' – meaning that this was a force of nature completely beyond human control.[11]

With the French Revolution, Rosenstock-Huessy argues, a new concept of revolution, the romantic concept, comes to the fore. Revolution is now seen as the heroic, romantic deed, as the assertion of human subjectivity, of man as the master of history. Before the Revolution, Voltaire and Condorcet had laid down the elements of this view; Robespierre became its spokesman and Blanqui and Buonarroti its dedicated disciples: the barricades of 1848 and the Blanquist faction in the Paris Commune of 1871 were its visible expression. In reality, however, the romantic period in Europe was short-lived. By 1850, it had lost most of its force. In the Italian Risorgimento, the realist Cavour replaced the romantic Mazzini; Germany moved into the age of Bismarck; the Republican opposition in the France of the Second Empire falls under the

[11] Cited by Sigmund Neumann, discussing Rosenstock-Heussy, in his 'The International Civil War', *World Politics*, I (1948–9), 336. Arthur Hatto, providing brief but independent confirmation of some of Rosenstock-Huessy's findings in his 'Revolution: an Inquiry into the Usefulness of a Historical Term' *Mind*, 58 (1949), 495–517, notes that Clarendon calls the events in England of 1660 a 'revolution' in the sense of a restoration, of the wheel of fortune returning to the rightful order of things (p. 505). For the opposing party, 1688 was the return or restoration, occurring, they were delighted to note, precisely 100 years after the expulsion of the Papists from England; it was their 'revolution' – the Glorious Revolution that marked the restoration of their fortunes.

sway of the Comtean positivist Gambetta; the working-class movement replaces the anarchist conspiracy. We enter a new period in the history of the idea of revolution, the general trend of which is only confirmed by the defeat of the Paris Commune. It is the period of the realist concept of revolutions.

Rosenstock-Huessy is in the Hegelian tradition; he sees the realist phase as the dialectical negation and synthesis (*Aufhebung*) of the two previous phases. In the realist phase, revolution is no longer seen as an unpredictable result of superhuman forces; to that extent, naturalism is overcome. But revolutions are seen as dependent on objective conditions; they come when the time is ripe for them. To that extent, naturalism is preserved. Neither, for the realist, are revolutions the product of the bare human will; they can occur only in a revolutionary situation. Thus, romanticism is overcome. For the revolutionary situation to become effective, however, there must be a class ready to do its work, or a decided leadership able to recognize, articulate, and direct the revolutionary forces of the time. Thus, romanticism, the importance of subjectivity, is also preserved. Karl Marx, the outstanding 'realist', combined and yet transcended the naturalistic and romantic views of revolution; he and his disciples could therefore claim to be neither the astrologers nor the poets of revolution, but its scientists, going beyond the concept of the natural upheaval and the political coup d'état to that of the *social revolution*, without which a mere political overthrow was futile and meaningless. They based that science largely, if only implicitly, on their understanding, their appreciation and their criticism of the French Revolution and its early nineteenth-century historiography.

The realist theory of revolutions has one more important component, also drawn from the French Revolution and the Enlightenment. Die-hard Hegelians, no doubt, might interpret it as the *Aufhebung* of cyclical repetition and of lawless leaps into the future. This is the concept of progress. Revolutions, for the realist, are the milestones in humanity's inexorable march toward true freedom and true universality. Each revolution, Marx and Engels write in the *German Ideology*, is the work of a particular class, but during the revolution it appears as the representative of the whole society; it surpasses, if only for a moment of history, its sectional, egoistic particularity and thus strengthens a universal revolutionary tradition. Further, as we pass from the aristocracy to the bourgeoisie and from the bourgeoisie to the proletariat, we pass to an ever-broadening base of social power; each revolution is thus truly nearer universality than the last. It is along these lines that we can understand the upheavals in Asia and Africa, and the unrest in Western societies, as the working out of the logical implications of the French Revolution, as an attempt to universalize its assumptions both socially and geographically, to grasp and realize fully the universalistic implications of the slogan 'Liberty, Equality, Fraternity'.

The ascription of responsibility in history is governed by much the same psychological mechanisms as the ascription of responsibility in morals and law. A revolution, like a street accident, results from the interaction of a number of factors, each of them necessary but not sufficient to produce the result. We are constantly tempted to pick out as the cause the factor that we consider unusual or improper, the factor that lies outside the normal range of our expectations. The young Marx, accustomed to think of governments and social structures as rigid, and greatly impressed with the comparatively recent consciousness of the far-reaching economic changes taking place in society, saw revolution as caused by these changes. By the turn of the century, there was a new generation of Anglo-American thinkers, accustomed to think of far-reaching economic changes as the norm of social life: to them, the cause of revolutions seemed the rigidity of governments, the lack of social mobility and political flexibility, repression, and administrative incompetence. This, they thought, explained why revolutionary ideology was weakest in the Anglo-American world, where democracy had taught governments to give way.

Though the emphases differ, the position is basically the same. Revolution, says Marx, is the bursting of the integument by the repressed forces of economic and social development; revolution, say later sociologists as different as Ward, Ellwood, Pareto and Brooks Adams, is the conflict between advancing classes or groups or interests in a society and the rigid structure or elite that holds them back. From Macaulay to the recent present, the class theory of revolutions has been the dominant tool of those who study – and who make – revolutions, though recent and more detailed work puts greater and greater emphasis on the rôle of the contingent and treats the concept of progress – Whig and Marxist views of history – more sceptically.

Serious study of the French Revolution and of subsequent revolutions now has brought out both the complexity of classes and class interests and the inadequacy of the attempt to define them in terms of their position in the process of material production, of their relation to factors of production, the manner in which they appropriate surplus value. It has also shown that revolutions are as dependent on collapse at the top as on an uprising from below – financial incompetence, the effects of war, a split in the nobility and the clergy and a weak and indecisive king made the French Revolution possible. Max Weber's definition of classes as composed of those who share the same chance in life rests on a recognition of the fact that sectional solidarities and outlooks, even conflicts and revolutions, can be based on factors other than economic exploitation or Marxist economic classes – on race, religion, feelings of national identity etc. Revolutionaries, of course, prefer a single key to human misery and to human happiness. Only if there is such a single key is it plausible to believe that society can be totally reconstructed by a single revolutionary act that marks the triumph of reason in human affairs. Since modern revolutionaries speak and act in the name of 'the people', they are much less comfortable with another striking feature of the French Revolution and of subsequent revolutions: the role played in them by lawyers, by those who live by the pen or, more generally, by the class that nineteenth-century Russians came to call the *intelligentsia*. That class was initially not the bearer of its own economic interests; it was not held together by those. It was composed of people who saw a glaring and insupportable discrepancy between the values and possibilities inherent in the new and burgeoning secular education produced by the Enlightenment, of which they had acquired at least a smattering, and the social arrangements in which they lived, which they wanted changed. Their success, as Marx saw, depended on the existence of a material force or of material forces, or a material situation that rendered the old regime powerless and that produced disaffection wider than that found among portions of the educated and the semi-educated. But, as in the case of the Jacobins, it is this *intelligentsia* that provides the leaders of the revolution, those who determine or seek to determine its course by plans and projects, repression and propaganda from above – stepping into a secular society to replace the Calvins and Savonarolas of earlier times. There is no doubt that Marx was right in perceiving the extraordinary dynamic of capitalist industrial production and the extent to which it would undermine traditional authorities and traditional arrangements throughout the world. But Marx ignored – to some extent because he took it for granted – the equally extraordinary independent force of the ideas of the Enlightenment incorporated in the political slogans of the French Revolution. Education spread more quickly than industrialization, democracy or the so-called 'bourgeois revolution'. Whatever else they may have been, a whole series of revolutions and collapses in Eastern Europe, in Russia and in China, represented the belated French Revolution of their societies. The Marxism of *The Communist Manifesto* has lived, above all, in the struggle against the economically and socially backward old regimes of the world. It is here that the struggles of the Jacobin French Revolution, its hopes and ideals, remained most immediately relevant.

But the leaders of the revolution from below – Hébert and Chaumette – fell victims to Robespierre and his Committee of Public Safety after the law of Fourteenth Frimaire in December 1793 established a strongly centralized Jacobin government and subordinated the *sans-culottes* and their revolutionary committees of the Sections to the Committee of General Security at the centre. While Marxism continued to extol both the revolutionary intellectual and the mass movement from below but above all the 'proletarian' *party*, the Polish revolutionary Jan Waclaw Machajski was warning in his *The Intellectual Worker* (1905) that the revolutionary enterprise had fallen into the hands of a new class, the *intelligenti*. Formerly hirelings of feudalism and then of capitalism, they had become increasingly hostile to aristocratic and bourgeois rule. The new class's monopoly of education constituted, in modern conditions, a most powerful form of property. The interest of that new class lay entirely in a self-seeking attempt to mobilize workers in a socialist revolution that would give the *intelligenti* power, assure them of better jobs and higher salaries as representatives of the social, as opposed to the workers', interest. Marx's scientific socialism was their creed.

III

Like all social events, the French Revolution is part not of one history, nor of *the* history, but of many histories that reflect the infinite complexity of history and society and not merely differences of perspective or viewpoint in those who write up these histories. It is precisely for that reason that the French Revolution has been rightly seen as the seedbed of many things and as the progenitor of a remarkable range of often conflicting and competing *idées forces*: of nationalism, liberalism, socialism and communism (though the three latter terms came into use only in the first half of the nineteenth century), of modern democracy, 'modern' legal systems, modern administration, 'national' education and ministries of propaganda and enlightenment. Its clubs were the first modern political parties; the seats they chose in their parliament created for us the political concepts of left and right. Above all, however, the French Revolution gave a totally new meaning to an earlier conception of the contrast and conflict between the modern and the ancient. It marked, for the French Revolutionaries themselves, the dawn of a new era, the overthrow of a *féodalité* and an *ancien régime* incompatible with the progress, the dignity and the potential rationality of mankind. It represented the struggle of the future against the past. It is that belief which decisively distinguishes the revolutionary of all eras after the French Revolution from those who rebelled before, looking backward to an imagined era of 'natural' equality, Celtic, civic, peasant or Saxon liberties and ancient constitutions. In 'traditional' societies, as we now call them, from the Russia of the old regime to much of South America and Asia, but not always in Islam, the revolutionary, even today, presents himself as and is the consummator of an uncompleted French Revolution on behalf of liberty, equality, fraternity, of progress and enlightenment.

At one level, Marxism is a version and an attempted empirical exemplification of the doctrine of progress, of the radical French Revolutionaries' belief in the perfectibility of man (and woman) and in their capacity for rational control and understanding of nature and society. On this view, the French Revolution was a necessary and inevitable step in the progress of mankind – a practical overcoming in the realm of politics, of the medievalism, superstition and irrationality that the Enlightenment had exposed in books. Karl Kautsky found it astonishing, not that the Austro-Hungarian Empire had collapsed but rather that it had managed to totter on into the twentieth century. Part of the continuing appeal of the French Revolution and of French revolutionary rhetoric to nineteenth-century revolutionaries in Europe and South America and to twentieth-century revolutionaries in Asia, Africa and the Pacific lay precisely in their belief that their countries were being deprived of 'modernity', oppressed by 'traditional' or backward-looking regimes and authorities or excluded from enlightenment – education, progress, self-determination.

The Carbonari may have been formed in the struggle *against* Napoleon's invasion, as was the concept of the patriotic guerrilla. But in a world where Napoleon had long fallen, the French revolutionary slogan of 'Liberty, Equality, Fraternity' and the concept of revolutionary wars for democracy and national self-determination have reverberated with increasing strength. Insofar as most modern revolutionary movements, including socialist and Marxist ones, have at least formally elevated the rights of man, the sovereignty of the people, republicanism and democracy, progress and enlightenment, they have directly looked back to, or echoed the radical slogans and beliefs of, the French Revolution.

The populism of a Michelet, a Mazzini or a Mickiewicz (leaving out the latter's religious messianism) stood closer and was more sympathetic to the French Revolution than the socialism of Marx, which saw the post-revolutionary development of industrial capitalism as the central fact of modern society. There is a certain tension in Marxism and in Marx's own thought between his stage theory of history based on changes in the mode of production, i.e. his (complex) technological determinism, and his constant, if implicit, recognition of the continued interest of the French Revolution, connected with his elevation of political activism, of the need for revolution and for revolutionary tactics. On the periodization view, western societies, at least, move from feudalism through capitalism and stand on the eve of a socialist revolution. The French Revolution is thus *not* a world-historical event at any level except that of ideology, for it reflects a wider economic and historical trend it did not fully understand. It is part – perhaps the most dramatic part – of a series of bourgeois revolutions that took place in Europe and America. From the point of view of socialism, from the point of view of any Marxist understanding of the nineteenth or twentieth centuries, it belongs to the past. That was Marx's main view and for the Marxists of the Second International the French Revolution was interesting in the same way as the Levellers and Diggers, the Anabaptists of Münster or the 'Communism' of the Essenes. Once their own revolution of October 1917 was over – and had allegedly launched mankind on a new historical stage – Bolshevik Soviet writers, too, relegated the French Revolution to a completed past, to the bourgeois period of history. They saw 1848 and 1871 not as reverberations of 1789, or 1793, but as inadequate, unconsummated, adumbrations of the proletarian revolutions of 1917 and 1918, or as belated bourgeois risings in backward countries – though even the latter were made quite different from the French Revolution by the presence and influence of a real, formed, if ultimately defeated proletariat on the streets of Paris, Berlin, Vienna.

Marx himself, curiously, was yet also conscious of the French Revolution as one that pointed beyond the bourgeois order he saw it as creating. Many of his most interesting insights into the French Revolution – and he was both perceptive and imaginative – do not square at all well with his underlying economic determinism. They suggest, on the contrary, a genuine appreciation of the relative independence of the political. France, as Marx sees it, is the country of political enthusiasm: this is why its 'bourgeois' revolution goes beyond bourgeois interests, displays a universal soul. He never explains why England should be the economic paradigm of bourgeois rule and France the political. But he does back up his recognition of a transcendent universal theme in the French Revolution with a general law of revolution. The class that makes a successful revolution confronts the old regime not as a specific class, but as the representative of all the rest of society. In this alliance, and in part in sheer revolutionary enthusiasm, it is driven beyond its sectional particularism, it becomes genuinely the representative of the rest of society. But enthusiasm is limited to the period of the decisive struggle against the old. After victory, the sectional interests of the new ruling class reassert themselves; the Thermidorian reaction sets in, the Constitution of 1793 is replaced by the Constitution of 1795. The Terror that destroyed the old counter-revolution is now turned against those who challenge the interests and particularism of the new ruling class. From this is born one of the most important Marxist insights and strategies concerning revolution: the belief that revolution itself creates the conditions and opportunities for further radicalization, for creating a revolution *en permanence*. The theory came alive again, and was developed by Trotsky and Helphand-Parvus, in the discussion of the appropriate strategies to be adopted by Marxist social democrats in Russia at the beginning of the twentieth century, when the hope for revolution could only see it beginning as a bourgeois revolution against an *ancien régime*. Socialists, indeed, the line ran, must support that revolution, but not by taking power and responsibility themselves in the task of inaugurating a bourgeois order. They must use every opportunity to radicalize the bourgeois revolution, to mobilize the masses into pushing the revolution further than the bourgeoisie wants it to go, to maintain and use both revolutionary enthusiasm and the universal slogans that revolutionary leaders are forced to adopt. M. N. Roy took the same view of the relationship between the limited 'revolutionary' demands of the Indian 'national bourgeoisie' that the British quit India and the genuinely revolutionary demands of the peasant masses seeking social justice and relief from poverty as well. Here, the radicalization of the French Revolution between 1789 and 1793 as power passed from the

National Assembly to the Convention, from constitutional monarchists through the Gironde to the Jacobins and even, briefly, to the 'people of Paris' was clearly a model and inspiration, directly for the Russians, indirectly (through Comintern discussion) for Roy. More recently, and especially since the 'events' of 1968, a more voluntarist generation of Marxists has begun arguing that 'revolutionary situations' arise at the beginning and not only at the end of a new social order. They may thus create the opportunity through the mobilization of revolutionary enthusiasm to skip a stage of history or to shorten it, as Lenin did in 1917, and as Asian and African revolutionaries have allegedly done since. The witch-doctor, sang a bad Polish poet in the 1960s, points the bone to socialism!

Karl Marx, though siding with the Jacobins against the Gironde, with the (for him still inadequate) Constitution of 1793 against the Constitutions of 1791 and 1795, was not an admirer of Robespierre. He saw the Terror and the Committee of Public Safety as bringing out the fundamental limitations of the French Revolution: its proclamation of Liberty, Equality, Fraternity as a political slogan while it liberated, in fact, the greed, conflict and exploitation, and the resultant dependence and alienation, of civil society. Before that civil society and its particularism, the pretended universality of the state was in fact powerless: it could seek to suppress conflict, division and inequality only by despotic inroads, by terror. For traditional Marxists since then, Jacobinism has been a term of abuse, a manifestation of the false belief that human will, rather than economic realities, could shape history, a reversion to the romantic subjectivity of pre-Marxian revolutionary endeavour.

Nevertheless, Marx's conception of the socialist revolution was deeply influenced by the Jacobinism of the French Revolution and by Blanqui in two further respects: in his insistence that revolution required the seizure or creation of a centralized state apparatus and in his insistence that the revolutionary government must act firmly against counter-revolutionaries at home and abroad, establish, as he sometimes put it, an initial dictatorship of the proletariat to safeguard the revolution and its achievements.

In Lenin, widely regarded and denounced as a Jacobin by critics within and outside the socialist movement of his time (also including Trotsky at one period), the impact of the French Revolution is more pervasive and more direct, though – unlike Trotsky – he refers to Russian revolutionary traditions rather than to the French. For Lenin as a professional revolutionary, concerned to make revolution rather than wait for economic forces to burst the integument, the French Revolution was, though not consciously, an obvious primer, and the Jacobins, as individuals and as a party, the obvious prototypes for the professional and dedicated revolutionary vanguard.

The parallels between the October Revolution of 1917 and the French Revolution of 1789 onward are indeed most striking. Theorists of revolution have had no difficulty in showing similar forces at work in both societies on the eve of revolutionary outbreak – including half-hearted attempts at reform that raised expectations that were then sharply dashed. The interplay of contingent factors and of wider social climates and developments is equally striking in both; so is the incompetence of the ruler, the division in the upper orders and the 'alienation' of the *intelligentsia*. There is a similar concentration on the capital, a similarly important role played by mass violence before and after the transfer or power. But the parallels grow even more striking as the revolution pursues its course. Power passes rapidly from one group to another in the direction of increased radicalization – from constitutional monarchists to republican democrats to revolutionaries seeking to reshape the whole of society. It does so under pressure from (sections of) the masses. It moves rapidly toward centralized, dictatorial and pervasive rule from the centre, using terror and committees of public safety. It persecutes and proscribes on the basis of class origin. It censors the press (even the revolutionary press), suppresses 'oppositionist' clubs and societies (parties in the modern case) and arrests and condemns (in show trials of the most blatant political motivation) not only counter-revolutionaries, aristocrats and 'liberals', but its own fellow-revolutionaries. The revolution eats its children. When the country grows weary of the terror, when the tasks of stabilization and routinized mobilization of the population have to be faced, there is a consolidation of state power through one-man rule and a reversion to the traditional trappings and coercive foundations of authority. The Directory gives way to Napoleon; the Council of People's Commissars to the Father of the Proletariat, I. V. Stalin.[12]

It is in these circumstances that the French Revolution began once more to acquire a totally new significance, summed up in Franz Borkenau's Law of the Twofold Development of Revolution.[13] Every great revolution has destroyed the state apparatus which it found in a wave of anarchist sentiment and after much vacillation and experimentation has put another, even more powerful one, in its place and suppressed all free mass movements, all spontaneity from below. Bolshevik revolutionaries had embarked on a path that was most significantly similar to that of the Jacobins – they wanted, by force and revolutionary enthusiam, to reconstruct society from the top. Lenin's opponents, even within Marxism, denounced him as a Jacobin seeking to shape history by will from the very start. His followers, in the early years, never lost sight of the lessons to be learnt from the French Revolution: of the dangers of counter-revolution, from outside and from within, of the need to kill symbols of alternative legitimacy (Louis XVI and the Tsar), of the danger from revolutionary factions and from spontaneous 'undisciplined' actions from below (the Hébertistes and the Kronstadt sailors, Danton and the Left Social Revolutionaries). They feared also both restoration and Thermidorian reaction – a slackening of revolutionary will, a re-emergence of 'moderate' (in reality, counter-revolutionary) elements – a reason, it is said, for Stalin's expulsion of Trotsky and a basis for criticism of Bukharin.

If the Bolshevik revolutionaries in power in the Soviet Union were all too conscious of the French Revolution, their critics, especially those who were or had been Marxists, also became increasingly so. Trotsky, forced to explain from exile how a historically inevitable revolution could have been betrayed, developed his theory of the danger of a Soviet Thermidor. Thermidor, he argued, was not a period of reaction in general, a weakening of

[12] George Lichtheim, *The Origins of Socialism* (New York, 1969), 4.
[13] Franz Borkenau, 'State and Revolution in the Paris Commune, the Russian Revolution and the Spanish Civil War', *Sociological Review*, 27 (1937), 67.

revolutionary positions. It was the direct transfer of power into the hands of a different class, after which the revolutionary class cannot regain power except through an armed uprising. The forces for Thermidor in the Soviet Union, Trotsky believed, were concentrated in the *Kulak* class of the peasantry and in institutions such as the army and the diplomatic corps, assisted by persons in the Party, above all Stalin, who were making Thermidor more likely objectively, whatever their subjective intentions. The Mensheviks had already been quite happy to brand the Stalinist course as Thermidorian and to say that Thermidor had occurred. Trotsky vacillated, insisting to the end of his life that the Soviet Union was still a socialist state at the economic and therefore determining level because it had socialized ownership of the means of production, distribution and exchange. But at the political and administrative level, it was undergoing what he saw as counter-revolutionary tendencies and bureaucratic deformations. Sometimes he saw these as Thermidorian, sometimes – as Stalin's preeminence grew greater – as Bonapartist. Sometimes he even argued that the Thermidorian and the Bonapartist stages were being conflated into one.[14]

In the revolutionary tradition and in revolutionary ideology, then, the French Revolution lives – its lessons contradictory, but still urgent, its significance still emphasized by friend and foe of revolutionary ideology. The enormously more careful and detailed study of the events of and circumstances surrounding the French Revolution has led to much more differentiated and sophisticated treatments of causation in history, of classes and estates, of institutions and of the realities of economic life. It has not led to any general agreement about the significance of the French Revolution. Some see in it, as Jacob Talmon has done, the origin of totalitarianism as the working out and brutal imposition on society of the Jacobin urge to perfectibility and power. Others, like Hannah Arendt, have argued that the French Revolution was a failure,

[14] For an excellent summary and analysis of Trotsky's use of analogies from the French Revolution and a demonstration of the lack of any consistent theory behind them, see Jay Bergman, 'The Perils of Historical Analogy: Leon Trotsky and the French Revolution', *Journal of the History of Ideas*, XLVIII (1987), 73–98.

while the American Revolution was a success, because the former tried to reconstruct the whole of society while the latter contented itself with creating a political framework for liberty. For a new generation of post-Stalinist Marxists, the French Revolution, like the Paris Commune of 1871, is an inspiration to those who believe in participation, spontaneity and the masses, the masses who will not always be defeated even if so far they have been.

Yet, the appeal and significance of the French Revolution may also fade, like that of Clovis, if three of its central conceptions – the belief in progress, in modernity and in rationality – continue to be weakened in a new post-industrial radicalism and anti-modernizing fundamentalism that fears instead of welcoming 'the future', that sees rationality as external determination and elevates the nomad-hunter, the *mullah*, and the passive surrender to nature. But the man who predicts the future, Marx once warned, is a reactionary – for he can do so only in terms of the past, while the future produces genuine novelty. Whereof one cannot speak with confidence, one should be silent. The fashion of the decade is rarely, if ever, the truth of the century. Yet in Asia, Africa and Latin America, and in much of our own lives, the French Revolution lives.

The French Revolution and Human Rights

GEOFFREY BEST

Because it began with a ringing declaration of the rights of man and the citizen, because it presented itself to the world as an act on behalf of humankind at large, and because many besides the French people themselves have ever since assumed that it actually was so, the French Revolution has a reputation as the prime source and fountain-spring of human rights in the modern world. In this belief there is some truth, some error. This essay aims to sort out the facts from the fiction.

Reckoning the extent of the French Revolution's responsibility for the promotion of human rights in the world has to begin with reference to the rival claims of '1776' and '1689'. Not much of a specific kind need be added to my general comments in the Introduction. '1789', through more than the century that followed, had an altogether superior cutting edge because of its combination of bold expansive universalism with exceptional political dynamism. What it proclaimed about human rights (that is, what we have come to know as human rights but which were first trumpeted around the world in the form of the revolutionary Declaration of the Rights of Man and the Citizen) was however in itself not so original.

The essential core of civil and political rights, which has remained unchanged into our own day, was already secured to the subjects of the English crown by the 1689 Bill of Rights. Similar fundamental rights and liberties were secured to the citizens of the soon-to-be-United States of America in their several Bills and

Declarations of 1776. To those transatlantic versions was added the gloss and emphasis of universalist affirmation. That of course made the American event at once world-historically significant in a way the English event could not be. The latter's lack of universalist consciousness would not in the long run diminish its appeal and value to the movement for human rights – what was perceived over a long course of time to work well in practice could, after all, seem more worth emulation than what simply sounded good – but its prototype rights were cast within so unique a national mould that it was all but impossible for peoples beyond the British connection to benefit from their example. Whether any other peoples did so or not was a matter concerning which the complacent and insular English were largely indifferent. There was only one England, and all that could be said to envious foreigners was, hard luck!

The Americans, for their part, were more cosmopolitan-minded. Exulting in the virtuousness of their 'appeal to a candid world' and in what their constitution-makers declared to be the universal rightness of their principles, they were by no means indifferent to the effect of their example on the rest of their species; but they expected it to show primarily in the magnetic power which would draw freedom-loving people to them as immigrants to their (as it seemed) infinitely expansible land. There was only one United States of America, but it was open wide and welcome to all who wanted to be part of it.

The French, when it came to their turn to stir the pot, were even more universalistic than the Americans and – here came the Revolution's distinction – they had much clearer, even aggressive, visions of the spreading of their message. No more than England was their country one into which foreigners could be expected to move *en masse*, but their Revolution was a model which any other nation worth its salt could be expected, and encouraged, to follow. There was only one France, but its example and inspiration were generously available for the advantage and progress of humankind.

The excitement generated throughout the political universe by the Americans' revolutionary declarations was of course given a new lease of life when it became apparent that their enterprise had succeeded. Admiration for the United States' achievement had in

France the second dynamo, that without French military assistance the United States could not have won the war. There was much transatlantic coming and going of politicians, intellectuals and journalists; what had been done on *that* side offered blueprints and models for what might soon be done on *this*; so that when the French Revolution did get going, it seemed as natural and predictable that some who had fought in the recent war should now, with Lafayette at their head, become active revolutionaries and that some Americans (Jefferson, the best-known of them) should be there to offer experienced advice, as that the French Declarations, when they came, should turn out to be in some respects quite like the American. But those respects were superficial. At bottom, the French versions (at least four major texts have to be taken account of: those the National Assembly adopted on 26 August 1789 and 29 May 1793, the one the Convention put at the head of the constitution of 24 June 1793, and the one at the head of 'the constitution of An III', i.e. of August 1795) were substantially less ambitious and universal. Add to that a glance at French revolutionary practice at home and abroad, and a mighty caveat about the contradictory workings of the influence of Rousseau, and the persisting notion of French primacy or pre-eminence in the diffusion of human rights becomes a bit difficult to understand.

The very title of the French Declarations gives the game away. They are of the rights of man *and the citizen*, even (in the 1795 case) of the rights *and duties* of the man and the citizen: not of the rights of man anywhere at all but of the rights a citizen of France could expect according to the terms of whatever constitution was currently operative. This was a far cry from the rights of man as they appeared in the discourse of natural-law philosophers and publicists, and as they had been so boldly proclaimed in the American texts, and as indeed the French texts began by proclaiming – 'men are born free and remain free'. At the same time it was a lot more realistic and, even if unintentionally, more honest, for it faced up to the fact – a fact too often forgotten by human rights theorists – that rights in the abstract are politically of no effect or consequence. The only rights that human beings can hope to benefit from are those embodied in constitutions; and such rights can moreover only be relied on when such constitutions function as they are supposed to. Modern history is rich in instances of states with constitutions which read excellently, but in whose functioning there are hidden catches or practical failures which rubbish them so far as human rights go.

The French Declarations, seen in this perspective, were not intrinsically as misleading as the American. Only those of 1789 and June 1793 expressly mentioned natural rights, in their preambles, and then only once each; simply to record the French people's conviction that neglect of the natural rights of man, and indifference to them, were the prime causes of 'public misfortunes and the corruption of governments' (1789) and 'the misfortunes of mankind' (1793). The remainder of the preambles made it clear that the Declarations were aimed primarily at the French people themselves, to tell them what their civil rights and duties were and to provide a yardstick against which to measure the reciprocal observance of its rights and duties by the state. The emphasis was more on man-in-society and man-within-the-state than on man-as-individual. Subjected to the crude test question, Is this state made for man or is man made for this state?, one might conclude that these Declarations and constitutions got that difficult balance just about right, although it would be reasonable enough to reckon that the 1795 constitution came down more on the state side. Nor was their range of rights as great in absolute terms as it might have been. (Of course it was enormous in relation to the *ancien régime* – which, after all, was the main thing.) Slavery, the singular primordial blot on the panorama of United States rights, remained a blot on the French one until self-interest rather than altruism persuaded the Convention to abolish it in early 1794. Religious toleration was there from the start and in a practical sense freedom of belief also, but in 1794 there was state-sponsored worship of the Supreme Being, in 1796 Theophilanthropy, and something like a Catholic state church came back with the Empire, together with close regulation of Protestant and other sects. Rights thus politically manipulable have but scanty claim to the title of human rights. Equally tenuous, for other reasons, but momentous in their significance for the future, were the social-and-economic rights which made their first modern appearance in Article 21 of the June 1793 Declaration:

> Public assistance is a sacred obligation [*dette*]. Society owes subsistence to unfortunate citizens, whether in finding work for them or in assuring the means of survival to those incapable of working.

French citizens themselves were to some extent cushioned from awkward questions about the realities of their rights-regime by the impressive fact that out of their country's turmoil had come a degree of national solidarity and military strength which enabled it to beat up all but one of its neighbours and, under the flattering leadership of Napoleon Bonaparte, to become for ten glorious years the colossus of the continent. This was not quite what either original Revolutionaries or convinced republicans expected, but it needed exceptional qualities of firm principle and stoic self-denial to reject the bait. What made the bait easier to swallow was its coating of winning rhetoric of sacrifice and generosity. Even under the emperor, it was not beyond the powers of a reasonable Frenchman to believe that in overturning the old-established regimes of other countries and endowing them instead with French-style institutions, they were 'liberating' them, giving them rights they had not had before.

This brings us to one of the French Revolution's more incontestable contributions to the evolution of human rights, and it is one which has to be read between the lines of its Declarations, for by no means is it clear in them. 'The people of France' were declaring not only the particular points, item by item, in which their new regime was going to differ from their old one; they were also declaring, what was to the internationally aware among them something of immense importance, their right as one people, as a nation, to do what they collectively chose to do, without reference to other authorities past or present, French or foreign. And as to foreign reactions, they were not mistaken. Within three years France was at war with several counter-revolutionary foreign states, and the nationalism which in 1789 had not needed to be more than between the lines now came out clear and strong, like invisible-ink marks held to the fire. The most fundamental of all their rights, it turned out, was their collective right to be the nation they wanted to be, the nation (to adopt the language of the theorists who were not lacking to provide exalted rationales) they were designed and destined to be by (adopting the language of the new state which had recently set up across the ocean) the laws of nature and of nature's God. This has come to be known as the right of national self-determination.

This right or, as some have always argued and still do argue, this alleged but actually bogus right, would gain wide acceptance a century and a half later as not just a 'right' but explicitly a 'human right'. No one called it anything of the sort in the 1790s. They did not need to. 'Right' said it all. The French, a people deriving an unusual sense of national identity from the framework and spread of their national language and from their long experience of nation-statehood, were only in the political van of a movement then arousing all nationalities. The assertion of nationality became common form all over Europe and also, where it was less explicable, in Latin America. France played an ambivalent double role in promoting it. The example of the French people taking responsibility for their nation's management excited other peoples to follow suit. France in this light was a liberalizing and a liberating force. But in another light France was a bully and a parasite. Disagreeable experiences of invasion and occupation by French armies – *la grande nation*, in the form of *la nation armée* – had the effect of catalysing and militarizing national sentiment, to such effect that by the time France's armies were at last confined again to their homeland, Europe's nationalisms were more mature and violent than they might otherwise have been. In vain did French propagandists deploy the argument used later by the Soviet Union, that its protégés should be glad to make sacrifices to keep their only possible protector in business. What the French called liberation, and what, indeed, met with a welcome from Francophile minorities in most countries, was experienced by their national majorities as oppression and exploitation. Revolutionary rhetoric did not deceive them. Satirical parodies of the standard French liberation proclamation were not far from the truth: e.g., 'We have arrived and you are free. Anyone found on the street after sunset will be shot at sight.'

What seemed to be the French Revolution's main additions to national self-determination were a certain thickening of its theory, and an aggressive missionary twist to its practice. Theory after all had always been necessary even if only to justify what was being done and to win friends who might be badly needed. The French were rapidly brought to relish their identity as not just a people but, something more than that, a nation. Patriotism was important and there was plenty of it, but it was not enough. Something more was needed if a new France was to be made, if it was to be defended against foreign onslaught, and if the new man envisaged by revolutionary idealogues was to be created within it; and that something was nationalism. The French already formed more of a nation in the modern European senses (linguistic, cultural, 'organic') than had the Dutch in the later sixteenth century or than did the American colonists in the later eighteenth. The right to national self-determination suitable to such a case was correspondingly fierce. The original Monsieur Chauvin, who gave his name to some of it, was a soldier in the revolutionary armies before Bonaparte took them over.

The new missionary practice was correspondingly uncompromising. The French, it was soon discovered, had a mission, a calling, the duty as well as the right to give other peoples the benefits of the same experience they had given themselves. Beginning as 'liberation', it was in practice scarcely distinguishable from domination. In the course of such *realpolitik*-ings, admits Georges Lefebvre with regard to one of the worst of them, 'The rights of man were forgotten; or rather, the advantages which the annexed people were supposed to have derived therefrom masked the violence about to be done them.'[1]

*

[1] *The French Revolution from 1793 to 1799* (trans., London, 1967), II, 150.

This essay does not pretend to include a comprehensive history of human rights. Fortunately there is little need for any such thing with regard to the period between the French Revolution and the early twentieth century. What has to be said can be divided between what happened within that national frame wherein the revolution had firmly put them, and what happened at the international level. Let us be reminded that even the most perfect schemes of human beings' rights are nothing to do with human rights in our sense of the expression unless they extend beyond the national to an international or, better, supranational frame. Human rights means rights recognized in persons not by virtue of their being citizens of a state but simply because they are individual human persons, whatever state they do or do not belong to. Only in our later twentieth century has international society actually come to incorporate this explicit recognition in international law. If the later eighteenth century's declarations of the rights of men deserve a place in this story, as American and French writers above all claim that they do, it is because of their universalist pretensions. What was right for men in Britain's revolting colonies and in the kingdom, then republic, of France was right for men everywhere else. That was what was so novel and dramatic about their declarations. They spoke for humankind. But they weren't actually doing anything more for humankind in general than to excite and encourage it and to 'liberate' local bits of it, and, moreover, the other philosophical stream upon which the French Revolution was floated, the wild and eddying one springing from Rousseau, really had none of that sort of universalism in it at all. For Rousseauists, all rights were social creations, and the idea that individuals could have rights against society was dangerous nonsense. Anyone who talked that way had to be 'forced to be free' or, if that didn't work, got rid of. Rousseauists like Robespierre, Saint-Just and Barère put their own meaning on 'The Rights of Man and the Citizen', and it certainly was not that put by the Montesquieu-Voltairists!

How much revolutionary declarations actually did to enhance the enjoyment of rights within states (which is where alone implementation of rights could be hoped for) is a matter of debate. At the outset it may be remembered that of all the human rights that have been put on thc basic lists, only one – that concerning participation in the government of one's country – is not in principle attainable under non-representative regimes. Civil and political rights were observed and protected in pre-democratic Britain to a degree which won the admiration and envy of rights-seekers everywhere else. A right to political participation may or, according to circumstances, may not bring blessings with it. Many self-styled democracies since the Jacobins have ignored and extinguished it. There is, no doubt, much truth in the observation that democratic participation in government is a good way, perhaps the best way, for people to make sure they get the rights they are entitled to, but many have been the states whose proclaimed provisions for it have been effectively fraudulent. Fraudulence moreover has often gone beyond the right of political participation to infect all rights constitutionally declared. If to declare good things had been *ipso facto* to guarantee them, no peoples in the world could have been better off than those of Central and South America, where constitution-makers for all the new states vied to improve on the United States, Spanish and French models they worked from. There was fraudulence even in the ultra-democratic United States' grand array of citizens' rights. Slavery undid them from the start, and after slavery was apparently abolished (i.e. in federal law) its essentials were preserved for another century by the infra-federal states' uses (or abuses) of their legal rights and extra-legal opportunites. So long and so grossly did such abuses of human rights continue within the United States that when it came to the crunch after the Second World War, with the USA standing out like its own Statue of Liberty as human rights' global champion, it had to welsh on its initial promise to lead the promotion of a binding international covenant; second thoughts about The South and 'states' rights' drove the State Department to face the fact in 1948 that it could not deliver.

French experience was quite different. No problems of implementation in that supremely centralized military state! But not so many rights for its citizens either. The relatively limited range of the lists in the Revolution's declarations has often been remarked upon; and they were accompanied again and again, as French citizens' rights have been accompanied ever since, by forcible reminders of the obedience due to the law and to its agents. Thus, for example, in the 1789 Declaration:

> 7. No one can be accused, arrested or imprisoned except in cases determined by the law, and according to its prescribed forms. . . . Every citizen summoned or arrested by virtue of the law must instantly obey; resistance is an offence. . . .
>
> 12. The security of the rights of men and citizens depends on a public force . . . instituted for the general good. . . .

This fundamental principle has been kept fresh in popular consciousness above all by the powers allowed to the police by every French constitution since the Revolution (as before it) and by the arbitrary behaviour the police actually gets away with, which is something else. That the list of rights should alternately shrink and stretch in proportion with prevailing ideology was natural enough. That the biggest rumpus about rights – the Dreyfus affair – and the foundation at last of a *Ligue des Droits de l'Homme* should only come at the very end of the nineteenth century and when the prevailing ideology was that of the Third Republic, was perhaps less to be expected.

Within the British constitutional sphere of influence, the story is different again. Still eschewing formal statements of rights and tirelessly arguing that the rights of the right sort of people (viz. people with British standards and attitudes born or bred into them) were secure enough without needing to have them written down, the subjects of His and Her Majesty in Great Britain itself felt secure in a larger range of civil and political rights than could be found in any other European country. So did HM's subjects in the (more or less) self-governing dominions which Canada, Australia and New Zealand, one by one, became. Elsewhere within the British Empire, enjoyment of rights was more debatable – where people knew anything about them, which in these years was hardly at all outside Ireland and India.

In those turbulent countries, national self-determination was already by 1914 the crucial issue it was sooner or later to become everywhere else within the old empires, and was indeed spoken of as some sort of right. The British themselves had difficulty in understanding why. Were not certain most valuable basic rights secure wherever even-handed justice was impartially administered, and civil disorder firmly suppressed? Self-government in any case promised to be bad government; inefficient, factious and corrupt. Educated Irishmen and Indians were not so sure about that, and in any case were increasingly likely to feel that unless civil rights were married to comprehensive political rights, even fine lists of civil rights lacked the virtue the British attributed to them. It was an argument that perhaps seemed more persuasive then, before so many colonies gained their independence, than it does now, with the examples of all those newly independent states to go by.

More contributive towards the post-1945 flowering of human rights were their developments within the international frame made by the practice of states, the crystallizing of law and the operations of philanthropy and public opinion. 'Humanitarianism', not 'human rights', was the generic term by which these developments were known; but human rights law-books correctly discern in them some of their foundations: humanitarian intervention, in the occasional practice of which French motives seem to have been neither more disinterested nor more self-seeking than those of other major powers; the abolition of slavery, where reversals of policy lost France the lead it might have had; and racial non-discrimination, in the faltering international story of which France's contributions before 1940 have to be set against Vichy's complicities with Nazism between 1940 and 1944.

It was because of Nazism's racism and fascism's many other offences against humanity – part of the endeavour described by various of its leading figures as 'undoing the French Revolution' – that human rights achieved during the 1939–45 war the importance in the world they have retained ever since. They were discovered, one might almost say, as the best way to describe what the United Nations stood *for*, and what fascism in particular stood *against*. Introduced, it would seem, by President Roosevelt and regularly featured in the Western Allies' war-time proclamations, human rights were, in Winston Churchill's words, 'enthroned' in the foundation Charter of the United Nations Organization, and soon thereafter enshrined in its uniquely prestigious Universal Declaration of 1948. The part of France in these momentous transactions was unusual and important but not quite as important nor as singular as the French have come to believe. This part of the essay will be given to examining what actually happened, and to explaining why.

First, how human rights got into the UN in the first place. None of their three converging main roads was French. The United States' President and his State Department trod one road. President Roosevelt's end-of-war aims, the famous 'four freedoms' of his state-of-the-nation message of January and the Atlantic Charter of August 1941, did not use the term human rights, but it immediately came into use to describe them. A second road was Latin American. *Derechos humanos*, derived from *les droits de l'homme* (mostly via the Spanish constitution of 1812), had long been a big thing in Latin America, and particular rights – e.g. those of aliens and that of asylum – had been the subject of conventions drawn up by the succession of International Conferences of American States which had been meeting about every five years since 1890. It became for them a sort of race, to make a declaration of their own before the UN could do it, and to press the UN at every opportunity to fashion its declaration in the image of theirs. The third separate road by which human rights got into the foundations of the UN was of course the Jewish one.

If there was no French road over that first lap, it may have been to some extent because France's international position and status were so fragile from mid-1940 through 1944. For the USA and the Latin American states, it was for long an open question whether there was one France or two. As the liberation of France proceeded and the Vichy regime evaporated, the question settled itself; but by then, de Gaulle's France was too late to make it to Dumbarton Oaks, and although it was not too late to go to Yalta, where big decisions were made about the San Francisco conference to launch the UNO, de Gaulle wasn't invited. France therefore began its participation in the United Nations as a late starter with a chip on its shoulder and an urgent need to make its mark. Most of that chip had been removed by the Big Four's agreement before the conference began, that they should become 'the Big Five'. That need was satisfied, first, by France's successful insistence, even before the conference had got going, that French should join English (the official language most delegates would have preferred) as co-equal with it; and secondly, by taking a lead on the cultural side of the organization's development, a side which the Americans' natural first preoccupation with its political, legal and (at that hopeful stage) military sides had barely yet touched. It was an ideal as well as a necessary time to make the most of France's *mission civilatrice*; from which quickly resulted the conspicuousness of France's shares in the promotion of UNESCO (and its triumphant location in Paris), and of human rights; France being, it was claimed, *le pays des droits de l'homme*, and well-equipped to stand before the world as their best protagonist.

This standing was personified by the great Frenchman who was through the UN's first decade or so his country's chief representative on its social and economic side. That Frenchman was René Cassin. Already internationally distinguished by 1945, he was to become even more so in the course of the next thirty tireless years; of which no more need be said here than that they brought him the Nobel Peace Prize in 1968. If anyone represented human rights before the world, it was he. But he was not as singularly important in the making of the Universal Declaration of Human Rights as his admirers and his national government have claimed.

This most famous and elevating of UN texts, fixed at last in December 1948, would be outshone only by the Charter itself, and was in any case of greater immediate moral interest to most human beings. But they might find the story of its composition disillusioning and disappointing. What became presented in the end as a sort of Decalogue for a brave and better new world, and a quasi-religious text, actually took shape during a tangled tale of international diplomacy and national politics replete with the usual measure of accidents and absurdities. Not only were the contents of the

Universal Declaration uncertain until the last few days of three years' fairly intensive work, the very title of the document was for long unsettled. Bill, Covenant or Declaration? The State Department planners conceived it as an international 'bill' of rights. They shifted to 'declaration' in order to avoid confusion with their own national 'bill' and in order to make more of an appeal to Europeans, whom they supposed to think, as certainly did Latin Americans, in terms of the French '*déclaration*'. The Quai d'Orsay's planners of course thought in no other terms. Whitehall's planners thought primarily of a 'bill' and yielded only under the weight of pressure gathered behind the hardening American-French idea of splitting its contents between a covenant/*pacte* (intended to be legally binding) and a declaration (assumed to be morally so).

What was to be in the declaration? Content could not be separated from form. The USSR's readiness to accept anything that might be thought to bind 'western' states was accounted for in Washington and Whitehall (I am not sure about Paris) by its scarcely concealed resolve not to be bound itself. Washington and Whitehall stood at opposite poles in their interpretation of the declaration's force. Americans, of North and South alike, had become accustomed to declarations of ideals that might not in practice mean much, but could always be justified as inspirational descriptions of the directions state and societies would like to move in. The British view was quite different. Distrustful of what are now called 'gesture politics' and, although much more ready in 1946–7 than the Americans for a covenant that would really commit states to something, determined not to be committed to anything they could not carry out, the men of Whitehall at first viewed this solitary declaration as a second best and liked to rub in at every public opportunity the fact that it had no more than moral force.

Cassin's view fell interestingly between the two just sketched. I will call it equally 'Cassin's view' and 'the French view' although, as Quai d'Orsay archives show clearly enough, there were plenty of *nuances* of difference between the members of the French preparatory committee and it might not even be certain how exactly Cassin's arguments entirely represented the wishes of his nominal employers, who were at that time embroiled in the turmoil of national reconstruction, and considerably divided among themselves.[2] But no trace of any such dissonance ever then appeared at the UN where, on these matters, René Cassin was France and France was glad to make the most of him. Cassin did not pretend that the Universal Declaration of Human Rights had the full binding force of the covenant which, after its separation from the declaration in mid-1948, was going to have to be taken up later; but neither would he assert with the British and (less straightforwardly) the Americans that it had no more than moral force. The difference of opinion that emerged that autumn was immensely instructive. To the UK the declaration as it issued from the drafting committee was in the main

> a satisfactory document. Its purpose, merely to state aims and ideals, is clearly shown in the preamble. . . . Furthermore, its possible usefulness as a moral force ought not to be overlooked, and its adoption by the Assembly will be regarded by many as an achievement for the UN, which is bound to do some of its work by this very method of enunciating broad principles which exert a moral influence and in the long run produce results.

But, continued this draft brief for the delegation going to the Assembly, it was important to watch the French! Cassin was on record as saying that his government

> proposed to indicate to the Assembly the links existing between the Declaration and the Charter of the UN. It would be dangerous to say to the peoples that the Declaration did not have full validity and merely represented a beacon guiding humanity towards the final goal. The Declaration on Human Rights was a complement to the Charter of the UN which could not be included in it because of the lengthy preparation it required. It represented a clarification of the Charter and was an organic act of the UN having all the legal validity of such an act. . . . The French government reserved the right to

[2] Public Record Office, FO 371/72810, UNE 3183, Beckett's minute of 6 August 1948.

> propose that the General Assembly should (1) invite all States to take early action to bring all their laws and practices into line with the Declaration of Human Rights and to set up the administrative and judicial instances of appeal necessary for the respect of human rights. . . .[3]

The brief went on to list other objections to what the French were proposing (for example, a strong version of the right to asylum and provisions even for individuals' petitions to the Human Rights Commission) but all were minor compared with that radically different reading of the significance of the declaration. Cassin was of course not the only international lawyer of distinction to attribute to it and to the human rights undertakings of the Charter more weight than the British and Americans liked. Cassin's British counterpart, Hersh Lauterpacht, in fact went even further. The French/Cassin position was to one side of centre, but by no means extreme, and the wisdom of hindsight makes it look more like how the world has actually come to see the Universal Declaration than how the UK then wanted to see it. Cassin was indeed somehow persuaded to take a softer tone in the final debates, but he never let out of sight what the British and Americans by then were determined to deny: that the Universal Declaration of Human Rights was in some measure an instrument of *obligation* for all members of the United Nations Organization.[4]

Part and parcel of this was the substitution at a late stage of 'universal' for 'international' in its title. The change was significant for those with ears to hear. Cassin was the mover of this amendment which was accepted with surprisingly little comment; something more indeed than the familiar sort of multilateral treaty but intelligible and proper at that epoch as a new sort of commitment, absolute rather than reciprocal, spelling out certain political deductions from universal moral law which recent nightmares of Nazism and war had made to seem indispensable for human decency and peace. Seen in this light, the declaration took at once a leading place among the evidence of international law's recovery of its

[3] Ibid., 72811, UNE 3939.
[4] Ibid., 72811, UNE 4175.

original bonds with natural law, and the word universal spoke no more than truth. Implementation necessarily remained a matter mainly for states but the source of its authority was, as in the Charter, 'we the peoples of the United Nations . . .' and it started absolutely from first principles: Article 1, an affirmation of all human beings' natural dignity, rationality and moral capability; Article 2, reinforcement of those modes of equality by emphasis on non-discrimination; and Article 3, 'Everyone has the right to life, liberty and security of person.'

For Cassin, moreover, the right to life meant more than in the American and British drafts. 'It is not only the right not to be condemned to death by irregular tribunals or the right not to be assassinated,' he said in an interview to his principal biographer. 'It's also the right to eat!'[5] Here lay the key to those articles on social, economic and cultural rights (Articles 22–27) which gave the final version of the Universal Declaration of Human Rights quite a different character from the first; a key moreover which had been first forged in 1793. It did not appeal to the Anglo-Americans. Civil and political liberties, they argued, were intrinsically closer to the universal and the absolute, classically few in number, capable of precise definition; whereas the spectrum of social and economic rights was not only indefinitely extensible, its implementation depended on such variables as gross national product, population movements, the weather and so on. With them you left the *terra firma* of proved capacity and launched human rights towards the blue horizon. Why be more utopian than you had to be? The point was a valid one. Human rights have been more easily made to seem unreasonable and ridiculous by utopian elaborations on this side – 'the right to sunshine' and so on – than on the other, and the more they were lugged into the realms of the remotely possible and the theoretically ideal, the less chance had the original small basic list of civil political rights of retaining respect and engaging concern. This great inflation of social, economic and cultural rights, to which the UN committed itself in principle as early as 1950 – that is, well

[5] Marc Agi, *De l'idée de l'universalité comme fondatrice du concept du Droits de l'Homme d'après la vie et l'oeuvre de René Cassin* (Antibes, 1980).

before the 'Third World' inflation of membership came to compound the problem – can easily be seen as one of the UN's more lamentable indulgences in posturing, at the expense of people. That this happened, however, can hardly be laid at René Cassin's door. He was the principal architect of the Article 22 which prefaced this batch of items and sought to put them within a frame of universal acceptability. His own description of it can hardly be bettered:

> At that moment I was fortunate enough to propose an 'umbrella' text covering the totality of rights in the category under discussion; this text envisages the human person as a 'member of society' and declares that he is 'entitled to realization, through national effort and international co-operation, of the economic, social and cultural rights indispensable for his dignity and the free development of his personality.' The text, completed by a final amendment proposed by Mrs Roosevelt: 'and in accordance with the organization and resources of each State', was adopted as one that justly took into account the concerns of each member of the Commission and rendered superfluous particular restrictive clauses which might appear to suggest that a hierarchy was being established to the advantage of permissive freedoms and to the prejudice of the newly consecrated rights entailing possible obligations on society.[6]

Enough has been said to show how large a share was that of France and its distinguished son in the making of the Universal Declaration of Human Rights; a share which is inconceivable without France's original Revolution and French myths about it. Cassin repeatedly said and evidently really believed that his country was uniquely fitted to take the lead in such a business. Words and phrases like *tache spirituelle, mission, vocation, phares de l'humanité* and of course *mission civilatrice* flowed easily from him – and what an orator he was! A patriot through and through (but absolutely not

[6] Cassin's essay on 'The text of the Declaration' in *Lumen Vitae. An International Review of Religious Education* (English edition), 24 (1969), 24–5.

a nationalist), he had made his own and perfected his own version of the familiar stuff about his national culture's genius for elucidating and expressing universal truths, about France as the chivalrous battler for the salvation of humanity and so on. Hence, the lack of any sense of contradiction in his mind about being simultaneously, in the UN-centred transactions under scrutiny, both delegate of his state and *l'avocat de l'homme lui-même*, 'spokesman for humankind'. British and American observers of his performances there (it was often remarked by such that he tended to go on too long and that he was a better orator than a debater) were sometimes amused by him and sometimes bored, but they were impressed and fascinated too. Human rights needed a René Cassin at that juncture, as cold-war ice began to freeze most of the generous and hopeful ideas which at first filled the UN. And, given that René Cassin was unthinkable without his beloved *patrie*, it may be said that human rights benefited from the powerful support France was then pleased to give them; the more credibly, for the testimony given of its commitment by the incorporation of an updated declaration in the Fourth Republic's new constitution.

That there were elements of mythologizing and of self-deception in French ideas about their country's role and performance in relation to human rights is hardly to be denied, and hardly matters. The French Revolution's specific contributions were ambiguous. French culture as a magnificent phenomenon-in-general certainly bore some essential human-rights principles along with it, but so did every other Christian-rooted culture of any significance. The French constitutions of the nineteenth and early twentieth centuries and, more important perhaps, the liberal political culture enveloping them protected human rights better than most others in the world, but came to such an inglorious end in 1940 that survivors of the debacle might well feel in 1944/5, as Cassin himself did, that much of the national edifice needed reconstruction from scratch and, besides, the bracing support of a new and better international order. French endeavours directly after the war may be read as, in part, the repair of a revolutionary tradition which self-evidently had gone wrong.

It can hardly be said to have gone, since then, self-evidently right. The most notable and world-influencing Frenchman of the period has been more reminiscent of Napoleon Bonaparte and of Louis XIV than of Mirabeau and Danton. René Cassin found himself surprised and disappointed by his national leaders' indifference to the great issue; de Gaulle's, not least. Two instances will suffice to make the point. First, the Council of Europe's Convention on Human Rights; conceived in 1948, formulated in 1950, and of effect among committed states since 1953. Cassin himself had mixed feelings about it. On the one hand it was a good convention in its exclusively civil-and-political way, and it contained those elements of supranationality which were, for him, a *sine qua non* of serious progress. On the other hand, it studiously set aside social-economic-and-cultural concerns, and as a regional institution it fell far short of his universalist goal. He feared it would be (what some of its sponsors certainly meant it to be) a privileged region's way of dodging global, UN-created commitments. He could approve and support while nourishing certain reservations. But that his own France should for long stand out as the one great power of Europe that would not ratify it, shocked him. That national resistance to (the old shibboleth!) 'surrender of sovereignty' was not merely Gaullist; it began before de Gaulle resumed the purple, it ended in 1973, after he doffed it. More directly due to de Gaulle were other acts of state that gave Cassin cause to wonder why his idea of the meaning of France-in-the-world was not shared by the most famous Frenchman of the age. De Gaulle's essential nationalism never depressed Cassin more than when it prompted that inflammatory nationalist cry from that balcony above the St Lawrence: 'Vive le Quebec libre!' But what in his president's foreign policy upset him most, and continued to darken his days to their very end, was, from 1967, its resolute hostility to Israel, which Cassin (himself prominent in the French Jewish community) keenly supported. Just where that left the Palestinians, we need not here inquire. The point is made merely to illustrate how independent he could be of a national party line, and how even so profound an internationalist knew where to draw lines of necessary force.

*

Only for a few years, then, did René Cassin and France speak on human rights with, apparently, the same voice. The *patrie* he revered as the primordial patron of human rights fell below his expectations. He had to battle for them at home as well as abroad. There were therefore rich elements of irony, not to say humbug, in the French government's request that the tenth anniversary of the Universal Declaration of Human Rights should be marked by the display at the UN of the early draft of it in Cassin's own hand, dated 16 Juin 1947. Photographic reproductions subsequently, and Cassin's own account of the matter in his last years, helped, in the words of one of the few persons in a better position to know about it, to 'create the myth that Cassin was the father of the Declaration'.[7] That person was the Director of Human Rights in the UN's Department of Social Affairs, the Montreal jurist John Humphrey. His memoirs make frequent reference, generally admiring, to Cassin, but it is pretty evident that the quiet Canadian found the higher-flying Parisian sometimes too much to take. His estimate of Cassin's significance is perhaps more grudging than it should be. But on this point concerning what has by now become canonized as the *Avant-projet Cassin*, he is surely right.[8] The UK delegate's report at the time is of exceptional relevance. 'It had been my understanding, and the understanding of others,' he wrote on 18 June, that Cassin's share of their week-end home-work was to draw up a *resumé* of rights-stuff 'not ripe for inclusion in a convention. To my horror however I found that Cassin had produced a draft [declaration] which amounted to little more than a re-arrangement of the document originally produced by the Secretariat.'[9] And that is exactly what Humphrey said it was. The importance of the *Avant-projet Cassin* has been misunderstood; not least, perhaps, by the inflexible, excitable Frenchman himself. Its importance lay not in its contents – Cassin had not in fact done much more than reshuffle cards already in the UN Secretariat's pack – but in its aim and timing. This turned out to be exactly what

[7] John Humphrey, *Human Rights and the UN: a Great Adventure* (Dobbs Ferry, 1984), 43.
[8] See Agi, *op. cit.*, 321–6.
[9] FO 371/67606, UNE 776.

the convention-preferring UK feared it would be; the moment when the declaration idea launched into self-sustained flight towards the General Assembly whose resolution of endorsement would make it 'morally if not legally, binding on all members'. But what the UK did not like (as prospectively 'a perpetual source of mischief'), the USA preferred.[10] From this moment, the declaration was destined to become the more significant document, and only the resourceful pertinacity of its British backer kept the convention panting in the race until it had to be pulled out twelve months later; *reculer pour mieux sauter* in the form of the second covenant of 1966.

What has happened to human rights since the later 1940s? A great deal, not all of it to the clear advantage of humankind. The chickens released upon the world a century and a half earlier have at last come home to roost; and a mixed brood they turn out to be. Not much of this could have been foreseen in 1948, though some might have been hoped for and some feared. Human rights have become a big thing in the world. They are the banner under which many national and intra-national battles are fought, the *lingua franca* of one of its most active and influential transnational communities and the subject of a big new branch of international law. They have also become inflated and overused to an extent that has been counterproductive, and in several crucial respects have taken up positions that contrast strangely with their earlier postulates and can be considered as incompatible with them. How much of this explosive vogueishness is to be interpreted as part of our Permanent Revolution, is impossible exactly to measure. Its proximate sources need not be traced beyond the UN, the stimulus and opportunity given by that parliament and forum of humankind to so wide a range of world-serving projects. To the extent however that those projects themselves have developed around the universalist ideas boosted by the men of '89, and given that these projects

[10] Ibid.

have relied heavily on their trust in social and (one might add) mental engineering, they must clearly be considered as part of the revolutionary inheritance, whose mixed and contradictory character they rather strikingly express.

On the one hand, the flag of universalism – genuine transnational universalism with supra-national implications – has kept flying with more credit and acceptance than sceptics and pessimists thought possible. While much of the human rights standard-setting that has luxuriated around the original 1948 tree has to be discounted as variously utopian, pretentious and irresponsible, that tree itself still stands and has in fact grown ever bigger and broader-rooted. The status of the Universal Declaration has done nothing but strengthen. What began as a text from which its most optimistic backers could not hope for more than strong moral persuasion has astonishingly developed into an instrument of quasi-legal obligation.[11]

As has already been intimated, it was not the declaration from which such force was originally expected to emanate, but the convention/covenant which was then intended to accompany it. The history of the covenant instructively sums up the other side of the human rights story. Shunted into a siding in 1948 to let the declaration through, its reappearance in the UN's legislative lists was seized upon as their golden opportunity by all those parties who thought the Universal Declaration too heavily weighted on the civil and political side. By 1952 the General Assembly was instructing the Human Rights Commission to draft two covenants; and when at last, after fourteen more years of argument and bargaining, the two texts were ready to go through the General Assembly, primacy was accorded to the one entitled the International Covenant on Economic, Social and Cultural Rights. Thus has the emphasis shifted away from where it had been time out of mind, on political freedoms and civil liberties, into the larger, vaguer, socio-economic field for which the UN was proving a mighty hothouse; and thus also did it shift from a relatively small, select band of rights that any state could be expected to respect, to a virtually

[11] See, e.g., Ian Brownlie, *Basic Documents on Human Rights* (2nd edition, Oxford, 1981), 21, and A. H. Robertson, *Human Rights in the World* (2nd edition, New York, 1982), 28.

limitless broad band that very few states could manage, even if only because of considerations of cost, to respect in their entirety. These are rights (so far as they *are* 'rights' in the classic sense, which may be doubted) of a different order from the classic ones. But no more than those classic ones do they lack a share in the French Revolution's ambiguous legacy. Its universalism was something of a smoke-screen. The hand might be the hand of Montesquieu, but the voice was often the voice of Rousseau.

The voice of Rousseau is heard in the other big way in which the human rights' movement has gone through its own rapid revolution since the Second World War. That is by transferring its focus from the individual to the group. This is not simply a shift of emphasis, it is a shift of base and foundations; and its explanation is much more political than philosophical. Indeed the Universal Declaration, like the major rights-of-man texts which preceded it, left the door open to the criticism that it was not quite as explicit and firm as it might have been about the individual's social origins and the obligations he might consequently be expected to acknowledge. René Cassin had (as we saw) played a leading part in inserting into it the relatively minor element there was of that tendency, and to him and others in the classic tradition it was enough. That tradition, Judaeo-Christian in moral sensitivity, denied that the complete adult human being was simply a social product. He and she were *himself* and *herself*, innately valuable as such. That was what human rights were about; the protection of the individual's ability to become his and her full *self* and fully to be that singular person, within whatever frame of conditions might politically be stipulated. Those conditions, it was admitted, might be more or less demanding or restrictive, especially at seasons of national emergency; but to the imposition of demands and restrictions an absolute limit was understood to be set by the religious and philosophical presuppositions of the classic human rights doctrine which saw Man, not Society or the State, as their most precious and primary object of concern.

It came therefore as an unwelcome shock when this long-standing preference for the individual suffered through the 1950s and early 1960s a double deplacement. It was bad enough that civil-and-political rights should be placed second to the others. It was worse that in *both* lists pride of place should be given to what by classic criteria was not a 'human right' at all: 'the right of self-determination'. This was made right number one in both of the 1966 International Covenants:

> All peoples have the right of self-determination. By virtue of that status they freely determine their political status and freely pursue their economic, social and cultural development.

This could not be considered a proper human right on at least these grounds: first, it submerged the individual in a group; second, clarity of meaning and therefore the possibility of judicial scrutiny collapsed around the vagueness of the concept of 'a people'; third, insofar as any element of 'right' was present, it was not a human right as hitherto understood but the sort of right spoken of in political and military science – right asserted by might and/or conceded by the controlling mechanisms of the international system. That was all it had been in the American Rebellion and the French Revolution. History since then was amply to show, as experience in our own age continues to show, how partial, arbitrary and conflict-causing the definition of peoples/nations actually is, and how the satisfaction of one claim very often involves the rebuff of another. The UN's definition in the 1960s was a purely political one, determined by the anti-imperialist de-colonizing passion that then dominated the General Assembly. Self-determination was quickly discovered to be a one-shot game with rules heavily loaded on the side of the successor regime, whether it was succeeding as new state to former colony or as revolutionary regime to former empire. Biafrans found that they benefited from it as little vis-à-vis Nigeria or as Eritreans vis-à-vis Ethiopia, Kurds vis-à-vis Turkey, Iran and Iraq, etc. etc.

Such politicization added insult to the injury already inflicted on human rights by insisting on self-determination's inclusion among them. The post-1945 profit-and-loss account has other debits to record. The gaseous inflation of the lists of economic, social and cultural aspirations, already referred to, owed much of its energy and relish to its convenience as a stick to beat the consciences and money-bags of the developed countries. The ethical seriousness at the heart of the human rights debate could not but be demeaned by the shameless political bargaining and sovereignty-claiming which for many years helped to shield bad cases from the Human Rights Commission's spotlights. Worst of all, perhaps, were the damages inflicted by the hypocritical double-standardry which used human rights simply as a one-sided weapon in the endless war of words for which the UN, in one of its less attractive aspects, provided such generous facilities.

All was not loss, however. Against these politicizations and abuses can be set solid gains. The proponents of the Universal Declaration were right, after all. It has asserted a moral ascendancy which has enabled the civil-and-political concept of human rights to survive even such manipulations. The UN's Human Rights Commission has moved into a more creditable phase, and its Human Rights Committee set up by the 1966 Covenant goes annually through a batch of reports dutifully submitted by signatory states and critically analyses them. Within their respective regions, the analogous acts of the Inter-American and European Commissions on Human Rights carry great weight, and the European Court of Human Rights provides steady proof of the viability of a supra-national judiciary. Amnesty International and the International Committee of the Red Cross, each with its distinctive human rights preoccupations, stand high in public esteem the world over and prove that the organized moral concern of humankind has some influence on what governments do, even if mainly on how they like to be seen. There is not yet the International Court of Human Rights which some states sought at the outset, nor the UN High Commissioner for Human Rights who has more recently come to seem another good way forward. But the 1984 UN Convention against Torture etc. seems set to turn a crucial corner, by making that most abominable of human rights transgressors, the torturer, as generally recognized a common enemy of humankind as used to be the pirate; a person for whom ultimately no state offers refuge.

*

To sum up: such juxtaposition of pros and cons, of gains and losses, is the best one can do to depict the status of human rights in the world today. That it should be so mixed and ambiguous ought to surprise no one, not least because there had been so much ambiguity about these rights ever since the French Revolution launched them (under their earlier names) upon the tide of modern and contemporary history. The strengths and weaknesses of the human rights idea have been apparent ever since that start. 1789 after all turns out to have been more significant a year than 1776 or 1689. The men of 1689 had no interest in anyone else's rights. The men of 1776, although some of them professed such an interest and although they liked to be thought to have it, were in no position to do anything about it. But the French not only professed such an interest, in some part of their hearts and minds they really meant it and they actively exported it, seeking to share with the rest of mankind their own good fortune and superior virtue. Within the short space of a few action-packed years the revolutionary kaleidoscope had spot-lighted pretty well all the awkward questions that pursuit of human rights has raised ever since: notably, do they really mean the same for women as for men, to Muslims and Hindus as to Christians and atheists? Which of them, in hard times, takes priority? Have some categories of people more human rights than others? Have some categories of people, perhaps, no human rights at all? And lastly, has the State or the Nation or the People a right that trumps them all?

Aspects of Counter-revolution

GEORGE STEINER

No revolution is unanimous. The very concept of revolution entails that of opposition or counter-revolution. In the French Revolution, attempts at opposition and reversal are evident from the outset. Counter-revolution generates both political doctrines and political action, rhetoric and violence, opposition of a public and constitutional kind on the one hand and of clandestine conspiracy and subversion on the other. The spectrum of ideology and of public and private sensibility at the source of these diverse counter-revolutionary responses is as wide as political consciousness itself.

At one extreme, we find ultra-conservative positions of an essentially theocratic order, positions which not only repudiate the Revolution itself but those 'weaknesses' in the *ancien régime* which had allowed it to erupt and develop. At the other, notably in 1795–6, we find ultra-radical and proto-socialist or, indeed, communist or *communard* critiques and embryonic movements of resistance for whom the French Revolution is an incompleted, aborted act of emancipation whose inherent economic-social opportunism has brought gains only to the *bourgeoisie*. Between these polarities, the shadings of doctrine and of counter-revolutionary practice are of the utmost variousness and complexity. They comprise the constitutionalists and *monarchiens* who look to the precedent of the Glorious Revolution in Britain in 1688 and, more immediately, to that of the American Revolution and the instauration of the American balance of powers. This large, fluctuating body of opinion aims at the preservation or restoration of monarchy in France, but of a more or less parliamentary monarchy and of judicial restraints on the executive powers of the throne. There are moderate republicans whose ideal, often indistinctly formulated, is that of a bi-cameral system based on limited suffrage. Here the point of reference, often mythological or metaphorical, is that of Periclean Athens or republican Rome. Within this diffuse position, a small Spartan core does, from time to time, surface. It is that which postulates a communitarian republic under the dictatorial aegis of virtue and military excellence. Ironically, it will be this image, held fitfully and by few, that will, in fact, prevail in Bonapartism and the Consulate.

Within Jacobinism, the nuances of opposition are almost bewilderingly shifting and intricate. Historical analysis and archival scholarship have cast deepening doubt on the very notion of a planned Jacobin hegemony. It would seem that even the more radical aspects of Jacobinism, such as the Terror, were, in significant measure, reflexes of unwilled tactical immediacy, *ad hoc* developments in a situation whose pressures and complications outstripped considered control. We know now, though important gaps remain in our documentation, of the constant contacts between Jacobin personalitites and even members of the Committee of Public Safety on the one hand, and various centres of *monarchien* and conservative-royalist opposition on the other. We know of the profound ambiguities which beset and, in a surprisingly brief span of time, exhausted Robespierre's vision and policies in respect of the meaning and destiny of the Revolution. How was it to be brought to an end? Well before Trotsky, there were those who understood that the posing of this question is the counter-revolutionary act in essence. It is, moreover, out of these ambiguities at the heart of the crisis of 1793–4, out of the dialectic which knits revolution so closly to counter-revolution, which makes the motivations of a Sieyès or a Fouché opaque to this day, that will spring the transitory logic of ambiguity in the Directoire and the readiness of the Bonapartist solution.

For the Revolutionaries themselves, for the people of France at large, counter-revolution did mean ideological debate and institutional conflict. Was not the peril of counter-revolution the shibboleth of each successive wave of repression, parliamentary exclusion and administrative governance? Did it not bring to the scaffold monarchist and Girondin, Danton and Babeuf? But the counter-revolution that mattered, and most evidently beyond the confines of Paris, was that of actual insurgence. It was that of the Vendée and of south-eastern France, of Lyon and of Toulon. There were moments when the Republic seemed hemmed in by hostile armies both from within and without, when the restoration of the Bourbons by force looked to be the most realistic prospect. As in the Russian Revolution (the analogy has often been drawn) the 'white' armies out of the Catholic-royalist west and those of the foreign powers streaming across France's eastern borders seemed set to strangle revolution in its cradle.

How serious was the actual threat? The monographic literature on different regional aspects of armed counter-revolution and foreign incursion is voluminous. But imponderables remain. In terms of the numbers involved and of its duration – incidents are reported as early as 1791 and sporadic violence will continue almost until the consolidation of the Napoleonic empire – it is the civil war in the Vendée and throughout Brittany which looms largest. It involved a number of set battles and sieges, innumerable local skirmishes and guerrilla warfare and repression both of which rapidly took on a character of peculiar ferocity. Defeated in December 1793, the peasant-armies of the Vendée rose again in the spring and summer of 1795. Feebly supported by an English fleet, in large measure abandoned by the *émigrés* to whom they had looked for leadership and equipment, the insurgents were crushed by the republican forces at Quiberon in late July 1795. But it had taken the generalship of Hoche and a very considerable economic and military investment by the Directoire to arrive at pacification. And even this concept, as I noted, remained relative for some years to come. The *chouannerie*, this is to say the small-scale warfare of ambush and rapine, continued in the *bocage*-country and in the more remote areas of Brittany and the Normandy marches till 1803–4.

Readily accessible to counter-revolutionary regimes in Spain and the Austrian provinces of Italy, open to constant infiltration from the Rhineland and Switzerland, the south-east, and Lyon in particular, were a natural focus for reaction. Potentially, the Lyon uprising in the late spring and summer of 1793 was one of the most menacing to confront the Convention. The wealth of the great city, its easy proximity to *émigré* forces based in the Kingdom of Savoy, the possibility of coordinated insurrectionary movements throughout the Jura, the Rhone Valley and the Alpes Maritimes, seemed to afford counter-revolution its golden opportunity. The vigour of the republican riposte, however, and dissensions inside Lyon itself, brought a rapid conclusion. On 9 October, the remnants of the royalist troops and their most compromised supporters evacuated the city. Repression was of appalling savagery. The National Assembly decreed: 'Lyon has waged war on liberty; Lyon is no more.'

This draconian fate did not, however, arrest other counter-revolution conspiracies and uprisings through the south-east and along the Mediterranean coasts. Jacobins, moderates and outright royalists fought murderous internecine actions in Provence, notably at Aix, in Marseille and Avignon. Revolutionary Paris went in some fear of a junction between counter-revolutionary forces in Lyon and Marseille. The occupation of Toulon by Anglo-Spanish naval units and the royalists who had invited them into the harbour and city lasted throughout the autumn and winter of 1793. Notoriously, it took the gunner's eye of one Lieutenant Bonaparte to bring the siege to a victorious end.

Of a more formal and spectacular kind was the actual invasion of republican France by Austro-Prussian regulars and *émigré* 'legions' under the command of the Duke of Brunswick in the late summer and autumn of 1792. Goethe's eyewitness account, in his *Campaign in France*, remains a classic of political irony and disenchantment. The repulse of Brunswick's motley host at Valmy on 20 September gave to the French Republic an enduring and talismanic icon. It sanctioned, with consequences that have altered and dehumanized the history of national, ideological conflicts, the concept of mobilization, of the *levée en masse* as against that of the professional constraints and merciful mendacities of eighteenth-century warfare. But in itself, Valmy was only the logical and, from a strictly military point of view, minor, epilogue to an invasion that had already crumbled into mud and dissolution.

Historians and political scientists ask why the manifold and repeated counter-revolutionary movements, which extended from 1791 to the Paris rising of October 1795 (the insurrection of Vendémiare), should have failed so miserably. There is no simple answer. No faction had a monopoly on hatred, courage or tactical boldness. After the murky death of the Dauphin (Louis XVII), the comte de Provence, now self-proclaimed Louis XVIII, might have rallied moderate and weary sentiments to his side. He chose, instead, to espouse a policy of vindictive retribution. All he promised was the restoration of absolute monarchy tempered by certain limited acts of royal pardon. Chateaubriand's analysis of the long folly of Bourbon policy remains exemplary. Foreign support for counter-revolutionary actions tended to be fitful and merely opportunistic. Had there been a 'Wellingtonian' presence and intervention at the height of the Vendée as there was to be in Spain in 1809, the tale might well have been a different one. Prussia, the principalities and kingdoms of the Holy Roman Empire, Austria, Sardinia and the Russia of Catherine, may have shared certain fundamental counter-revolutionary impulses. But their several political and territorial aims were divided and, at cardinal points, mutually hostile. Protestant England did not view the dangers posed by the French Revolution in quite the same light as did Catholic Vienna or Orthodox St Petersburg. Centralization and the stern talents of desperation lay on the side of Paris and the Republic. Each of these factors and the interactions between them matter.

In essence, one conjectures, two elements were decisive in defeating the attempts at royalist counter-revolution. Even moderates, who certainly constituted the great majority of the politically literate in metropolitan France, did not wish for the return of absolute monarchy. Secondly, the French Revolution was able to harness nascent strengths and imaginings of nationhood, of nationalist pride and fidelity new to modern history. Neither 1688 nor 1776 are significant dates in the rise of nationalism, of militant and ideologically marshalled chauvinism as we have come to know them. 1789 is a crucial date. What fell with the Bastille was a Europe of castes and monarchic-aristocratic family alliances, of mundane and intellectual civilities across often ephemeral frontiers, of mercenary armies and peregrine academicians, financiers or mountebanks. It was the Europe of Voltaire, of Diderot, of Necker, of Casanova and Cagliostro. The French Revolution woke into fierce being and enlisted within its energies that most trenchant of modern emotions: the tribalism of the nation-state.

In fact, the defeat of the counter-revolution remained partial. It is at this crucial point that our theme reaches, with costly intensity, into the present. Even as there are certain features of the internal struggles of 1791–7 which relate to the religious and civil broils of the sixteenth century, so the conflict between revolution and counter-revolution continues throughout modern French history and political allegiance. Himself a conservative historian of the French Revolution, Thiers will preside over the humiliation of Paris and the massacre of the Communards in 1871. Both he and Marx fully perceived the symbolic and the socio-political continuity of hatreds which connected the Commune and its bloody suppression to the September massacres of 1792 and to the counter-revolutionary terrorism of Thermidor. In the profound antagonisms between Paris and the rest of France (there was more than allegoric symmetry in the fact that Thiers's army was based in Versailles, in the very seat of humbled and slain royalty), the savagery of 1871 had its source and logic. The deeply incised lines of force and fundamental polemic which had divided revolution from counter-revolution cut, once again, across the manifold intricacies of the Dreyfus affair and the emergence of the French right in its twentieth-century guise.

If we do not recognize the strength and internal consistency of this division, we cannot make sense of the meanings either of Vichy or of the liberation. Explicitly in its rhetoric, in its educational revisionism, in its agrarian-Catholic repudiation of Paris, in its authentically nationalist Jew-hatred; implicitly in the image it revived and fostered of French regionalism and of France's destiny as a bulwark against anarchic libertarianism, the world of Vichy and Pétain was that dreamt, fought for by the counter-revolutionaries of 1793 and 1795. It was the world of Jeanne d'Arc, of the *ancien régime*, of Bossuet – the high master of a theological and conservative historicism – seeking to eradicate that of Voltaire, of Jaurès and of republican and Jacobin utopia. Vichy, as a concept, as a functional structure, was 'triggered' by German military victory; but its essence is rooted utterly within France itself, within the vengeful patience of the Vendée and the counter-revolutionary fury of the south-central and south-eastern *départements*. The ideological-sociological fabric of the pro-Vichy *milice* closely echoes that of the White Terror and of the *Compagnie de Jésus* after the fall of Robespierre. Almost eerily, numerous of the most homicidal and implacable armed clashes between *milice* and Resistance in 1945, as well as many of the worst episodes of the *épuration*, of the vengeance of the left on those who had hunted and decimated it under Vichy, occurred in those very regions and communities which had witnessed the combats and vendettas, the prison-massacres and show-trials of 1792–7. It is neither hyperbole nor oversimplification to see in the history of French political life and sensibility since 1789 an essential continuity of conflict between revolution and counter-revolution. In July 1987, France celebrated the thousandth anniversary of the foundation of the Capetian monarchy; in July 1989 it celebrates the two-hundredth anniversary of Bastille Day. Both anniversaries have their immediacy. As Chateaubriand noted, the 'justice of civil war' is always latent in the politics of modern France.

As we shall see, the most rigorous foundation for a doctrine of counter-revolution is theological. In spirit and expression, however, most counter-revolutionary manifestos and diagnoses are anti-theoretical. It is precisely abstract political theory and attempts to impose analytic and systematic projections on the essentially irrational, instinctual, contingent flux of human affairs which the counter-revolutionary scorns and repudiates. The psychological and stylistic components of the counter-revolutionary sensibility are those of an ardent remembrance (often embellished and arcadian) of things past; of a profound distrust of voluntarist, cerebrally inspired innovations in the inherited weave of communal life; they are of those of instinctive *pietas* and of an intuition of the organic in the very pulse and structure of history. In Edmund Burke all those components are most vividly felt and articulate.

The *Reflections on the Revolution in France* are the classical statement of an 'organicist' position. They belong to that particular lineage of conservative imagining, of the custodianship of threatened private and civic values, which relates the political-religious writings of Richard Hooker, John Henry Newman and T. S. Eliot. Burke's celebrated rhetoric, with its alternance between pathos and irony, baroque organ-flights and sober, closely arrayed discourse, is, at every point, meant to persuade. The *Reflections* are a tract, intended most explicitly for the times. They are hortatory, didactic propaganda in the sense in which Milton (a constant stylistic model) understood that term and intent. It is never Burke's aim to offer a dispassionate analysis of the late events in neighbouring France. He seeks to turn French readers from their fatal course; he seeks, above all else, to expose the blindness, the potential self-destructive folly of those who, in Britain, were voicing enthusiasm for the revolutionary cause in France itself and, potentially, on home ground. Literally haunted by his deep intimations of crisis, of the utter fragility of civic order and progress in Ireland, Edmund Burke felt the awesome tremors from across the Channel. Only that hauntedness and the unmistakable strain of violence – in imagination, in idiom, in his evolving political stance – can account for the clairvoyance of the *Reflections*, for the graphic prevision of horrors and armageddon to come as it is set out, well before the facts, in the benign, seemingly conciliatory ambience of 1790. It was as if Burke had in some sense willed the spectres he saw rising on the horizon (the Miltonic–Gothick armature of the spectral and the satanic plays a significant part in Burke's imagery).

Burke detests the 'new political Men of Letters', the landless, urbanized clerisy of the *philosophes*, of the publicists who had undermined the stability of traditional intellectual and political values. It is these libertines of meliorist thought who had, in their purported love of their fellow men, in the purported critique of feudal injustice and ecclesiastical repression, brought on a despotism far worse. It was they who had laid the foundations for what Burke, in a lashing phrase, calls the 'homicidal philanthropy of

France'. What the Revolution would, inevitably, generate is 'a perfect democracy', which is to say 'the most shameless thing in the world'. Freed from the constraints of religion and social hierarchy, the 'lust of selfish will', the anarchic play of intellectuality and of material greed, must bring on the *régime* of the mob. It, in turn, compels the establishment of a dictatorship based, solely, on the spurious legitimacy of the gun. Intuitive, fuelled by metaphor, contemptuous of any such empty concept as that of 'laws of history' or 'economic determinants', Burke's exposition was wholly prophetic; he saw Bonapartism coming out of the very matrix of what looked, in 1790, to be a gradual ripening towards constitutional monarchy and the rule of law.

Like any great orator and propagandist, Burke knows how to pull together the urgent strands of his case into central, cadenced moments of summation. A number of these passages have been often quoted and anthologized. But they richen with reiteration:

> Society is indeed a contract. Subordinate contracts for objects of mere occasional interest may be dissolved at pleasure – but the state ought not to be considered as nothing better than a partnership agreement in a trade of pepper and coffee, callico or tobacco, or some such low concern to be taken up for a little temporary interest, and to be dissolved by the fancy of the parties. It is to be looked on with other reverence: because it is not a partnership for things subservient only to the gross animal existence of a temporary and perishable nature. It is a partnership in all science; a partnership in all art; a partnership in every virtue, and in all perfection. As the end of such a partnership cannot be obtained in many generations, it becomes a partnership not only between those who are living, but between those who are living, those who are dead, and those who are to be born. Each contract of each particular state is but a clause in the great primaeval contract of eternal society, linking the lower with the higher natures, connecting the visible and invisible world, according to a fixed compact sanctioned by the inviolable oath which holds all physical and all moral natures, each in their appointed place. This law is

> not subject to the will of those, who by an obligation above them, and infinitely superior, are bound to submit their will to that law. The municipal corporations of that universal kingdom are not morally at liberty at their pleasure, and on their speculations of a contingent improvement, wholly to separate and tear asunder, the bands of their subordinate community, and to dissolve it into an unsocial, uncivil, unconnected chaos of elementary principles. It is the first and supreme necessity only, a necessity that is not chosen but chooses, a necessity paramount to deliberation, that admits no discussion, and demands no evidence, which alone can justify a resort to anarchy. This necessity is no exception to the rule: because this necessity itself is a part too of that moral and physical disposition of things to which man must be obedient by consent or force; but if that which is only submission to necessity should be made the object of choice, the law is broken, nature is disobeyed, and the rebellious are outlawed, cast forth, and exiled from this world of reason, and order, and peace, and virtue, and fruitful penitence, into the antagonist world of madness, discord, vice, confusion, and unavailing sorrow.

Together with Plato's hymn to cosmic order and ordinance in the *Timaeus*, together with Dante's meditation on eternal hierarchy in the *Paradiso* and T. S. Eliot's interweaving of the live, ordering past into the hazard and menace of the present in the *Four Quartets*, this page in Burke's *Reflections* is one of the touchstones of counter-revolution. Turning on an *intelligentsia* which attends only 'to the shell and husk of history' (Yeats will himself re-enact that angry motion in his poems on the Irish civil war), turning on the anarchic opportunists of innovation and the mob which they, unavoidably, unleash, Burke sets out the covenant of an acceptance, of an observant – note the religious intimation in the phrase 'fruitful penitence' – at-homeness of man in the immanent and in the transcendent world. The true revolutions are those of the celestial bodies and of the seasons. The authentic 'tree of liberty' is the 'great blossomer' rooted in the mystery and logic of the immemorial. Torn from the earth, that tree will become the dead firebrand of the terrorist and the *ad hoc* tyrant.

Burke was scarcely read in revolutionary France. His influence elsewhere on the continent was only gradual. In Britain, the progress of the French Revolution towards deepening violence and expansionist aggression gave to the *Reflections* the prestige, the persuasiveness of verification. In the nineteenth century, via the political analyses and histories of de Tocqueville and of Taine, Burke's reading of the meaning and potential of 1789 acquires seminal force. Marx's *Eighteenth Brumaire* is in many regards a satiric riposte to Burke. The bones of contention remain fiercely alive. Like Goya in his mesmerizing etching, Burke had seen arising, out of the dreams of reason, the swarming nightmare of civil massacre and warfare between nations on an unprecedented scale. His case is not one which our own times can, with any facility, dismiss.

The assertion put forward by Friedrich Schlegel in his *Charakteristiken und Kritiken* of 1796–1801 is arresting. Schlegel posits the French Revolution, Fichte's *Wissenschaftslehre* and Goethe's novel *Wilhelm Meister* as the three greatest 'impulses' or 'currents' of the age. The Revolution may, indeed, be 'loud and material'. But this or that 'small book', of which the clamorous multitude takes no notice at the time, may come to play a greater role in human affairs and in the history of human consciousness than the external events which seem so overwhelming.

The part of the French Revolution in the genesis and development of German Idealism is at once ubiquitous and complex. We can dissociate no key element, no internal transmutations in the thought of Kant, Fichte, Schlegel, Hegel and Schelling or in that of Hölderlin, the most metaphysically inspired of poets, from the successive phases of the French Revolution and from the incursions, ideological and political, of that Revolution into the fate of Germany and of reactive German self-consciousness. To delineate the German philosophic reception and response as a motion from jubilant welcome to dark reaction – a motion parallel to that which we can observe in Wordsworth and in Coleridge – would be both true and oversimplified. No complex of thought and sentiment felt more acutely than German Idealism what it took to be the self-betrayal of French revolutionary ideals and practices. None formulated with more intellectual and emotive strength a second or counter-revolution, which is to say an epistemological and heuristic programme for the emancipation of the human subject. It is towards this internalization of revolution, towards this liberation and legitimization of the human spirit and, in Hegel's *Phenomenology* of the Spirit *per se*, that Friedrich Schlegel points in his challenging dictum. At the font of both the French Revolution and of the 'greater, more lasting' revolution brought on by Kant and his successors, lie the work and emblematic figure of Rousseau. But it is, argues German Idealism, in Kant's ethics, in the pedagogic psychology of Goethe's *Bildungsroman*, in the perception of animate nature as we experience it in Hölderlin, in the organic conception of the state as we find it, though in different modes, in Hegel and in Schelling, that Rousseauism is given its authentic legacy.

No sequence of responses to the events of 1789–97 is more various and difficult to outline than that of Goethe. Countless nuances of reflection and of judgement mark the spectrum between enthusiasm for the Promethean fire of revolutionary insurgence and profound abhorrence. Even at his most negative, Goethe fully recognizes the immensity of the event, its pivotal and determinant position in modern history. But it is as 'the most terrible of all occurrences' that he will come to envisage it. Almost against his will, Goethe finds himself compelled to the conclusion – itself charged with a desolate violence – that injustice is preferable to disorder, that the imperial solution enacted by Napoleon can, alone, repair something of the ravages to the condition of civilized man perpetrated by the Revolution in France and the anarchic embers it scattered across Europe.

Goethe tells of the 'limitless effort' which he devoted, throughout the 1790s, to an attempt to 'master poetically', to give imaginative-rational embodiment to, his understanding of revolutionary events. We owe to this endeavour not only Goethe's account of Brunswick's ill-fated foray into France, to which I have already referred, but a series of somewhat bizarre satiric or allegoric dramas and dramatic fragments: *Der Grosskophta*(1790–2), *Der Büngergeneral* (1793), *Die Aufgeregten* (1793–4) and *Das Mädchen von Oberkirch* of 1795–6. We owe to it as well innumerable decisive touches in such masterworks as *Iphigenia* and *Tasso* and the allegoric-ironic examination of power and rebellion in *Faust* II. But the essential impulse is not that of satire. In contrast to Burke, the counter-revolutionary critique in Goethe is not, primarily, political. The counter-values set into play (this is, very distinctly, Schlegel's point) are those of human inwardness, of the inviolate privacy of human spirituality. They are those of abstention and renunciation, as these will find crowning realization in Faust. The chaos which Goethe apprehends is, in a sense related to Burke's polemic, that of the world-order and the *polis*; but it is, more decisively, that which threatens to take possession of man's identity and make of him a stranger to felt being.

Goethe planned to set forth his oblique but nonetheless fundamental dissent from the French Revolution in a trilogy of dramas on the model of the *Oresteia*. What we have is only the first of the intended triptych and Goethe's notes and sketches for the project as a whole. *Die natürliche Tochter* (1803) is based on the curious *Mémoires historiques de Stephanie-Louise de Bourbon-Conti* to which Schiller had drawn Goethe's notice in 1799. From this tale of persecution and falsification in the France of Louis XV (whether or not the lady, was, in fact, the high personage she claimed to be remains, to this day, in dispute), Goethe drew one of his most veiled and portentous inventions. Much in the two dramas which were to follow, and which would have involved the characters in the actual events of the fall of the monarchy and the execution of Louis XVI, would have clarified Goethe's meaning. In the prologue, the repudiation of the Revolution is implicit in an almost private language of lyric-philosophic symbols and of cross-references to others of Goethe's works. What is palpable is two-fold: the evocation, metaphysical in depth, of the loss which society and civility must incur through revolutionary action, and the dialectic between external political crises on the one hand and the attendant transformations of personal consciousness on the other.

The exalted milieu of absolute monarchy and historical allegiance in which the beginning of the action is situated, is threatened both by obscure agencies of disorder and by intrigue and corruption sprung from within itself. The very genius of an *ancien régime* is, for Goethe, hedged with mystery (even as in Shakespeare, such mystery attends upon kingship and high lineage). The trope of the garden, of the arcadian enclosure, articulates Goethe's sense of a system of comeliness, of 'order and degree' which is vulnerable precisely because it seeks to marginalize, to distance itself from, the ineluctable metamorphoses of time. Outside the park teem those men and women who are 'terrible' because they have nothing to lose, who have no stake but bitterness in the conservation of remembrance. But inside the park, a fatality of ambition, of nearly theatrical spuriousness, mines the sanctity and perpetuation of the dynastic continuity. (A closely comparable vision haunts Yeats's depiction of the great houses of Ireland on the brink of violence and dissolution.) The Arcady of order and ceremonious wisdom must fall. Goethe has no illusions on this point. The pressures from without and the poisons from within (had Goethe in mind the obstinate rumours that intrigues by Louis of Orleans had brought on the Revolution?) will, fatally, prevail. But the balance-sheet is of the most uncertain kind. Anticipating the 'theses on history' of Walter Benjamin, himself steeped in Goethe, *Die natürliche Tochter* dramatizes the inviolate aura of the defeated, the rights and claims upon our understanding and our imagining of that which the logic of violence has swept away. Images of ruin, of waste, of unrecapturable worth, abound in the play. Closely related to antique tragedy, Goethe's strange dramatic allegory is, by virtue of its very form and lyric-philosophic elevation, an act of counter-revolution, a rebuke to the prosaic tumult of the revolutionary proposal. The climactic simile is that of a noble harbour shattered by earth-tremors and, then, silted into desolation, a Claude Lorrain harbour, as it were, ruined by 'sand and mud' – a pairing which, in turn, relates to Goethe's view of the revolutionary crowd and its suffocating, tidal ingress. 'Each ruin points to a grave.' A wearied humanity can no longer 'master the elements' (we recall the reclamation of land from wasteful sea at the crux of *Faust* II).

Subtler, more difficult to paraphrase, is Goethe's rejection of revolution in the name of privacy. Goethe takes the ultimate significance of the French Revolution to be one of *politicization*. An *ancien régime* is one in which ordinary men and women conduct their lives within their social caste, locale and profession. The making, the suffering of history is, in essence, the business of the few. Even as traditional warfare is the business of the aristocrat and the mercenary. What the French Revolution has done is to abolish the millennial barriers between common life and the enormities of the historical. Past the hedge and gate of even the humblest garden march the bayonets of political ideology and historical conflict. The consequence is not only that of a quantum leap in the scale, ferocity and unpredictability of political-historical events: it is a reduction, ontological as well as psychological, in the inner space, in the inner temporality of private being. The leisure, the fundamental quietude needed for men and women to come to know themselves, the *dignitas* of discretion within *domesticity*, are swept away by the ephemeral relevance of public news (one remembers that harsh scorn for the 'journalistic' voiced in the Prologue to *Faust*). Under stress of political totality, the individual can no longer hear himself think and feel. What is gravest: he can no longer ripen towards the authenticity of his own private person. And for Goethe (this is the theme Schlegel adduces), such ripening outweighs all external liberations. Hence the radically counter-political utopia expressed by the *Gerichtsrat* in the play (he was to become the protagonist of the trilogy). Only one way of life can hope to escape from the 'raw surge' of the politicized crowd, from the 'embittered libels' and ephemerally raucous clamour of partisan pronouncements: it is that of the 'holiness' of one's hearth. There, alone, man is master of himself and of his promises. There, alone, he can experience the supreme revolution which is that of a coming to maturity. The tranquil imperative in Goethe's counter-revolutionary programme is formidable: for if it has its antecedents in the symbolism of the Edenic and in the Horatian turn from the factitious claims of public affairs, it is rooted no less in Goethe's specific sense of the biological, in his central intuition of the organic, evolutionary nature of human truth. What greater revolution can there be than to come home to oneself?

Summarily expressed, the terms of reference in Burke's counter-revolutionary position are political and social; those in Goethe's are of the order of philosophic psychology. Both critiques are, in the final analysis, underwritten by metaphysical intuitions concerning the relations between eternity and historical time, between a cosmic concordance and the destiny of the individual within the social process. Both these intuitions and *a priori* determinants are only implicit or metaphorized. It is the virtue of Joseph de Maistre to have articulated with uncompromising clarity and consequence the metaphysical-theological axioms inherent in any fundamental repudiation of the French Revolution. If we have difficulty, today, in apprising the full force and logic of Maistre's argument, it is just because he meant every word of what he said, and said in a prose of the most luminous and lapidary quality. Being perfectly consequent, this 'prophet of the past' and writer of genius represents the counter-revolution in essence.

The entirety of Maistre's work (much of it as yet unpublished) can be understood as a single, unbroken Phillipic against the misreading of the crises in France. Be it a study of the political edifice of the German states, a defence of Papal hegemony and infallibility, a treatise on capital punishment or the famous *Soirées de Saint-Petersbourg* (one of the masterpieces of philosophic debate and wit in the history of Western dialogue), the underlying argument remains the same: and it is addressed to the cataclysm of 1789. But it is in the early *Considérations sur la France*, most probably published in 1796 (there is some doubt as to the date and locale of the first edition), that Maistre's critical and predictive procedures can be seen in their sharpest light.

Maistre takes it as self-evident that divine providence commands the lives of nations and of individuals. A 'supple chain' binds man to God's throne. He is, as Augustine and Aquinas have taught, at liberty to will and carry out his personal and public acts within the mystery of God's foreknowledge and final purpose. It is, therefore, puerile to regard the French Revolution or any event of comparable magnitude in human history as somehow accidental, as the more or less contingent product of conspiracy, of secular error or mischance. God has allowed (willed) the new apocalypse and it is in the sombre light of that fatality that political conflicts and developments must be understood. As are so many other major crises and devastations in history, both ancient and modern, so the French Revolution is an embodiment of divine retribution, of God's chastisement of mutinous and unbelieving mankind. Blinded by opulence, indifferent to moral justice, self-destructive in its frivolous toleration of the deism or outright atheism of the *philosophes*, the *ancien régime* was ripening towards divine anger. It is, paradoxically, the very powers unleashed by the fall of the Bastille, the turbulent dynamism of the revolutionary thrust across France and neighbouring Europe, which allow us to gauge the corresponding strength of God's wrath. Where the 'sovereignty of religion' has been trivalized into empty pomp, where the 'execrable sect' of free-thinkers and libertarians has been licensed to 'bring pestilence to Europe', the whirlwind shall and must be reaped. The Revolution has in it a fearful symmetry of response to 'a century of blasphemy'. How could any thinking man be astonished at or bewildered by its eruption?

What is Maistre's evidence for this theological fatalism? None other than the very course of the events from July 1789 onward. The so-called agents and leaders of the successive revolutionary movements and legislatures, whom Joseph de Maistre judges to be a pack of rabid mediocrities and loud-mouthed mountebanks, are, in fact, mere puppets. In a series of mordant passages, Maistre points to the strangely 'passive and mechanical' tenor of their purported deeds and decisions. 'One cannot repeat it too often: it is not men who lead the Revolution; it is the Revolution that makes use of men.' If divine providence makes employ of such vile instruments, it is, as we shall see, towards regenerative ends. But such regeneration must be preceded by the most sanguinary trials. It is in the manifest logic of God's design that the French Revolution should devour, in turn, each of its deluded, indeed crazed, children (again, Goya's images of cyclical destruction and of history as Saturn lie close to hand). Each in turn, the Girondins regicides, Danton and the killers of September, Robespierre and his murdering pack, are ground to bloodstained dust by the very engines of factitious law and corrupt judgement which they themselves had instituted and visited upon their predecessors. Each, in turn, Mirabeau, Danton, Robespierre, Saint-Just and the petty despots of the Directoire see their cunning plans turn to suicidal folly. Dark tides of transcendental finality and chastisement carry these hollow men into the abyss. Though their systematic premises are antithetical, Maistre and Trotsky are the two great visionaries of the ineluctable, of the necessitarian imperative of the historical as it confounds and crushes the vanity of political agents.

Now comes the brilliant, once more paradoxical, turn in the argument. The France of Louis XVI, rules Maistre, was enfeebled, mined from inside, impotent at its frontiers. That of the French Revolution has, in Coleridge's image, the limbs of a 'giant upreared'. All Europe trembles before the might and discipline of the Revolutionary and Bonapartist battalions. France is emerging triumphantly from the hideous divisions of class hatreds and civil broils. Such a renascence is wholly characteristic and revelatory of God's intent and secret presence. The entirety of the French Revolution is, fundamentally, one of self-contradiction (Marx will adapt this dialectical analytic to his own purposes). Unknowing, the regicides and the men of Thermidor have served the cause of the crown. 'All the monsters brought to birth by the Revolution have laboured only for royalty'. Their wild, demonic accomplishments at home and abroad have surrounded France with an aura of victory. It is this aura, together with the purged strength and historical genius of the French nation, which restored royalty shall inherit. It is, via the hands that have wrought the martyrdom of Louis XVI and Louis XVII, that Louis XVIII shall reascend his throne 'with all its *éclat* and all its puissance and even, it may be, with might augmented'. No true adherent to religion, to royalism and legitimacy, would want the Revolution undone.

That the Restoration will follow on the Revolution and on its Napoleonic epilogue, was to Maistre an axiomatic certainty.

Though he could not foresee the interlude of empire, Maistre spelt out, in his inspired tract of 1796, the actual developments of 1814 and 1815. He clearly envisioned a France, at once exhausted and glorious, turning, almost unanimously, towards its Bourbon monarch and the traditional intimacies between church and state. Drawing on Burke's *Reflections*, Maistre's *Considérations* cite the illustrious precedent of the restoration of the English crown after Cromwell. Once before, a great European nation, steeped in history and the world-view of Christian civilization, had passed through the purging grime of revolution, regicide and civil conflict in order to give to monarchy an even sounder, more resplendent basis. Maistre's programme was not, to be sure, one of parliamentary rule and constitutional limitation. What he counselled the fugitive Louis XVIII was absolutism tempered by pardon and made just and efficacious by its devotion to God and to the embodiment of divine historicity in the nation. Anything less would be betrayal of the very possibilities sprung from the fiery furnace of 1789. Hailed as a clairvoyant when the actual Restoration came to pass, Maistre soon found himself in wholly eccentric isolation. The concessions made by Louis XVIII to post-revolutionary and post-Napoleonic France, the *Charte*, seemed to Maistre a fatal weakness. With perfect accuracy (here he saw far more deeply than Chateaubriand), Maistre foretold the coming of new political and social crises from within a system no longer at the level of its own destiny and obligations. 1830 and 1848 were to confirm his solitary alarm.

The validation of Maistre's counter-revolutionary arguments was theocratic. The consequences of practical, political application would have been those of an intransigent atavism. As a result, the actual influence of the *Considérations* and of Maistre's subsequent writings has been almost subterranean. Nevertheless, they have known a constant legacy. Baudelaire's vision of human culpability derives from Maistre. Maistre's bracing pessimism and lucid sense of the infernal in history and politics are decisively present in the *Action française* and Maurras, in the philosophic monarchism of Pierre Boutang, in the apocalyptic nihilism of Cioran (who has modelled his prose on that of Maistre). Maistre's thought also lies at the foundation of the theological politics of Carl Schmitt, the German conservative jurist.

But an even more salient parallel relates the vision of the *Considérations* and of the *Soirées* to our own moment. The conception of revolution as a divinely occasioned act of political self-chastisement, the summons to the restoration of a religious-political *auctoritas* in a fundamentally theocratic state and society, are those of Solzhenitsyn. His total rejection of the Russian Revolution in the name of the Christ of Byzantine majesty and suffering, his detestation of the uprooted *intelligentsia* which brought on the crises of 1917, his incomparable image of the cannibalism, of the self-devouring which are the iron law of a Bolshevist utopia, make of Solzhenitsyn a close counterpart to Maistre.

It is this parallel that leads to the heart of our theme.

A counter-revolutionary position, where it is more than political opportunism or *ressentiment*, entails a particular reading of the meaning of history and of social institutions. A Maistre, a Solzhenitsyn postulate, literally and metaphorically, the fact of original sin, of some primordial guilt in the nature of mortal man. History as we know and live it, the never-ending sequence of injustice, public and private *misère*, warfare and devastation, are the direct, palpable reflection and realization of man's fallen state, of what is, in the true sense of the word, his 'disgrace'. A secular meliorism, of which actual revolution is the most radical and logical manifestation, is a capital sin. It is a rebellion not so much against contingent institutions, but against a world-order whose recurrently oppressive and irrational weight veritably incarnates man's 'fall into history'. From this fall there can be no pragmatic, immanent escape. The only true revolution will be that of the messianic, of the apocalyptic in the light prefigured by the Book of Revelation. At that day of judgement, the inhumanities, the absurdities, the injustices wrought by man on man, will be resolved in a finality of punishment and of recompense. The endeavour of mundane revolutions, of revolutionary tribunals, to anticipate that last judgement, to enforce upon history and social relations some man-made code of equity are, in the strictest and most concrete connotations, blasphemy.

It follows that they are futile, or worse. The 'love of man' preached by egalitarian and socialist dreamers, the levelling of class differences prescribed by Jacobin or Marxist dreamers and terrorists, ends, must necessarily and eternally end, in what Burke called 'homicidal philanthropy'. The September butcheries and the Terror in Paris, the Gulag Archipelago as it extends across the empire created by the Russian Revolution, are no accident. It is not the despotic or paranoid sensibilities of a Robespierre, of a Lenin or of a Stalin which deflect revolutions from their liberating course. The attempts to institute on earth 'kingdoms of justice', to legislate the messianic in secular terms, go not only against the grain of human nature (fallen man is a rapacious, cowardly, materialistic creature): they go against the grain of divine providence and of the transcendental pendulum-swing from fall to resurrection which, alone, generates and makes evidential a meaning to history. It is in the first and last nature of the human condition, in the alpha and omega of politics and history, that those who plant 'trees of liberty' shall, rapidly, make of them the gate-posts to prisons and to death-camps.

This, in essence, defines the counter-revolutionary case. Being theological and prophetic, it is not debatable or negotiable on positivist and ideological terms where ideology is purely secular or, to use the revelatory claim of Marxism, where it is 'scientific'. The politics of counter-revolutionary transcendence have their exposition in Plato's *Republic*, in Dante's ascription of the killers of Caesar to the ultimate circle of Hell, in Shakespeare on 'order and degree' in *Troilus and Cressida*. It is Maistre's eminence to have applied these archetypal intimations to a modern circumstance, that of 1789, and to have opened his clairvoyance to the proof of ensuing events. Has the blood-stained history of nineteenth- and of twentieth-century Europe, Asia or Latin America refuted his indictment?

Questions of this synoptic kind admit of no rational answer. Nor is there any plausible method for assessing the total balance-sheet of the results of the French Revolution. Phenomena of the range and complication of that Revolution or of the Industrial Revolution, whose vital interactions with the drama of 1789 remain, at numerous points, yet to be elucidated, humble all attempts at comprehensive analytical judgement. There is a sense beyond simile in which they share the seeming ineluctability of natural catastrophes or of the movement of geological forces. As Voltaire stressed, in a text seminal to the Enlightenment and to pre-revolutionary intimations of the fragility of social institutions, explanatory reason and moral judgement are equally impotent in the face of an earthquake.

Talleyrand observed that those who, in Europe, had not known life prior to the fall of the Bastille had never known true felicity. The rejoinder that this arcadian retrospection pertains only to the privileged and that the existence of the populace at large was often an utterly wretched one, is both cogent and facile. It was far more than economic and social advantage, it was far more than exploitative mundanity that Talleyrand was invoking. The French Revolution unleashed opportunities for, and demands upon, privacy of a kind unprecedented since Sparta and republican Rome. It destroyed, so far as we can tell permanently, spaces and temporalities of private, personal consciousness. In a sense both unmistakable and very difficult to define, the cataclysm of 1789–1815 accelerated the fundamental *tempi* of perception and imagining. That acceleration is patent in the music of Beethoven or the narrative cadence of the modern novel no less than in the mechanics of industrial production and communication. Correspondingly evident and resistant to definition are the alterations, the magnifications of public space brought on by the Revolution and the Napoleonic adventure. Men who had ridden or marched from Lisbon to Moscow, from Cairo to Copenhagen, never came home to the parishes and bounded acres of common life under an *ancien régime*. Stendhal is our eminent witness to this transformation. In ways which no preceding historical phenomenon had accomplished, the French Revolution mobilized historicity itself, seeing itself as historical, as transformative of the basic conditions of human possibility, as invasive of the individual person. With hindsight we can make out that Rousseau was far less a begetter of 1789 than he was a pessimistic visionary seeking (in vain) to define and preserve for certain men and women, for certain localities, the rudiments of solitude. Irresistibly, the tidal impact of the Revolution turned the daily into the journalistic. Our present culture, if that is not too flattering a word, is the direct product of this mutation.

More specifically, the *levée en masse* to which I have already referred, Carnot's rationalization of the manufacture of armaments, the resort of both the revolutionary and the Napoleonic invasions to ideological and economic modes of attack, altered profoundly the nature of war. They made of war that recurrent instrument of foreign policy, that almost statutory component of international relations, which it is to this day. Clausewitz was the observant theoretician of the new totality. I have already adduced the exponential growth of nationalism, of the enlistment of patriotism and chauvinism as these were fostered by the men of 1792. Having routed the catholicities of ancient privilege, which had prevailed across boundaries, having largely eradicated the ecumenism of *civilitas* in the European church and aristocracy, the Revolution crystallized the myth and practice of the nation-state. Here, again, our current parlous situation is its direct heir. It is after Valmy and after Waterloo that ordinary men, conscripted into diverse forms of national service, have died in the modern way for bits of coloured cloth which we call flags.

The barest enumeration of some of the principal consequences of 1789 enforces the realization that the world as we know it today, and not only in the essentially democratized and industrialized west, is the composite of reflexes, political assumptions and structures, rhetorical postulates, bred by the French Revolution. More than arguably, for it entails subsequent, so often mimetic revolutionary movements and struggles across the rest of the planet, the French Revolution is the pivotal historical-social date after that of the foundation of Christianity. Far more than an arrogant conceit or piece of propaganda inhabits the revolutionary calender, the dating of *l'An un*. Time itself, the cycle of lived history, was deemed to have begun a second time.

The counter-revolution prevailed neither in action nor in its critiques. In political practice, counter-revolutionary convictions, as we find them, for example, in the *Action française*, in royalist factions, in such regional atavisms as Breton separatism or in the more conservative spheres of Roman Catholicism, lead a tenebrous, mainly literary existence. When they do surface, it is, more often than not, under the dubious aegis of proto-fascisms or outright fascism. This reality does not refute Burke or Goethe; it does not cancel out Joseph de Maistre's clear-sightedness or the tragic grandeur of his dissent. But it does convey something of the organic logic, of the natural validity of the Revolution itself. It does make very nearly self-evident the fact that the French Revolution and the changes it brought with it were respondent to overwhelming needs within modern rationality, within a post-religious and scientific sense of the human status, and within the nascent dynamics of mass production and mass consumption. To sing, as does the French round, as do, in many respects, Burke or Maistre or Maurras, 'C'est la faute à Voltaire/c'est la faute à Rousseau', is childish. The clocks could not be turned back. They could only be started anew. That the times they have told have proved both creative and destructive, both liberating and tyrannical, beyond even the dawn-prophecies of a Saint-Just or the nightmares of a Maistre, is simply another way of saying that 1789 continues to be now.

Bibliographical Note

Somewhat surprisingly, the counter-revolution has not been the object of major historical consideration. Monographs on this or that aspect of the civil conflicts and counter-Terror in France are numerous. Jacques Godechot's *La Contre-révolution* (1961) provides a lucid survey and lists both primary and secondary sources. But the work which would combine into a persuasive synthesis the practice of counter-revolution on the one hand, and the philosophical-literary refusals of, dissents from, the events of 1789 on the other, remains to be written. Hippolyte Taine's great study of the origins of modern France is the nearest we have to such a master-text. It is, one suspects, little read.

The following are of great interest: R. R. Palmer, *The Age of the Democratic Revolution*, I (*The Challenge*) (1959); J. L. Talmon, *Origins of Totalitarian Democracy* (1961); Barrington Moore; *The Social Origins of Dictatorship and Democracy* (1966); F. Furet, *Penser la révolution* (1978).

Anyone reading Burke's *Reflections* will be indebted to the magisterial introduction by Dr Conor Cruise O'Brien in the Penguin English Library edition of 1982 (the Pelican edition, now out of print, appeared in 1968). Professor B. Böschenstein has generously put at my disposal his material on the historical and philosphical background to *Die Natürliche Tochter*. Neither C.-J. Gignoux's *Joseph de Maistre, prophète du passé* (1963) nor Robert Triomphe's *Joseph de Maistre* (1968) is satisfactory. E.-M. Cioran's preface to Maistre's *Du Pape et autres textes* (1957) is characteristically stylish and idiosyncratic. George Orwell's polemic considerations of Dickens's role in stimulating a counter-revolutionary liberal-bourgeois mythology of the French Revolution ('Charles Dickens', 1940) is a malicious classic.

The Nineteenth-century Fallout

EUGEN WEBER

'France is revolutionary,' declared Lamartine in 1847, 'or she is nothing at all. The Revolution of 1789 is her political religion.' Whence this peculiar assertion? There were several revolutions two hundred years ago – not least the American one. French involvement in transatlantic revolution aggravated the economic crisis that eventually led to the calling of the Estates General, and, thence, by exciting stages, to the beginning of what the French, with characteristic self-centredness, describe as contemporary history. Yet only in France did the Revolution become a national obsession: a tradition to be played out over and over, like a Passion Play, to which it might be compared because both genres express elevated aspirations closely related to very immediate interests, rather like the famous fourteenth-century Shepherds Play in which the nativity is collocated with a contemporary case of sheep-stealing.

Immediate interests and elevated aspirations account for the fact that no revolution which includes both is ever complete. Every revolution, even when it has been successful, leaves behind unfulfilled expectations, newly suggested aspirations. Yet most traditional revolutions were directed at fairly limited ends. The French were first to suggest that the ends could be practically unlimited, that revolution could become a manner of government, a crucial component of politics. Since the revolutionary agenda was so extensive, it was never exhausted. Rather, it suggested reasons for further revolution, principles to be carried to their logical conclusion – conclusions which some regarded as excess. Revolutionary excess (forcing people to be free, and so on) led to reaction, reprisal, repression, followed by counter-explosions. So that, almost ritually, every revolutionary upheaval was followed by multiple aftershocks; every political revolution inspired a social follow-up; and every repression of social revolution suggested the revolutionary resurgence to follow.

Very roughly speaking, this is what we call nineteenth-century French history: the liberal Revolution of 1789 drifting into Terror by 1793, repression in 1794, Napoleon's coup of 1799 and his fifteen-year dictatorship. The liberal revolution of 1830, followed by radical aftershocks in 1831, 1832, 1834, 1839 and ever more radical repression. The liberal revolution of February 1848, followed by the radical aftershock of June 1848, the reactionary drift thereafter, Louis Napoleon's coup in 1851. The liberal revolution of September 1870, followed by the radical rising of the Paris Commune the following spring, its bloody repression in May 1871; and then, only a few years later, what looked remarkably like another attempted coup when, on 16 May 1877, the President of the Republic, Marshal MacMahon, dismissed parliament and tried to govern with a minority government. This didn't work out, but since the First Republic had foundered on the Eighteenth Brumaire (9 November 1799) and the Second on 2 December 1851, there was no way of knowing, then, that the Third Republic wouldn't do as much on 16 May.

That it didn't, and how come it didn't, deserves serious consideration. But, first, I have to establish how strong by 1877 the revolutionary tradition had become in France, and how much a part of normal experience. This kind of political script, once registered, became part of historical memory, part of history, in other words part of current assumptions and current debate, in which participants in one revolution identify their situation and themselves in relation to their predecessors, one generation keeps quoting another, and the more self-conscious actually realize that they are repeating the words and the gestures of their great forerunners. Which is what Jules Michelet felt in 1848; and Gustave Courbet in 1871, when he told his fellow-Communards who were just setting up a Committee of Public Safety that they were plagiarists, imitating the bloodier and more effective committee of the same name four score years before.

Revolutionaries imitate revolutionaries, and revolutions repeat each other, because a lot of history is being written after 1820 (not least Lamartine's *History of the Girondins*, published in 1847): lyrical evidence that the road to the guillotine is paved with good intentions, because the Girondins are the prototypical liberals turned revolutionary turned radical, fated to be overtaken and decimated by still more radical revolutionaries, hence to be looked on with favour by similarly idealistic and indecisive chips off the old block. But revolutions also repeat each other because this is the age of romantic historical drama, which affects more than the elite reading public of history books. And one example may illustrate this.

In 1847, Alexandre Dumas, always trying to make money, took over the Théatre Historique on the Boulevard Saint Martin; and one of the first plays he gave there was *Le Chevalier de Maison-Rouge*, which is about an attempt to save Marie-Antoinette from the guillotine by getting her out of prison. The play, which was a great success, included a chorus of embattled Girondins, which was going to become famous: 'Mourir pour la patrie, c'est le sort le plus beau, le plus digne d'envie,' which might be loosely translated as

> There's nothing so fine, no fate I so cherish,
> Than a suitable chance for my country to perish.

It also included a riot, for which Dumas recruited the raging mob daily, personally directing their savage surges and songs and cries – apparently to great stage effect. Contemporaries alleged that, by so doing, Dumas taught a lot of workers and street urchins the rituals of rebellion, and that the play inspired the sack of the Tuileries in February 1848.[1] Even if the exercise was not directly related to the crowds breaking into the royal palace (sacking the Tuileries was another revolutionary tradition), it played its part in illustrating and revigorating historical memories.

This sort of thing would not have mattered if historical memory had not been reinforced by personal memory – which it was,

[1] Germain Bapst, *Essai sur l'histoire du théatre* (Paris, 1893), 563–4.

because most people living in those days had gone through not one but two or three revolutions; and those that they had not experienced, they had heard about from parents or neighbours or friends. So the civil war, once it had been fought in 1789–94, would be re-enacted on subsequent occasions by people whose familiarity with the script acted as one more inspiration for self-fulfilling prophecies. Which explains why the Lyonnais and Marseillais and especially the Parisians had what Maurice Agulhon calls '*la barricade facile*' (took to barricades easily).

But which reminds us also that when the French weren't making revolutions, they were expecting them to happen. In April 1831, an eight-year-old boy is given a gym lesson in his parents' apartment, and his instructor (who is an old soldier) orders him to shoulder arms. As they hear his voice raised in command, the whole house falls into a panic, thinking that it is soldiers in the street, and that another insurrection has begun.[2] A few months later it would begin in earnest: September 1831 would be full of riots; and one literary young man notes in his diary: 'National Guards and Horse Guards charging on the Boulevard des Capucines. I went up to my little fairy's apartment. From there you have a wonderful view of the riot.'[3]

Fairies pass but the riots go on. It's at this time that the staid *Revue des deux mondes* changed the title of a regular feature ('The Fortnight's Chronicle'/*Chronique de la quinzaine*) to 'The Fortnight's Revolutions' (*Les Révolutions de la quinzaine*). The title would be changed back in 1832, but riots, rebellions and revolts continued through the 1830s, some of them very bloody indeed; and just when things seemed to settle down, here came February 1848, quite unexpectedly, because most people agreed with the king that you do not make revolutions in winter, when the weather is bad. But now they had learnt to make them in all seasons; and, after 1848, the next few years were also very nervous.

By 1851, everybody was talking about civil war in 1852, when Louis-Napoleon's term as President of the Republic expired, and

[2] Eugène Mouton, *Le XIXe siècle vécu par deux français* (Paris, n.d., 1899?), 154; also 149.
[3] Antoine Fontaney, *Journal intime* (Paris, 1925), 40.

when they expected more fighting in the streets. One gentleman noted in his diary that people waited for 1852 the way they waited for the year 1000, which had been supposed to usher in the end of the world. And Walter Bagehot, visiting Paris, heard a big fat housewife referring as a matter of course to 'when the Revolution comes next May'.[4]

It did not come in May because the president forestalled it in December. But once Louis-Napoleon's coup had been successfully executed in December 1851, the sense of insecurity persisted; and just when the anxious mood was passing in the 1860s, the revolutionary drama was duly played out again in 1870. And remember that 4 September 1870 was no further from 2 December 1851 than the Vietnam War is from us today.

In countries where they are endemic, revolutions are like dysentery: they have a brief incubation period, but the convalescence drags on and on. Which is why, three years after the Commune, Walter Bagehot commented that 'the Frenchman lives in the constant presence of a revolutionary force, and is always imagining an outbreak of it – they are so used to it, that they now are scared at any shadow.'[5]

Bagehot was in Paris during the coup in 1851, and he returned there frequently. I shall have occasion to quote him several times, not only because an observation rings with greater authority when it is made by a man or a woman who is dead, or because Bagehot was editor of the *Economist* and an eminently Eminent Victorian; but because he had personal experience of what French revolutions were like. He even helped to build a barricade. But the French had lived in this atmosphere for eighty-five years and three generations, which in the United States would be the equivalent of the period since 1901 and the murder of President McKinley: plenty of time for traditions to form, and habits, and expectations based on experience – especially when revolutionary experience was so intimately tied to everyday life.

[4] *Mémoires du Comte Horace de Viel-Castel sur le règne de Napoléon III*, I (Paris, 1943), 78; Walter Bagehot, *Collected Works*, ed. Norman St John-Stevas, IV (London, 1968), 29.
[5] Bagehot, *op. cit.*, IV, 169.

Take Alexandre Dumas, whose Historical Theatre is on the rocks because revolutionary times are hell on theatres, seizing on Louis-Napoleon's coup of December 1851 to exile himself to Brussels, less to escape Louis-Napoleon's police than to get away from his creditors. Or another insolvent thespian – Etienne Arago, youngest of a great republican clan – who helps to set off the revolution of 1830 by handing out the weapons used as props in the theatre he managed, who then has to hide from the police for trying to make revolution after it was supposed to stop, and who does so in Western France, when he makes friends with a local doctor, Benjamin Clemenceau. In 1848 Arago is part of the Provisional Government, in 1849 he has to take refuge abroad, in 1870, after the September revolution, he becomes mayor of Paris; in which guise he appoints as mayor of the 18th district his radical friend's even more radical son – Georges.

Everybody who was anybody (or was going to be somebody) was there in 1830. Dumas had a great time shooting and being shot at. Auguste Comte, a perennial student at the Ecole Polytechnique, was helping Lafayette at the Hotel de Ville. Hector Berlioz was taking the examination for the Prix de Rome; but as soon as he could get out, he picked up a pistol and joined in the fun. And then, a few days later, walking through the Palais Royal gardens, Berlioz comes across a sort of barbershop octet singing a martial hymn of his composition, and joins in, and ends by leading a large crowd in singing the 'Marseillaise', which he had just orchestrated for two choirs and orchestra. Stendhal is seeing his *Red and Black* through the press, so he's holed up in the Rue de Richelieu correcting proof, but he enjoys the 'agitation sympathique' even though the printers have knocked off to go and riot. Tocqueville, on the other hand, who is a junior magistrate twenty-five years old, is so embarrassed at having to take the loyalty oath to the new king that he looks for an excuse to leave the country, and finds it, and sails off for America in February 1831 – from which he was going to return with a book.

And everybody seems to be around again in 1848.

So the history that people knew was the history that they had lived. Their own personal and family history. And it hasn't been sufficiently remarked that revolutions were also family affairs, which meant that (like the actors at Oberammergau) you inherited a family tradition that cast you in a certain role, whether you liked it or not. It was not only on the 'right' that the French had hereditary opinions. Lots of people were hereditarily 'red' or 'blue', like poor Dr Mie, who played an important role in the politics of Périgueux, in 1848, and about whom a local paper explained that not his instincts not his political principles, but his family connections, made him despite himself the leader of the red party.[6]

This is not an exceptional situation. France was full of families which had felt the impact of revolution or reaction in their fortunes and in their lives. Guizot had been orphaned by the Terror. Tocqueville's family had been decimated by it, his parents imprisoned and permanently marked by the experience. Thiers had been initiated into the secret revolutionary society of the Carbonari (so had Louis-Napoleon). They had sworn the death of kings and simulated regicide by plunging a dagger into the breast of a straw mannikin. Blanqui, the prototypical revolutionary, was the son of a Napoleonic official destituted and ruined after 1815. Godefroy Cavaignac, the son of a deputy to the convention, a regicide, plotted against Louis-Philippe who had filched the revolution of 1830 from the people. When he was arrested and brought to court in 1832, he moved even his judges when he spoke about his filial love for the Revolution.[7] Cavaignac died in 1845, but his brother lived to head the Second Republic – very briefly, in June 1848. And his grandson refused to accept a prize from the hands of the Prince Imperial, whose father had killed that republic.

Family traditions. Family feuds. You were red or white or blue, bitterly for or against the Revolution, the monarchy, the Republic, the Empire, because your property had been confiscated or your ancestors had bought National Property. Losing your fortune to inflation and paper money, or making a fortune by speculating in them; going to a church served by a constitutional priest or refusing

[6] Georges Rocal, *1848 en Dordogne* (Paris, 1934), I, 125.
[7] Claude Nicolet, *L'Idée républicaine en France* (Paris, 1982), 92.

to do so; holding an office or a commission from this or that regime; any of these could mark a family, a clan, a village, for generations.

A small Breton village which goes along with the revolutionary decrees and accepts a constitutional priest in the 1790s, is 'punished' for its political conformity after the Restoration, in 1815, and it turns red for over a hundred years. A carpenter in a village near Avignon volunteers for the Republican armies in the 1790s and is persecuted after 1815. His son, Agricol Perdiguier, becomes a Republican, and a deputy in 1848. A village teacher in central France is ill-treated under the Second Empire: his whole clan turns red.[8]

Which reminds us that the actual revolutions were not the only times when circumstances marked people. After the murder of the Duc de Berry in 1820, after Fieschi's attempt to murder Louis-Philippe in 1835, after Orsini's attempt to murder Louis-Napoleon in 1858, thousands were arrested, persecuted, humiliated, and hundreds were deported or sent into exile – reminding them that the account was not closed; and that politics were not about principles alone, but about personal security, dignity, honour, hatred. In 1858, when Dr Clemenceau of Nantes is arrested and about to be transported to Algeria, his seventeen-year-old son Georges visits him in prison and declares, 'I will avenge you.'[9] Political and family history go together.

No wonder that, when some kind of peace was re-established in France after the Commune, Bagehot called it a rickety structure; and a French publicist wondered how the peace would be able to resist such powerful memories and resentments as had been built up over time.[10]

This raises a question. Not why or how the fallout of the great Revolution engendered three subsequent revivals, because that is not surprising in the light of its agenda and its effects. But why the

[8] André Burguière, *Bretons de Plozévet* (Paris, 1977), 212–16; Agricol Perdiguier, *Mémoires d'un compagnon* (Paris, 1964), 24, 53, 55, 60; Lucien Gachon in J. Fauvet and P. Mendras, *Les Paysans et la politique* (Paris, 1958), 409.

[9] David R. Watson, *Georges Clemenceau* (New York, 1974), 19.

[10] Bagehot, *op. cit.*, VIII (London, 1974), 235, 249: Dupont-White quoted with approval in Daniel Halévy, *La Fin des notables* (Paris, 1930), 74.

tradition was broken, why there were no more revolutions after 1871. More to the point: why there were no more revolutions when everybody for a long time continued to expect them to occur, and when revolutionary situations were no more lacking in 1877 with MacMahon, in 1889 with Boulanger, in 1898 with Dreyfus, than they had been in 1830 or 1848.

If we want to explain this break in tradition we should listen to Edmond de Goncourt who, just a few days after the debacle of the Commune, notes with grim satisfaction that 'repression had bled white the rebellious section of the people, putting a new revolution off by one generation'; and who concludes that 'we can expect about twenty years of quiet.'[11] Precisely because Goncourt is a nasty piece of work, it is interesting to see how his judgement coincides with that of the more attractive Bagehot, who finds the defeat of those he calls the City Reds 'the preliminary to a decent government,' and who hopes that it 'may be twenty years till the next eruption of the ever-burning volcano'.[12]

So both for Goncourt and for Bagehot their optimism of 1871 is mitigated: the volcano continues to burn, its next eruption could be put off, but hardly avoided. The trouble with the French is that they do not have the sense to behave like the English. If they could only organize a real responsible opposition (not a volcano, now erupting, now capped) then 'we should no longer fear periodic spasms of revolutionary ardour.' Which is rather like the wish George Sand expressed in 1871, that the new regime might last long enough for us (French) to learn to debate without starting a revolution.[13]

At any rate, there we are in the 1870s, and the thorough sweep effected during the Bloody Week of May 1871 provides just such a chance. Especially when it is backed by solid police and security work, and by the determination never again to let rebellion turn into revolution. But repression could go only just so far. Tocqueville, who hated the workers' rising of June 1848, nevertheless understood that the men and women who fought in it perceived

[11] Edmond and Jules de Goncourt, *Journal*, II (Paris, 1956), 819.
[12] Bagehot, *op. cit.*, VIII, 201.
[13] Bagehot, *op. cit.*, VIII, 225, 226; Halévy, *op. cit.*, 82.

society to be founded on injustice, and wanted this to change. 'This is the sort of revolutionary religion,' said Tocqueville, 'that our cannon and our bayonets will not destroy.'[14]

So what happened to the revolutionary religion after 1870? To answer that question, we might as well start with economic determinism. It will not give us the answer, but it will provide the beginnings of one.

All the French revolutions had a background of economic crisis, hunger, misery. On 14 July 1789 the price of bread in Paris was higher than on any other day in the eighteenth century. The years 1826–30 were years of financial crisis, unemployment, rotten harvests and dear bread. 1846–8 were even worse. And March 1871, when the Commune broke out, was a time of terrible economic dislocation following a winter of extreme cold, hunger – and, of course, defeat in war.

It is true that many Revolutionaries agreed with Robespierre that the people should not riot for bread, but for some more worthy purpose. But it is unlikely that Revolutionaries would have found much of a following if the vast majority had been adequately fed and fully employed. And the first thing to say about the modern economy – the railroad economy – is that after the 1850s there are no more bread riots in France, and that there is less and less of that bleak, concentrated misery which was the sporadic bane of the old economic order.

But Tocqueville's revolutionary religion was still there; and true religions, and true believers, know neither tolerance nor compromise. As Bagehot complained, 'the "Red" character is incapable of compromise, and . . . prides itself . . . on its bigoted adherence to a few abstract formulae.'[15]

The abstract formulae were going to change, and I shall come back to that. But even true believers were not entirely hung up on abstractions. Politics are about give and take: all parties concede something, all gain something, all lose something. That could not

[14] Tocqueville to Eugène Stoeffels, 21 July 1848. Quoted by John C. Cairns, in his introduction to J. S. Mill, *Essays on French History and Historians* (Toronto, 1985), xxi.

[15] Bagehot, *op. cit.*, IV, 133.

work as long as the mass of people were excluded by definition from the political bargaining. As long as those who had were disinclined to concede anything, those who wanted what they had would not concede anything either: it was all or nothing on both sides.

In this context, it makes perfect sense to find the revolutionary socialists of the mid-nineteenth century trying to destroy existing society, 'to expropriate the present for the sake of the future'.[16] But the situation which justified this point of view was evolving under the Second Empire and it improved still more under the Republicans; until, by 1890, not even professed revolutionaries really wanted to sacrifice the present to anything.

Revolutions are made by those who have nothing to lose for those who have something to gain. By 1890 (which is where Goncourt's and Bagehot's twenty-year respite takes us) there were few left in France who had nothing to lose, and there were lots who had made modest but significant gains. Even among those communards who had survived death sentences (commuted) or exile, there were plenty who chose henceforth to battle the regime from the inside: they became deputies, senators, municipal councillors, members of the Legion of Honour. One of them, Adrien Lucipia, became President of the Paris Municipal Council in 1899, just in time to inaugurate the International Exhibition of 1900.[17] One cannot imagine Blanqui or Louis Blanc thus coming to terms with those who had crushed their revolts.

But something more fundamental had happened than the integration of a few individuals. Unexpectedly, the conflict had shifted from the street into Parliament. The parties of revolution had become the parties of reform, because the parties of government had become parties of integration and assimilation.

The first revolution had been about popular sovereignty, which implied universal suffrage. Universal suffrage had been achieved in 1848, only to be limited and restricted two years later by a frightened reactionary Assembly. Re-established in 1871, it would

[16] Nicolet, *op. cit.*, 87.
[17] See Bernard Noël, *Dictionnaire de la commune* (Paris, 1978), *passim*.

never be questioned again. So, now, in theory at least, democracy could embrace all social classes – even the poor, the disinherited, the proletariat. And part of the proletariat came to say so, even to think so.

Under the new Republic, society could be peacefully transformed through the democratic process: meaning pretty much the electoral process, supplemented by schooling. The major socialist leader, Jean Jaurès, was the first to say so, and then even a dogmatic Marxist like Jules Guesde came around.[18] And, if this happened, Marxism had a lot to do with it; because it replaced the bloody-minded revolutionary religion of violence and barricades with a new creed of scientifically determined social – hence political – revolution. As Paul Lafargue had it, who was Marx's son-in-law, 'the economic contradictions of capitalist production are leading us inevitably to communism.' If this was so, bloody revolution could only be counterproductive. It wasn't possible, said Jaurès, to 'predict exactly when and how capitalism would collapse'. But one had to 'work for those reforms which would prepare the way'.[19]

The only revolutionaries who still held out were the syndicalists, who wanted direct action. But their direct action was industrial action, and when Georges Sorel reflected on violence and concluded that you could not have the revolution without violence, the violence he recommended consisted of strikes, culminating in a general strike. That may have been because the police were more efficient, but it was also because, now, unions were legal, and strikes and political action were legal too. And if social equality was only a little greater that it had been a hundred years before, the dignity of the individual/citizen/elector was an established fact. The First Republic called for primary instruction, the Second legislated it, the Third turned it into reality. And schooling produced another crucial effect: perhaps the crucial factor in the change that I described, because it rewrote the republican foundation myth in a more moderate vein.

[18] Harvey Goldberg, *The Life of Jean Jaurès* (Madison, 1962), 120; also Daniel Ligou, *Histoire du socialisme en France* (Paris, 1962), 54–5.
[19] Jean Jaurès and Paul Lafargue, *Idéalisme et matérialisme dans la conception de l'histoire* (Paris, 1895), 34; Goldberg, *op. cit.*, 114, 262.

Myths are accounts that bear on the origin and nature of the world, of society, and of their proper order, and on actions supposed to realize that order or undo it. The revolutionary religion, the religion of the barricades, was this sort of myth: a kind of morality tale that set up criteria for judgement and action. To the myth of the revolution, the schools of the Republic (and not just schools, but all the agencies of public discourse: speeches, statuary, every sort of public art) proposed an alternative. Not a counter-myth, but a modification, a qualification, an elaboration, presented as realization and based on the argument that the Revolution now lived in the Republic which realized its belief in social and individual perfectibility.

By assimilating the Revolution and reaffirming its general values, the new reformism legitimized the different conventions by which social life would henceforth be regulated or assessed. One myth of enlarged human possibilities had modified another, and largely replaced it. A radical change was presented as conservative of the original values under changed circumstances. Louis-Philippe had tried to do this in the 1830s and Louis-Napoleon had tried to juggle away the Revolution in the 1860s. If this worked after the 1870s it must have been because circumstances had changed, and could be perceived to be changing.

Which brings me back to the beginnings of the Third Republic in the bloodbath of the last French Revolution.

The Paris Commune had been crushed by Adolphe Thiers, who had been born in 1797, two years before Napoleon's coup of Eighteenth Brumaire put an end to the First Republic. The home in which Thiers grew up was poor, because both his parents' families had lost comfortable fortunes in the first years of the Revolution; so Thiers had no love for revolution, indeed he had little love for anything but himself. His career, like that of his fictional contemporary, Eugène de Rastignac, is the career of an opportunist. Rastignac says, 'there is no virtue, there are only circumstances.' Thiers lives by that creed. He joins the revolutionary Carbonari, he gets on under the patronage of Talleyrand, he serves as a minister under Louis-Philippe, he knows no principles, only interests.

After 1871, Thiers' interest is that the fragile Republic should last, and for that he is as willing to court the masses as he is willing to murder them (those of them that rebel). The masses are not the destitute. They are the peasants, shopkeepers, artisans – the little people who had made the revolutions of the past because their stake in society wasn't complemented by a say in society. We know that the Third Republic would be their Republic: *petits gens*, *petits bourgeois*, *petits employés*, *petits soldats*, *petits commerçants*, reading the *Petit Journal* and the *Petit Parisien*, earning petty profits, committing petty larceny, pursuing their petty interests.

Ernest Renan, the philosopher, had run for election in 1869 – which was neither very philosophical nor very successful. His impression of an electorate of petty bourgeois was that this sort of people were determined to make no sacrifice for interests that were not concrete.[20] It was the wonderful perception of Thiers and of Gambetta (who was first his rival, then his ally) that in these people lay the crucial stabilizing force, to be mobilized not by appealing to ideals (although these had their uses), but to interests: concrete, immediate, and wildly exciting only when they affect you, your business, your home, your shop, your family. In 1846, when suffrage was still restricted, the most influential electors of a small town called Pézenas had gone to the Prefect in Montpellier and assured him that they would elect whomever he liked, even his horse, if only the railway could pass through their town.[21] This was a story that Thiers and his successors remembered, and it was an attitude that most electors retained and have retained since.

I shall quote Bagehot for the last time, because he has something to say on this. 'I do myself think,' he had written in the wake of the December coup, 'that a due and regular consideration of the knotty points of paving and lighting . . . is a valuable discipline of national character. It exercises people's minds on points they know, in things of which there is a test. Very few people are good judges of a good constitution; but everybody's eyes are excellent judges of good light, every man's feet are profound in the theory of agreeable

[20] Halévy, *op. cit.*, 141.
[21] Procureur Général, Montpellier, 24 July 1846. Archives Nationales, BB[18] 1442.

stones.' Bagehot took issue with Mazzini, who sneered at the selfishness of shopkeepers: 'I am for the shopkeepers against him. . . . The selling of figs, the cobbling of shoes, the manufacturing of nails – these are the essence of life.'[22] One might add that being engaged in this sort of business keeps most people too busy to mess around much with other people's lives.

The Third Republic was largely about this sort of petty concern, and this was widely deplored at the time, and it has provided the crux of many derogatory interpretations of the Republic since. But this self-regard, however unenlightened, was going to create a broad underlying consensus that no disturbance managed to destroy.

Charles Péguy, who was disgusted at the way the Revolutionaries abandoned their revolutionary ideals for a mess of *potage*, warned against the way mystique deteriorates into politique. The shift from principle to practice need not be seen as a deterioration, but rather as an evolution. As more social groups are integrated, as modern communications put an end to local famines, as German Marxism replaces French Jacobinism, violence becomes less appropriate because politics is sublimated violence. Political debate no longer excludes petty interests, but integrates them; and politics is recognized to be (as it should be) a jigsaw of high principles and trivial pursuits. The concrete aspects of the mystique provide a passageway towards the politique: the province of everyday concerns, where we can make our revolutions in the realm of lighting and taxes and school, which is common to all.

Revolutionaries continued to talk about expropriating the expropriators, but now this was supposed to happen without bloodshed because, to quote the preface to the memoirs of one professional Revolutionary who died with the century, 'the era of violences, regicides, barricades, armed strikes, was closed.'[23]

As this happened, the physical geography of insurrectionist display shifted: the rituals of revolution were themselves marginalized. The 1790s had grafted a new political ritual on the old

[22] Bagehot, *op. cit.*, IV, 82, 84.

[23] Lucien Descaves, preface to Gustave Lefrançais, *Souvenirs d'un révolutionnaire* (Bruxelles, 1902), vii.

tradition of popular effervescence: bread riot, tax riot and so on. They displaced action from the place de Grève or the great markets, to the political centre of Paris. After 1792, the ritual of revolution involved plunder of the Tuileries, invasion of the National Assembly, the proclamation of a new regime at the Hotel de Ville. But, after 1871, the Tuileries and the Hotel de Ville were no more. They had been burnt down by Communards determined to eliminate their symbolism. Sedition evolved new ceremonial patterns peripheral to the political centre: at the Mur des Fédérés where the last Communards had been shot, but above all anchored to the two great squares around which working-class life of northeast Paris turns: the Place de la Bastille and the Place de la Nation.

The first of these held the Colonne de Juillet, memorial to the dead – first of the July Revolution, then of the June rising of 1848.

The second pole of revolutionary remembrance developed in the Place de la Nation, a few minutes' walk away, where the Paris Municipal Council decided to celebrate the triumph of the Republic (that is, of the Revolution tamed) with a majestic sculpture moulded by Jules Dalou, another Communard: director of the Louvre under the Commune, condemned to forced labour for life in 1871, amnestied in 1879.

Dalou's plaster cast of the Triomphe de la Republique was inaugurated on 22 September 1889, nearly a hundred years after the First Republic had been proclaimed in the wake of the September Massacres. The final bronze was inaugurated in November 1899, just a few days from the centennial of Bonaparte's coup of Eighteen Brumaire – a coincidence which wasn't mentioned by the President of the Republic or the other eminent speakers who watched hundreds of thousands of workers march past under red banners and sometimes under black ones.

Dalou's biographer summed up the general impression: 'Never did a day resemble more the great days of the Revolution. Only this time the People had come into the street not to overthrow the Government, but to affirm its will to defend it. With all the outward appearance of an inssurrection, it was exactly the contrary of an insurrection.'[24]

[24] Maurice Dreyfous, *Dalou, sa vie et son oeuvre* (Paris, 1903), 287.

So the revolutionary quest, swallowed by the Republic, was not exactly laid to rest with the century, but made more eccentric to real life and real politics. Revolution had always gone with rhetoric; now it was increasingly consigned *to* rhetoric, and to the sort of history which is rhetoric stuffed and served with a contemporary sauce. Revolutionary rituals continued to be observed, revolutionary models to be copied, as in February 1934, May 1968, December 1986. But – as *Le Temps* observed when, in May 1885, the first demonstrators sought to march to the Mur des Fédérés – universal suffrage had killed the barricades.[25]

Yet the revolutionary experience bequeathed many more things than barricades. The Revolution had many faces. Conservative, constitutional, then defensively bellicose and bloodily humanitarian, it raced and lurched from rational argument into confused enthusiasm, violence, panic, terror, war, reaction, tyranny – separately, together, and in no particular order: a Yellow Pages of political references. Uncomfortable effects were felt at once and for a long time after. After 1789, instability, inflation, price controls, ever heavier taxes, civil and foreign war, discouraged investment and trade, and set the French economy back by a generation. *Assignats* also gave paper money a bad name and kept several suspicious generations from accepting it, depriving the economy of nineteenth-century France of a precious source of legal tender, and encouraging the tradition of hoarding silver and gold. The fears born in the 1790s were confirmed in 1848. In the 1860s, still, the great French economic problem remained credit – that is, confidence in the future. 'All discussions on currency,' noted the *Economist*, 'come back to *cours forcé* . . . making convertible notes irrefusable tender during a revolution. If you propose the simplest credit operation to a French banker, he says: "You do not remember 1848; *I* do."'[26] Could this be why Flaubert's *Dictionary of Commonplaces* explains that while republicans are not all thieves, thieves are all republicans?

One man's thievery is another man's redistributive justice.

[25] *Le Temps*, 23 May 1885, quoted Madeleine Rébérioux in Pierre Nora, ed., *Les Lieux de mémoire*, I, *La République* (Paris, 1984), 625.
[26] Bagehot, *op. cit.*, IV, 115, 119.

Possessions of enemies of the state and other *émigrés*, seized and resold as National Property in the 1790s, made many a fortune and started many a long-running feud. The Catholic Church also became a sort of national property. Reorganized on a national basis in 1790, it also lost much of its wealth and most of its privileges. After 1791, whatever the vagaries of his clergy, God sat firmly on the right. Friction between the reason[s] of a secular state and the interest of an embattled church at odds with the nineteenth-century spirit seared French society, and politics too. Like their compatriots, French churchmen fought their fellow-citizens and each other, now seeking to enlist the state, now calling for freedom from it: one more sourcc of division, instability, ambiguity.

French ambivalence about state intervention goes back well before 1789 which (as Tocqueville insisted) simply perfected many a royal enterprise. French patriotism, on the other hand, is a creation of the Revolution, perfected by the schooling system that was another revolutionary legacy. Most French combine a highly critical attitude toward their state and their fellow-French with ardent love for France itself. It would be a soldier of the Empire, Nicolas Chauvin, who gave his name to the exacerbated love of country we call chauvinism. Unflinching patriotism, often oblivious to experience, can infuriate foreign observers; it remains a source of strength to French foreign policy and to the nation. Nor does the enthusiasm affect the French alone. To this day, to paraphrase an American journalist, France remains a cultural superpower 'based firmly and squarely on illusion'. Having killed millions in revolutionary wars of conquest, it continues a symbol of liberty, equality and fraternity, because it believes it is one.[27]

There were other memories (and concrete gains) without which the image of revolution would not have survived. Much was accomplished in 1789 and after. The liberal ideal in action abolished restrictive survivals, declared caste and privilege at an end and men equal before the law, emancipated Protestants and Jews, freed peasants from clerical tithes and surviving feudal rights. Internal trade was freed, the national market united, a legally

[27] Mort Rosenblum, *Mission to Civilize* (New York, 1986), 4.

diverse country was unified by a common constitution, the uniform administration of a new and rational departmental structure, a common language, a common coinage and a common (metric) system of weights and measures.

Not all the changes of the early 1790s, nor even of the Empire (like the franc) passed from principle to practice very soon. One rationalization proved short-lived: the radical revolutionary calender, introduced in 1792, lasted only twelve years, two months, twenty-seven days. It was finally abolished in 1806, leaving behind a few useless watches with dials divided into ten, not twelve, hours, and the memory of events that took place in months that are hard to place, like Thermidor or Brumaire. Some innovations, like linguistic unity, took most of the century to be realized. Others, like education for all, had to be revived over and over before being implemented. Yet the generation of 1789 set the benchmarks of expectation and aspiration for the century that followed; and that was no mean achievement.

Lesser accomplishments deserve a shred of remembrance: the tricolour flag, which combined the royal white with the red and blue colours of democratic Paris; the opening to the general public of museums like the Louvre and also of *ménageries*, the ancestors of our zoos (not to mention access of all artists to the annual Salon of paintings); the reaction to revolutionary vandalism (a term coined in 1794) which invented the notion of 'historical monuments' and the modern interest in their preservation; the creation of the first real 'restaurants' by chefs left at loose ends when their noble employers left Paris for exile. French cuisine – at least in its more public and accessible forms – may be counted part of the fallout of revolution. So, perhaps, may be the tradition of public banquets: great feasts of collective harmony, destined to set off the revolution of 1848, and culminating during the celebration of the first centenary of the Revolution in the gigantic banquet of 15,000 mayors of French communes on 18 August 1889.

Even when things went wrong, French revolutions set up signposts for the future. In 1789, Royalists bunched on the right of the President of the National Assembly, so Republicans placed themselves on his left. Right and left have been with us since. So has conscription: the comprehensive, nationwide, universal, compulsory military service of a given age group for a set number of years, instituted by the Republic to service its wars and institutionalized by Napoleon to fuel his.

It is not irrelevant that in 1952 a French economist could coin the term 'Third World' by reference to the Third Estate and its revolutionary self-affirmation.[28] More immediately, slavery, abolished in 1794, re-established in 1802 after bloody conflict had torn the West Indies apart, was finally ended in 1848. In 1850, the first law against cruelty to animals, introduced by a cavalry officer concerned for the wellbeing of our equine friends, was designed to diminish popular cruelty and bloodthirstiness, and spurred by the hope of avoiding more bloodshed on the barricades. Two years earlier, in February 1848, fears of revolutionary terror being repeated had led to abolition of the death penalty for political offences.

Yearning for a purifying bout of terror, dread of its return, were yet more legacies of the Revolution. In the first quarter of the twentieth century, the Bolsheviks put up a statue to Robespierre, named one of their cruisers *Marat*, another one after the Paris Commune. By today's standards, the Terror appears a small affair. More French died in one of Napoleon's futile battles than the 17,000 executed at the height of the Terror, between May 1793 and July 1794. But half a million persons were imprisoned during those fifteen months – one man, woman or child for every three score French – in improvised, inadequate, unsanitary quarters.[29] Almost as many lived in hiding, in exile, even more lived in fear. Many were ruined, many lost their health.

Others, however, may have found equality in action cheering or, at least, edifying. In December 1793, didacticism and democracy combined to inspire the Decree of 6 Nivôse An II, which provided that women could attend the sittings of the Revolutionary Tribunal 'with their husbands and their children and knit': hence the *tricoteuses*.

[28] Alfred Sauvy in *L'Observateur*, 14 August 1952.

[29] Donald Greer, *The Incidence of Terror during the French Revolution* (Cambridge, Mass., 1935), 26–7, 143.

It was in 1794, after Robespierre's fall, that two new nouns enriched the vocabulary: *terrorisme*, meant to designate the policy of Terror during the past two years, and *terroriste*, for those who had applied it. In 1796, the verb *terroriser* (to terrorize) was coined to describe the politics and activities of those frightened years. Meant to characterize events that were past, all three were destined for heavy service in the future. And all the while, between 1793 and 1796, the civil war in Vendée alone slaughtered over 200,000 more: a disaster of Vietnam proportions, right at home.

It was Madame de Staël, daughter of the Finance Minister whose dismissal precipitated the fourteenth of July, who noted that to understand everything makes one very indulgent (a thought that makes more sense than its misquotation).[30] But there is not all that much we really understand. Historical analysis of revolution and of terror softens reality, because it offers reasonable explanations for circumstances and actions in which reason contends against sharper passions. In 1789, 1848, 1871, the coincidence of economic problems and of revolution suggests plausible causal connections. But in the end, as Saint-Just confirmed, it was the force of circumstances that led men on. Revolutions are less about misery than they are about power. In the French case, as in many others, about the power to forge a better world and a better humanity within it. But high aspirations carried to logical conclusions lead to impossible extremes. Having declared all men equal in their rights, which they should be, and equal by nature, which they are not, some revolutionaries decided that only equality of conditions would satisfy that ideal: equality not just of property, but of appearance and manners. Better still of ability: that 'absurd fear' of better minds Madame de Staël bemoaned.[31]

> Shorten giants by the neck
> Raise the small up – what the heck!

[30] *Corrine ou l'Italie* (1807), Book 18, ch. V. The original, generally misquoted, is 'Tout comprendre rend très indulgent.'

[31] Baronne de Staël, *Des Circonstances actuelles qui peuvent terminer la révolution et des principes qui doivent fonder la république en France* (1799 ms, ed. John Viénot, Paris, 1906), 82.

Everyone at the same height
That's true happiness and light.

It was to rail against this levelling spirit that the satirist Antoine de Rivarol proposed a bill for the equalization of climate throughout the world, limiting temperature variations, excluding longer or shorter days and nights, prohibiting floods and other natural catastrophes, permitting hail and lightning only over forests where they would not harm the crops. If this sounds ridiculous, what should we make of 'Gracchus' Babeuf's insistence that social institutions must prevent any individual from becoming richer, more powerful, or more distinguished by his lights, than any other? Or Jules Michelet's demand in 1848 that everyone should be made to wear identical dress? Against such purism, when it is armed, there is little one can do except try to keep out of the way. But this is just what revolution is designed to prevent.

What had begun as a contest over practical interests became a war fuelled by the will to dominate hearts and minds, hence by ever sharper demands for ideological conformity. The idea that perfection was possible here on earth suggested a bureaucracy to enforce it, exasperating those affected and equating non-conformity with rebellion. The belief that only good will was needed to attain good ends engendered hatred of those who seemed to lack the will, or to doubt the efficacy of measures taken, to attain the end.

Finally, the evident justice of the revolutionary cause suggested that only selfish conspiracy could account for opposition to it, that behind open argument darker motives lay, as they sometimes did. It followed that open argument should be stifled, and conspiracy with it. But two could play at that delusion. While revolutionaries hunted for conspirators (and sometimes found them), their enemies did the same. By 1796, the Swiss publicist Mallet du Pan, no less intelligent for being an enemy of the Revolution, rued the new 'coalition of fanatics and fools who, if they could, would forbid man to see and think'. Shortly, John Robinson's *Proofs of Conspiracy* (London, 1798) inspired the House of Commons to set up a parliamentary commission to inquire into subversive activities. 'Simple causes accessible to the laziest and most superficial minds have been substituted to very complicated ones,' remarked a French observer. Modern politics had come to stay.

Michelet's moving account of the French Revolution, often simply silly, reproves the massacres of revolutionary terror, but reproduces all its fables. This allows us to note the high ideals that justified butchery: 'the idea of a great and radical moral purge, the hope to purify the world by the absolute expurgation of evil,' thieves, gamblers, prostitutes, as well as aristocrats.[32] How serious was this? In April 1793, like many fellow-Frenchmen, the villagers of Sémelay, in the newly created department of the Nièvre, took a public oath to 'the death of tyrants, the execration of despots', and swore 'to exterminate whoever should support monarchy directly or indirectly, and to denounce those who should speak in its favour. . . .'[33] Though most of them probably did not mean it (the village priest also took the oath), there were those who took such rhetoric seriously. After the massacres of September 1792, Marat had to reassure a man who came to him in tears, confessing that he had spared an aristocrat. The Friend of the People spoke kindly to his visitor and absolved his weakness; but, says Michelet, 'the man could not forgive himself, could find no consolation.'[34]

Men had to be forced to be free. National unity would be achieved by exclusion, national regeneration by terror, civil peace by excluding unbelievers as well as counter-revolutionaries of the left and right; doubters, wait-and-seers, moderates, radicals, took their turn beneath Dr Guillotin's humanitarian invention, the executioners of today were purged tomorrow, and the purgers then purged in turn, precariousness became a way of life, everyone felt threatened, surviving, reprieved, from one day to the other. The best answer one could offer to the question, 'What did you do during the Revolution?' would be the Abbé Sieyès's 'I survived.'

Survival also ensured the perpetuation of the feuds, the hatreds, and the will to vengeance generated in those dangerous times. Against these, and against the ideology that furnished public

[32] Jules Michelet, *Histoire de la Révolution française*, Book 7, ch. III.
[33] André Thuillier, 'Sémelay de 1793 à 1795', in *Actes du 87e Congrès des Sciences Sociales* (Paris, 1963), 241.
[34] Michelet, *loc. cit.*

warrant for private vendettas, the machinery of repression developed. Set up in 1796, the Ministry of Police was abolished in 1820; the police lived on, frightening, restrictive, intrusive. Even without a ministry to represent it, French nineteenth-century history testified to the belief that a policed state could only survive as a police state. French public opinion teetered between condemnation of police interference and demands for more effective police intervention. After 2 December 1851, no government underrated the vital importance of political intelligence or undercover agents. Determined to withstand insurrection and, if need be, to crush it, the Second Empire is unlikely to have been swept out but for a national disaster like Sedan. The Third Republic, whose political police was even more finely honed, succumbed to none of the political threats *it* faced, and perished like its predecessor of incurable humiliation inflicted in war.

We have no study of the police activities that constitute a major contribution of the Revolution and of its successors; any more than we have prosopographic or genealogical studies that show how clan and community-memory affect political stance. I have already suggested that both of these played significant roles in perpetuating political hostilities. The revolutionary inheritance also affected another kind of discord, not peculiarly French, but peculiarly bitter there: generational conflict and, more generally, family strife.

We might start off with a characteristic scene that takes place in Grenoble, in January 1793. Henri Beyle is not quite ten years old when he hears the news of Louis XVI's execution. 'It is done,' says his father with a heavy sigh, 'they have murdered him.' The future Stendhal experiences 'one of the sharpest feelings of joy I have ever felt in my life'.[35]

That killing the king is killing the father becomes even clearer in the equally well-known story of Baudelaire on the barricades of February 1848, brandishing a rifle and crying, 'We must go and shoot General Aupick' – his stepfather.[36] General Aupick, then commanding the Ecole Polytechnique, survived. But a few months

[35] Stendhal, *Vie de Henri Brulard*, ch. XI.
[36] Maurice Agulhon, *Les Quarante-huitards* (Paris, 1975), 93.

later the workers' rising of June 1848 would be put down in good part by members of a new-style militia: the *gardes mobiles*, recruited largely among young workmen and apprentices. One explanation of the enthusiasm with which these *gamins de Paris* went after their fellows was advanced at the time: their resentment of the *brimades* (ragging, bullying, persecution) they suffered at the hands of older journeymen.

That sort of explanation may be no more than an argument against class identity. It is more difficult to dismiss André Gide's wide-echoing cry of 1897: 'Familles, je vous hais.' [37]

Intriguingly, the chief French regicides of the century were both orphans at odds with their family. Louis-Pierre Louvel, executed in 1820 for murdering the Duc de Berry, was an orphan, brought up partly in an hospice, partly by an elder sister with whom no love was lost. Giuseppe Fieschi, executed in 1836 for trying to kill Louis-Philippe (he missed, but killed eighteen others and wounded many more), had been abandoned by his father; then, soon, by his mother as well. Ravachol, the notorious anarchist (and thief and murderer and grave-robber), executed in 1892, had been left with a wet-nurse till the age of three, then in a children's home till he was seven. His father, who worked in a rolling mill, regularly beat his mother and tried to get the boy to spy on her for him. When the father walked out on his wife and four children, Ravachol was put out again. He says he cried.

Young people did not wait for the Revolution to find adult society oppressive and family life frustrating or repressive. But the oppression, the repression, the frustrations that others suffered pending the opportunity to inflict them in their turn were, in France, denounced as counter to the rights of man (women were to wait a long time before they could hope to share these). Rights that applied in society could well apply in that mini-society we call a family. If political revolution fed on private grievances, private rebellions fed on public claims. An ideology that sharpened political and social frustrations and made awareness of deprivation keener, whetted resentment of injustice, unkindness, vexation in the home.

[37] André Gide, *Les Nourritures terrestres* (Paris, 1897).

One aspect of social relations has always been their adversary quality. The Revolution aggravated this. Liberal enlightenment viewed the conflict of particular interests as contributing to the common good. The 1790s rejected such rationalization for a choice between black and white. Between right and wrong there could be no compromise. The French ideal shunned compromise and the ultimate harmony this promised, preferring unity – as imposed by a rational authority. Even as it proclaimed freedom of person, of conscience, above all of property rights, Napoleon's Civil Code (1804) was going to translate reason of state into concert of kindred, the authority of the state over its citizens into the authority of the father over his wife and children.

The repression and revolt built into such a system were reproduced at the family level, where adversary relations became less the result of incidental frictions and more the expectable result of irreconcilable norms. By 1840, Pierre Leroux[38], the socialist philosopher, voiced a widespread aspiration for families in which individuals could develop without being oppressed. One year later, Balzac's Laurence de Cinq-Cygne (another orphan who wants to kill the intrusive, oppressive, stepsire – the First Consul, Bonaparte) incarnates one model of survival: 'Nothing so tempers the spirit as constant dissembling in the bosom of one's family.'

Again, such relations were no monopoly of nineteenth-century France. But it is there that they appear to have left the deepest traces in literature as in national character.

In 1985 still, a Paris newspaper discussing a crime in the provinces found at its heart a family 'that tears itself apart . . . that ferociously [continues to] destroy itself. . . . For decades family hatreds have racked this village and these families . . . hatred is transmitted from generation to generation. . . .'[39] Autocracy tempered by rebellion was carved into family as into political life; political and family history mesh in more ways than one. In both spheres, antagonists learned that coexistence is a civil war in which no party accepts defeat short of coercion.

[38] Pierre Leroux, *De l'humanité* (1840), III, ch. I; Balzac, *Une ténébreuse affaire* (1841).

[39] Serge July, 'Le Miroir de Lepanges', *Libération*, 17 July 1985.

As public ideology colours private relations, so private scores can be settled in public life. Arthur Ranc (1831–1908), friend of Gambetta and of Clemenceau, revolutionary emeritus, died a radical senator. His great-grandfather, a younger son, had welcomed the Revolution because it abolished the primogeniture that deprived him of his inheritance. When little Arthur, at school in Poitiers where his father practised as solicitor, got into political hot water and his father's windows were broken in reprisal, the elder Ranc was not displeased: 'Blood will tell.'[40] Arthur became a Blanquist, and a communard. The country lives on, polarized in enclaves of reciprocal suspicion and disrelish in society as in the home.

Everybody, as Cavaignac had told his judges in 1832, was a son of the Revolution.[41] Or else of the counter-revolution. Is that what made Franco-French relations so prickly? Not fraternity but fratricide – and patricide and infanticide – were what the generations born after 1789 found in their cradles. Marx was wrong. When revolution repeats itself it becomes not farce, but tradition.

[40] Arthur Ranc, *Souvenirs, correspondance, 1831–1908* (Paris, 1913).

[41] And as Ledru-Rollin told the citizens of Chalons-sur-Saône on 19 December 1847. More immediately, Alexandre-Auguste Ledru-Rollin, known to some as Le Duc Rollin during his candidacy to the Presidency of the Second Republic in 1848, was the grandson of a famous physicist and prestidigitator, Dr Ledru, tutor of Louis XV's children and collaborator of Benjamin Franklin in his work to develop a lightning conductor.

The Twentieth Century: Recollection and Rejection

DOUGLAS JOHNSON

The history of France in the twentieth century is shot through with the recollection of the Revolution. It was at the beginning of the century that the *fête* of the fourteenth of July became firmly anchored in the habits of the French population. At a time of tension between church and state, schoolteachers, in their small towns and villages, were pleased to welcome an official celebration in which the church would not play a preponderant role. For once a festivity was rational, celebrating an important historical event, and was not connected with the Virgin, a saint, or local folk-lore and superstition. The mayors too were not displeased with a ceremony in which they would play a preponderant role. It was therefore celebrated with speeches, banquets, dancing, fairs and firework displays. In towns with garrisons or with a naval establishment it became customary to add a military element to the ceremony and, particularly after the war, 14 July became associated with patriotism and nationalism.

The fourteenth of July 1919 was the first great national celebration of victory; all the emphasis was on the triumphant French army. It was to remain like that. The processions of 1919 showed the world that the French army was the most powerful army in Europe, and future parades were meant to emphasize their efficiency and their equipment. 'It's tomorrow's army,' was the cry, when on 14 July 1936 two hundred planes flew over the avenue of the Champs Elysées, when a section of the infantry appeared in new uniform and when heavy tanks (damaging the streets with their caterpillar tracks) had their regimental numbers concealed because it was a military secret. When the age of jets came three fighters would fly low over the Arc de Triomphe, emitting trails of red, white and blue. There were always the *anciens combattants*, with their medals and their standards, the wounded with their sticks and crutches, or with an empty sleeve revealing the loss of an arm. Paul Léautaud recalls a patriotic society where ex-soldiers, *Grand mutilés de guerre*, used periodically to parade, 'True heroes they were. So many campaigns, and yet they wanted more. However badly injured, still they marched.'[1]

In the parades in the Champs Elysées, and in other places, colonial troops took part. One not only saw the Foreign Legion, with a goat as their mascot, but there were the Spahis with their baggy trousers, detachments from Indo-China, Africa, Madagascar and the Indian Ocean, and, lasting into the Fifth Republic, a small group of the legendary Touareg, immensely tall with their unmistakable mauve veils. On 14 July the French recalled that they were at the centre of an immense Empire.

And everyone in the Empire realized the importance of 14 July and were made to celebrate it whether they wished to or not. A centralized educational system meant that the same, or similar, textbooks were used throughout France and in many parts of the Empire. In history 1789 was the starting point. Officially, French contemporary history began at this date so that the significance of 1789 was seen as a part of the present. A widely read textbook in history, like the Malet-Isaac, explained how, on 14 July, the whole of the *ancien régime* collapsed, an entirely new political and social regime was constructed and from then the Revolution spread to Europe. In 1958, having assumed power for little more than a month, General de Gaulle took the occasion of the 14 July to speak to the French Empire. 'While France celebrates its national festival, the festival of Liberty, Equality and Fraternity,' he sent a particular message to La France d'outre-mer, to the five parts of the globe with which France had had links for so many years. 'What a

[1] Paul Léautaud, *Propos d'un jour* (Paris, 1947), 153.

blessing for the whole of mankind, gripped by so much hatred and pain but dreaming always of brotherhood.'[2]

The fourteenth of July also took on a particular social importance. It became the day when the summer term ended. After that day, the schoolchildren of France were on holiday, as were their teachers and, in many cases, their parents. As holidays grew in importance, especially after the introduction of holidays with pay by the Popular Front government of 1936, 14 July became the symbol of liberation. Although under the Fourth Republic, as attempts were made to stagger holidays and to meet the demands of the sea resorts that term should end sooner so as to lengthen the season, 14 July lost this privileged position, it nevertheless remains something of a turning-point, marking the accepted beginning of the holiday season, with shops and businesses closing down as the French rush away.

In schools, which traditionally had strict discipline, the end of term was often riotous. 'The plates explode, knives fly, jugs produce unexpected showers, the trolleys of grub are overturned, and the grub itself is transformed into missiles which fly from one end to the other of the refectory. The head refuses to be bothered, the monitors back away, whilst the kitchen staff of twenty people look startled and frightened upon this incomprehensible row.'[3]

Thus the souvenir of the 1789 Revolution, via the celebration of 14 July, has had two popular interpretations: that of patriotism and that of a festivity. Both fit in well with considered views of the Revolution. Anatole France, who, as Monsieur Bergeret, has often been thought of as a spokesman for the Third Republic, put forward his thoughts very clearly. 'It cannot be denied that feeling for one's country existed under the Ancien Regime. But what the Revolution brought to this was none the less immense. It added the idea of national unity and the idea of territorial unity. When it gave to peasants the right of ownership, the new regime imposed upon them, at the same time, the duty of defending their property, whether this property was already acquired or about to be acquired.

[2] Charles de Gaulle, *Discours et messages* (Paris, 1970), III, 24–5.
[3] *Libération*, 22 June 1977.

You have to take to arms if you have acquired land, or if you wish to do so. Hardly had the Frenchman established himself in the town or started to enjoy the sunshine on his land, but the armies of the European coalition sought to reduce him to his former slavery. Then the patriot turned soldier.'[4]

There was also present, as is now recognized, in the mentality of the pre-revolutionary and revolutionary era, the need for some sort of festivity which would bring people together, a dream of a community which would reaffirm its solidarity at regular intervals. It was present in Rousseau, in Saint-Just when he talked of the need for the Republic to affirm itself by means of collective commemorations and celebrations, in Michelet, and in Péguy when he wrote, 'In my time everybody sang.' When the flags flew, the bands played, the soldiers marched and the people danced, 'la communion sociale' was, perhaps, attained.[5]

The vocabulary of 1789 became a permanent feature of French political culture. The word 'revolution' was, and is, used with extraordinary facility. 'Vive la Révolution' was the cry of the mutineers of the French army in June 1917 as they marched through Châlons, and *Révolution* is still the title of a weekly paper published by the Parti Communiste Français, with the subtitle 'Ours is the age of revolutions'. Words like 'Jacobin', '*sans-coulotte*', '*brass-Nus*', 'Montagne', 'Thermidor', '*droits de l'homme*', '*États généraux*', have frequently been used in French politics and are still a constant part of current political coinage. Above all, 'Bastille' remains a word heavy with meaning. General de Gaulle, who saw himself during the war, and who has to be seen, as someone who

[4] Preface to Anatole France, *Jeanne d'Arc* (Paris, 1908), 2 vols.

[5] See the interesting reflections on this theme in Raoul Girardet, *Mythes et Mythologies Politiques* (Paris, 1986), 119 ff. See also the comments of Mona Ozouf. 'Le 14 juillet, c'est la jeunesse de la Révolution. Dans tant de fêtes et de discours commémoratifs consacrés au 14 juillet, on ne trouve nulle trace de lutte, ou même d'effort. Le 14 juillet est une danse, un chef d'oeuvre de pure activité, où les mouvements d'un peuple unanime s'ordonnent par miracle dans les figures d'un ballet gracieux et gratvit. C'est en dansant que "la nation francaise, ivre de liberté, brilliante d'ideés libérales, foule aux pieds les hochets du trône." Ou en chantant. . . .' 'Le Discours de la révolution sur elle-même', *Revue historique*, 493 (January–March 1970), 50.

was in the tradition of 1793 and who spoke of 'l'insurrection nationale', claimed before the Liberation that if there still were Bastilles in France then they should prepare to open their gates, and then in the struggle between the people and the Bastille, 'It's always the Bastille which is wrong.'[6] When the French observed the Russian Revolution of 1917, the historian Mathiez wrote newspaper articles in which he tried to identify individuals and parties in Russia with their equivalents in the French Revolution (it was Mathiez, Robespierriste and critic of the moderates in the French Revolution, who would apologize to a student who asked for a *rendez-vous* because he lived in the Vergniaud, named after a Girondin, but who would then cheer up, explaining that the student could take the 93 bus, a reference to the crucial year of the Revolution).[7] The Socialist Party Congress of October 1918 adopted a resolution, proposed by Longuet, Faure and Delépine, deploring the armed intervention of France (and other countries) in Russia and protesting 'against the policy of France and its allies towards the Russian Revolution, a policy which all too well recalls how the coalition of monarchs reacted towards the French one'.[8] Hostility to the revolution of the Soviets was easily assimilated to the counter-revolution that had existed in France.[9] Later in 1922, when Edouard Herriot, who was far from being a revolutionary but whose radicalism always claimed to be faithful to the great principles of 1789, made an assessment of the Russian Revolution, he clearly had the French traditions in mind. 'There is, at this time, a country to the east of Europe, whose people have launched upon a great experiment, one which they admit has not succeeded. . . . A whole people is emerging from a night which has been marked by suffering, violence, sacrifice, and this people turns towards the sun and asks for light. This light is freedom. We who are free should give them that freedom. This is the French tradition, our tradition.'[10]

[6] Jean Lacouture, *De Gaulle*, I, *Le Rebelle* (Paris, 1984), 656, 698.
[7] Jean Bruhat, *Il n'est jamais trop tard* (Paris, 1983), 39.
[8] Quoted in Pierre Durand, 'La Contre contre-révolution', *Révolution*, 389 (14–20 August 1987), 36.
[9] *L'Humanité*, 14 July 1918.
[10] *Congrès du parti radical et radical socialiste* (1922), 111, quoted in Serge Bernstein, *Edouard Herriot ou la république en personne* (Paris, 1985), 122.

The memory of the French Revolution could serve as a model which would help in understanding events. Thus the extreme left during the 1920s pondered the question of whether or not the expulsion of Trotsky from the Soviet Union was the equivalent of the death of Robespierre, whether or not Stalinism represented a Thermidorian reaction, whether or not revolution should be seen in terms of spontaneous insurrection rather than in terms of a bureaucratic machinery.[11] The analogy of the Revolution could take the form of a warning, as when Pierre Mendès France, addressing the Radical Party in September 1953, claimed that France was living in 1788.[12] It could be a means of associating a confused movement with a precise moment in history, as when in 1958 the disorganized and uncertain rebels in Algiers declared that they had formed a Committee of Public Safety and their example was hastily followed in other Algerian towns. Or the Revolution can provide simple figures of speech, as when a leading sporting newspaper reporting on the Tour de France as it reached the first mountainous stage, solemnly declared, 'A Bastille to be stormed.'[13] For André Malraux, France, the victor of Valmy and Jemappes, always had a mission in the world and without that mission, France could not be France and would suffer illness.[14]

The fourteenth of July also provides an opportunity to make a direct political argument. Thus the leader of the Communist Party in the Assemblée Nationale, and the designated candidate for his party in the presidential elections of 1988, recently claimed that the ideals of 1789 remained relevant. 'Two centuries later, the struggles of those peasants, those *sans-culottes*, those workers, do not belong to a distant path. In conditions which are naturally very different the ideals of 1789 remain the issues which cause the people to be in confrontation with the ruling classes. This is the

[11] See the discussion in Jean Rabaut, *Tout est possible* (Paris, 1974), and Donald Baker, 'The Politics of Social Protest in France: the Left Wing of the Socialist Party, 1921–1939', *Journal of Contemporary History*, 43, 1 (March 1971).

[12] Jean Lacouture, *Pierre Mendès France* (Paris, 1981), 212. After this speech Edouard Herriot compared Mendès France to Necker.

[13] *L'Equipe*, 14 July 1987.

[14] André Malraux spoke frequently in these terms, notably at a press conference in Paris, 25 October 1958.

case for liberty. Today there are new Bastilles to be stormed. This is the case where employers imagine that they have a divine right to dispose as they wish of those men and women who have to work in order to live. This is also the case with those institutions which are transforming France into an elective monarchy. As for the freedom of France, for the sovereignty of France which the revolutionaries of 1789 defended with passion, it has never been more in danger, threatened as it is by capitalist activity on a European and world scale.'[15]

This persistence of reference to 1789 has contributed to France's reputation as a country which is prone to revolutions, where reforms can only take place in the wake of revolutions, where excitable and excited politicians can lead an inherently conservative society into revolutionary postures and deeds. Often this contributed to the role which foreigners assumed that France would play in the world. Thus we learned that Chinese students came to France, both before 1914 and in the 1920s, because France was 'the country of revolution'. The students were convinced that 'it is France which holds the three mainsprings of modernity: the doctrine of the rights of man, the theory of evolution, and socialism.' Those who came who were already revolutionaries expected that they would learn 'the secret technique of every species of subversion'.[16] David Ben-Gurion was moved and heartened when he knew that French Jews were fighting against Hitler. This was special. 'When in Palestine we learned of the existence of a Jewish Resistance in France, we said to ourselves: the world of jewry will never be the same again.'[17] When Malraux went to see Nehru in order to arrange for an exhibition of Indian art to be held in Paris, he offered in exchange either an exhibition of Norman sculpture or one on the French Revolution. 'France', replied Nehru, 'means the Revolution. When Vivekananda discovered it,

[15] André Lajoinie, 'Une nouvelle révolution française', *L'Humanité*, 14 July 1987.
[16] Annie Kriegel, *Communismes au miroir française* (Paris, 1974), 82–3.
[17] Jacques Lazarus reported this remark in a colloqué held in October 1984, the proceeding of which are published in *Les Juifs dans la resistance et la libération, historie, témoignages, débats* (Paris, Editions du Scribe, 1985).

he passed the day with his friends shouting Vive la République. Do you know that *Les Misérables* is one of the most famous foreign books in India?' Malraux comments on this, 'I had already encountered and I was to encounter scores of times, this French presence. Soviet Russia has not removed it. In underdeveloped countries machines create skilled workers rather than a worker proletariat. And wherever the revolution is not brought about by the proletariat but by the people, the example of the French Revolution, the exaltation of the struggle for justice which has been passed from Saint-Just to Jaurès, via Michelet and above all via Victor Hugo, retains a prestige which is at least the equal of Marxism. In Africa, and in Latin America, even when the technique of the Revolution is Russian, its language remains French.'[18]

Nevertheless, in spite of the national and international persistence of 1789, and the uses which can be made of it both symbolically and practically, and its continued and consistent presence in the political and cultural life of the country, there is a simple observation which has to be made. The French Revolution remains a controversial subject which still divides the country; on the whole the Revolution is neither popular nor appreciated. As one of the leading historians of the moment, Pierre Goubert, has put it, 'You can never get French people, even the best educated of them, to agree about '89 and its aftermath.'[19] Or, in the words of another leading historian, Maurice Agulhon, 'There is still a lot of argument about the Revolution in France today.'[20]

In one sense the French Revolution ought to be easily accepted by everyone. It is widely agreed (as Agulhon argues) that 'men are born and remain free and equal before the law.' Sovereignty exists in the nation as a whole, no state needs an hereditary monarch, the state is dependent upon a system of law rather than on any arbitrary system, people have the right to vote, discussion should be free, the

[18] André Malraux, *Antimémoires* (Paris, 1967), 193–4.

[19] Pierre Goubert, *Le Nouvel Observateur*, 23–29 December 1983.

[20] Maurice Agulhon, 'La Révolution française au banc des accusés', *Vingtième siecle*, 5 (January–March 1985), 7–18. See also his articles 'Faut-il avoir peur de 1789?' *Le Debát*, 30 (May 1984), 27–9; and 'Le Grand debat sur la révolution française', *Magazine littéraire*, 239–240 (March 1987), 53–5.

state will not impose any religion upon its citizens. All these were the objectives and the attainments of the Revolution. Few would take exception to them. But when one wishes to commemorate the Revolution, whether in its one hundred and fiftieth or in its two hundredth anniversary, then the objections are stirred up, become vociferous, and one sees that after two centuries the Revolution still divides the nation. It is not possible to celebrate this bicentenary with the same ease as the bicentenaries of the American Revolution or of the discovery of Australia.

It had been relatively easy in 1889, the year which had seen the failure of General Boulanger to seize power, to claim that the principles of 1789 had been those of progress, and to suggest that the Third Republic was the natural successor to the Revolution. The statue of Danton, erected in the carrefour de l'Odéon, was the symbol of the Revolution, generous, courageous, patriotic and sacrificial.[21] But 1939 was different. The Minister of Finance did not want to give any money for a celebration. The committee which was set up to organize the ceremonies was presided over by Edouard Herriot, then the President of the National Assembly, who considered himself to be an expert on the history of the French Revolution and who, according to the Minister of Education, Jean Zay, neglected practical details and preferred to spend his time discoursing eloquently about controversial revolutionary events.[22] The President of the Republic, Albert Lebrun, was frightened of the idea, thinking that a parade would turn into a left-wing demonstration with red flags and clenched fists.[23] There was a total absence of any popular enthusiasm and, with the added misfortune of bad weather, most of the celebrations were considered to have been failures, even fiascos. When the ceremony was marked by speeches from 'les trois Presidents', the three most important people of the state, the President of the Republic, the President of the National Assembly, and the President of the

[21] See the article, '1789: trois commémorations', *Le Monde*, 2 September 1987, republished in Jean-Noel Jeanneney, *Concordances des temps* (Paris, 1987).

[22] Jean Zay, *Souvenirs et solitude* (Paris, 1945), 387–8.

[23] Pascal Ory, 'La Commémoration révolutionnaire en 1939', in René Remond and Janine Bourdin, eds, *La France et les Français en 1938 et 1939* (Paris, 1978), 117. See by the same author, 'Le Centenaire de la révolution française', in Pierre Nora, ed., *Les Lieux de mémoire*, I, *La République* (Paris, 1984), 523–60.

Council (or Prime Minister, then Édouard Daladier), the content of the speeches underlined the moderate nature of the Revolution, rejecting the idea that 'la Révolution est un bloc' (as Clemenceau had put it in his famous speech of 1891) and stressing the principles of liberty and justice rather than equality. Given the international situation (and the concluding celebrations of the anniversary, which had been planned for September, had to be cancelled because of the war), it is not surprising that the most enthusiastic praise was reserved for the patriotism of the Revolution and for its Anglo-American origins. On 14 July 1939 British troops took part in the parade in the Champs Elysées. With their presence, and with the presence of colonial battalions, all the emphasis was on the alliance, the Empire and the military strength of France. If, as was said, something like the 'communion nationale' of the Fête de la Fédération Nationale of 14 July 1790 was discovered, as was also pointed out by writers in *Le Figaro* and *La Croix*, the taking of the Bastille had been forgotten.

The preparation for 1989 began formally with the announcement, made by the President of the Republic, the socialist François Mitterrand, on 24 September 1981, that the bicentenary should be celebrated in a manner which would be worthy of its importance, 'both in the history of France and in the history of humanity'. Two missions were set up, the one by the Minister of Research and Technology (then Jean-Pierre Chevènement) who invited Professor Michel Vovelle to organize appropriate academic meetings and publications in France and throughout the world; the other, much later, by the Prime Minister, in agreement with the President (who had a historian and specialist on the French Revolution in his private cabinet, Claude Manceron), when a leading freemason, Michel Baroin, was made President of the Commission charged with celebrating 'the bicentenary of the French Revolution and the Declaration of the Rights of Man and Citizen'. When Baroin was killed in an accident he was replaced by a former Prime Minister of the Fourth Republic and Minister for Education in the Fifth Republic, Senator Edgar Faure (an appointment which aroused some constitutional controversy, since a senator should not preside over an official mission for more than six months and since this nomination emerged from the Council of Ministers, presided over by the President, and could not therefore be more official).[24]

However, there was soon opposition. The Mayor of Paris, Jacques Chirac (who was to become Prime Minister after the elections of March 1986), was opposed to grandiose schemes for celebration, and this opposition, along with the need to reduce government expenditure, meant that many ambitious plans were shelved, including that of an International Exhibition which should have been held in Paris in 1989 (and for which President Mitterrand had appointed a member of the municipal council of Paris, le Conseiller Bordaz). More particularly one can note the appearance of a number of tendencies which are significant. The one is in the original report presented to the Ministre de la Recherche et de la Technologie in July 1982, by Professor Michel Vovelle himself, in which he pointed out how there had been a certain recoil in the study of the Revolution. The days were past when history at the Sorbonne was dominated by such eminent specialists of the Revolution as Aulard and Mathiez, debating about Danton and Robespierre; one could not count upon an army of schoolteachers dedicated to the cause of laicity, 'les institutents laiques', and dedicated to the belief that the Revolution was the great event in French history; the teaching of history in schools had been mutilated by a number of educational reforms and the Revolution was in a *cul-de-sac*, or 'un print aveugle', whilst the professional historians who, in the provinces as well as in Paris, might have rectified that, were now influenced by considerations of long perspectives, *la longue durée*, so that an episode such as the Revolution became marginalized; and, perhaps more importantly, public opinion, or as Vovelle puts it, 'sensibilité collective', has become attached to regional identities, and their roots, which places this opinion in opposition to the concepts of Revolution-Jacobinism, Jacobinism-Centralisation.[25]

A second tendency appears in the statements made by those

[24] See *Le Monde*, 12 and 14 March 1987. For subsequent developments see note 69.

[25] *Rapport sur les formes de participation du Ministère de la Récherche et de la Technologie à l'organisation de la célèbration du bicentenaire de la révolution française*, by Michel Vovelle, Professeur à l'Université de Provence, Aix-en-Provence, 3 July 1982.

responsible for the organization of the less academic part of the celebrations. Thus when Michel Baroin was interviewed by *Le Monde*, in November 1986, on his plans, he explained that he saw his role as being the representative of general consensus about the Revolution, which for him is symbolized by the Constituent Assembly, the body which substituted for the old order of things a world where the individual counted. He saw a number of lines to follow up in the celebrations: the idea of universal fraternity; the need to establish a general ethic for the third millennium; the rights of man and of the citizen; and the Revolution as a creative force, in terms of art, costume, design and caricature for example. All in all, in 1989, the Revolution of 1789 should usher in another French Revolution, that of peace.[26] Monsieur Baroin's successor, Edgar Faure, in the course of many statements, has also stressed the word 'fraternity'. 'Two hundred years after the Declaration of the Rights of Man', he said in an interview to *Figaro-Magazine*, 'it is the right of France to propose the Declaration of human conscience, the manifesto of Millennium.' He envisaged an Arc of Fraternity (in the quartier of La Défense), a Collège d'Europe which will complete the Collège de France, and which will bring together the spirit of the *Encyclopèdie* and the *Aufklarung*. 'I see 1989', he declared, 'as being the year of Europe, of all the different Europes, that of the Community, that of the Council, that of the Continent. God willing, a thousand years after the baptism of Russia, a hundred years after the birth of General de Gaulle, we will celebrate Europe from the Atlantic to the Urals.'[27]

It is not necessary to point out how distant these views of the Revolution are from what are often thought of as the great achievements of the Revolution. The same cannot be said for a third tendency, which is downright hostility to the very idea of this anniversary, and which enters easily into certain details which suggest that the Revolution was a factor of division and civil war and should not be the subject of celebration. Naturally one can most easily find examples of this in right-wing publications such as

[26] *Le Monde* 16–17 November 1986.
[27] *Figaro-Magazine*, 10 July 1987, and more recently in *Le Monde*, 25 November 1987.

Figaro-Magazine. Thus in 1986, Christine Clerc, recalling how during the period of Vichy, Catholics and their bishops thought only of taking their revenge upon 'le petit père' Combes, of harassing the freemasons, of forcing the state schools to take up religious instruction and of closing down the *école normales* which were the breeding grounds of 'la laïcité', so she saw in the years 1984 to 1986 the French seeking to reanimate the war of the schools and to resuscitate Vendéens and Thermidorians, to play at the Revolution and at the Restoration. 'I dare not imagine', she wrote, 'what miserable excesses will take place at the celebrations for the bicentenary of 1789.'[28] Patrice de Plunkett recalled his school days, when history was far from neutral, when serious schoolteachers spoke as if every day they had to recapture the Bastille and when the fathers of the church behaved as if every day they had to avenge Marie-Antoinette,[29] whilst Louis Pauwels, in an editorial entitled 'Pour en finir avec le Révolution francaise', mocked those who believed, according to him, that if you did not adore Robespierre then you were in favour of Vichy and collaboration, or that if you believed that the war in the Vendée was an example of genocide, then you were ready to disbelieve in the gas-chambers and the martyrdom of the Jewish people. The object of Pauwel's virulence was Max Gallo's *Lettre ouverte à Robespierre*, and he concluded, 'poor Monsieur Gallo, it is the agreeable souvenir of the guillotine that has caused him to lose his head.'[30]

But this hostility to the Revolution is not always confined to right-wing publications. Thus, within a short space of time one can find in *Le Nouvel Observateur* one article by Jacques Julliard in which he suggests that the terrorism of the twentieth century owes its origins to the Terror of 1793,[31] and another by François Furet who argues that if the revolution of 1789 was a call to liberty, and a sublime revolt of a people against its history, 1793 saw the same people fall back into the absolutism of the *ancien régime* and the

[28] *Figaro-Magazine*, 6 December 1986.
[29] Ibid., 25 July 1987.
[30] Ibid., 11 October 1986. Jacques Julliard replied directly to the article by Pauwels in *Le Nouvel Observateur*, 17–23 October 1986.
[31] *Le Nouvel Observateur* 26 June–2 July 1987.

confiscation of liberty.[32] In the communist review, *Révolution*, it is common, whilst praising the revolutionary movement, to criticize the bourgeoisie and to see those moments in the Revolution when the principle of the Revolution seemed abandoned and when one bourgeoisie simply replaced another.[33]

This is all the more significant because in an enquiry, a *sondage*, organized by *Le Nouvel Observateur* in 1984, when asked who was the finest republican of all time, only 5 per cent proposed Robespierre, only 6 per cent Danton, and 10 per cent Bonaparte. It is de Gaulle who triumphs with 71 per cent. When asked what is the most glorious achievement of the Republic, only 2 per cent give the victory of Valmy, the most votes going for universal suffrage, for free state schools and compulsory education and for the Resistance. Obviously to draw conclusions from this would be foolish. It can come as no surprise that more people are familiar with universal suffrage or with the name of de Gaulle than with that of the battle of Valmy, or with the names of Robespierre and Danton. But the same enquiry also approached eight leading political figures and enquired of them what best symbolized the Republic, and there one finds that the symbol of the Revolution is very present. Valmy for Michel Rocard and Bernard Strasi, the Bastille for Jean-Pierre Chevènement and Pierre Mauroy, the 'Marseillaise' for Pierre Bérégovoy, and amongst those who are not left-wing it is noticeable that Jacques Chirac chose as the place which best incarnates the Republic the Hôtel de Ville (with reference to Louis XVI receiving the three-coloured cockade from the hands of Bailly, as well as with reference to events of 1848 and 1870) and as symbol, the three-coloured flag; Michel Debré chose as symbol the picture by Delacroix, 'Liberty Leading the People', and as personages not only Jules Ferry and de Gaulle, but also Lazare Carnot; Simone Veil writes about the Third Estate and the soldiers of the Year Two, the 'Marseillaise' and the 'Chant du Départ', but she also mentions the paving stones which are present beneath the asphalt,

[32] Ibid., 10–16 July 1987. Furet was reviewing Edgar Quinet, *La Révolution*, edited by Claude Lefort (Paris, 1987).
[33] See, for example, *Révolution*, 24 July 1987.

'les pavés' which can at any moment become barricades.[34] This suggests that the persistence of the French Revolution is more marked in the political culture of the leaders than in that of the population as a whole, but it also suggests that the symbolism is ritualistic rather than meaningful, well distant from the historical realities of financial crisis, the attack on feudalism and the rights of the church, violence and the class struggle, political instability and economic crises. Leaving on one side the references to the Bastille and to barricades, the only historical reality that percolates through is that of nationalism.

A fourth tendency is that of not taking the Revolution seriously. Thus we learn for example that the schoolchildren of Cloteaux-Brétigny, near to Rennes, were invited by the local Maison des Jeunes et de la Culture to simulate, in order the better to understand, the taking of the Bastille. One of the practical ways in which they got to grips with history was by constructing a guillotine. *Révolution* started a new competition, called 'Let them eat cake'. Just as Marie-Antoinette supposedly responded to the news that the people were starving because there was a shortage of bread, so readers of *Révolution* were asked to supply quotations in which present-day personalitites would respond to the contemporary crisis with remarks which appear to be equally *mal á-propos*. Thus, when Jacques Chirac was asked, in a television interview, if the alternative facing the French in their social security system was either to pay more in the way of contribution or to receive less in the way of reimbursements, Chirac supposedly replied 'or both at the same time'. François Dalle, a businessman, in a series of suggestions concerning employment, is supposed to have envisaged sending unsatisfactory schoolchildren out to work at the age of ten. And François Mitterrand, when inviting Edgar Faure to prepare the celebrations of the 1789 bicentenary, allegedly charged him to avoid all polemic on the question of whether or not the Revolution was a good thing.[35] A competition, named 'Inventer 89', rapidly received several hundred projected designs and artifacts which

[34] *Le Nouvel Observateur*, 7 December 1987.

[35] 'Brioche de la semaine: prix Marie-Antoinette'. See, for example, *Révolution*, 3 April, 19 June 1987.

could represent the bicentenary, and which were deposited at the Cité des Sciences et de l'Industrie de la Villette. It appears that amongst the proposed exhibits is one which features a fountain on which is written the words 'Égalité, Stupidité, Brutalité'. There is a proposal to dig a trench between Versailles and Paris (commemorating the march of the women of Paris to Versailles in October 1789) in which would be placed 6,000 urns, each containing urine. An architect plans to construct an immense tower on the place de Bastille, with bricks, each marked with a 'CC', to symbolize the bicentenary. On 14 July 1989 the population of Paris will be asked to remove this tower, brick by brick, each Parisian taking one brick home with him, thus symbolically re-enacting the historic scene.[36]

Of course, it is possible to find many examples of those who believe strongly in the importance of the French Revolution and the need to celebrate it properly. Leading historians conscious of the coincidence of two anniversaries, the thousandth anniversary of the accession of Hugues Capet, 'the first King of France', and the French Revolution, have claimed that the origins of France have two dates, 987 and 1789.[37] It is possible to produce, for a wide reading public, a traditional view of the Revolution, as Michel Vovelle and his collaborators have done, in which, with learning and subtlety, the necessity and the legitimacy of this popular movement is well argued.[38] Vovelle, as the seventh holder of the Chair of the History of the French Revolution at the University of Paris, stands well in the tradition of Aulard, whose inaugural lecture was given at the Sorbonne in 1886 in the presence of Clemenceau, of Lefebvre, who took over the Chair in 1937, and of the communist Albert Soboul, whom he succeeded in 1983. All, in their time, have invoked the memory of the Revolution as a means of inspiring their countrymen to patriotism or to aspirations for social justice.[39] It is common for young historians still to describe

[36] 'On trouve tout dans le bazar de la révolution', *Libération*, 13 October 1987.
[37] See the article by Jacques Le Goff in *La Quinzaine littéraire*, 491 (August 1987).
[38] See Michel Vovelle, Elisabeth Guibert-Sledziewski, Guy Lemarchand and Guy Besse, in *Révolution*, 6 February 1987.
[39] James Frigugliette, 'Michel Vovelle and the Revolutionary Succession', *Modern and Contemporary France*, 21 (March 1985), 42ff.

1789 as 'the crucial year' in French history[40] and it was possible to suggest, in the summer of 1987, that François Mitterrand would be determined to seek a second term as President of the Republic so that he would have the satisfaction of presiding over the ceremonies of 1989.[41]

Nevertheless one has to try to analyse the reasons why the persistence of the Revolution of 1789 in French political culture and comprehension has to be measured today against a considerable amount of coldness, which is the product at times of cynicism and indifference, at times of a certain hostility. The first reason is undoubtedly associated with the work of the historians. This is not the place to attempt to review how historians have revised their opinions concerning both the causes and the course of the Revolution. This has been done many times.[42] It is, of course, not surprising that an important event should be subject to the constant process of historical revision. Nor is it surprising that historians putting forward different interpretations and appreciations of the revolution should adjust their optic to the preoccupations of their own times. Thus both Aulard and Mathiez (who acted as the temporary holder of the Chair of the French Revolution in the absence of Sagnac) emphasized the patriotic devotion of the Revolutionaries; Labrousse, who studied price fluctuations and the periodicity of crises, was influenced by the apparently inexorable power of economic movements; Lefebvre and Soboul, in their emphasis on social classes, reflected the social conflicts of the Popular Front era and of the Liberation years. It could be, as Soboul has suggested, that the concept of the Atlantic Revolution, whereby the revolution in France was to be seen as only one of a series of social and political movements associated with countries which were situated on the Atlantic seaboard, coincided rather neatly with the Cold War.[43] Or it could be that those who have maintained that the manner in which the Revolution developed was an accident, that its move from its bourgeois constitutionality into a

[40] See, for example, Abel Poitineau, *Les Mythes révolutionnaires* (Paris, 1987), 177.
[41] Jean-Marie Jeanneney, *Le Monde*, 2 September 1987.
[42] See, for example, William Doyle, *Origins of the French Revolution* (Oxford, 1980).
[43] Avant propos in Claude Mazauric, *Sur la révolution française* (Paris, 1970).

more violent extremism was in no way necessary, have been influenced by their belief that in order to change the world revolution is neither necessary nor desirable in modern society.[44]

Yet the result is a considerable confusion. Erudite scholars have argued convincingly that the Revolution cannot be studied exclusively in Paris but must be considered in all its provincial dimensions, all of which are necessarily different the one from the other. It is no longer possible to use the words 'aristocracy', 'bourgeoisie', 'artisan' or 'worker', still less 'peasantry', because these words mean so much that we are overwhelmed by our knowledge. It is difficult to generalize about the revolutionary armies, the *sans-culottes*, the Third Estate, the Committee of Public Safety or any other institution, without having the feeling that the generalizations contain so many inaccuracies or inadequacies that they may well be useless. Students who are asked to discuss some famous remark about the French Revolution, such as (if they are British) 'The revolution came because the monarchy was unable to solve the question of privilege, was not strong enough, in a word, to overthrow the remains of feudalism',[45] or, more generally, 'The revolution is a great drama whose chief actors are the social classes',[46] can do little but say that there is some truth in these remarks, but that they are not completely convincing. It would seem that there is little about the Revolution that is now completely convincing to the conscientious and objective student of history.

But this is not all. Possibly because the French Revolution has been so readily seen as the model for all revolutions, and because the evolution which the Revolution followed has been so frequently compared to the development of other revolutionary movements, the idea that there is no discernible pattern in the French Revolution has become almost obsessive in the minds of those that hold it, all the more so because they are confident that no pattern acceptable to scholars can be imposed upon them. Therefore the

[44] This suggestion is made, for example, in Michel Vovelle, *Révolution*, 6 February 1987, 18.
[45] H. A. L. Fisher, *A History of Europe* (London, 1936 edition), 795.
[46] Jean Jaurès, 'La Petite république, 23 Mai 1899', quoted in *Actes du colloque Robespierre* (Paris, 1967), 191.

suggestion is that the Revolution is a tale of sound and fury, signifying, more often than not, nothing.

One can see this by taking the example of the fall and death of Robespierre. It has always puzzled historians, as well as contempories, that he did not defend himself more vigorously when attacked in Thermidor (late July 1794); some historians have talked about misunderstandings (Napoleon did not believe that Robespierre was seeking to extend the Terror, as was alleged, but rather that he was trying to end it) or about Robespierre deliberately courting martyrdom. But it has always been known that there were a good many rumours going around about Robespierre, some of which, fantastic as they were, must have weakened his position. One was the suggestion, after Robespierre had launched a new civic religion, the Cult of the Supreme Being, that he saw himself as a religious pontiff, a suggestion which gained some credibility when a religious zealot, who claimed to have had visions of Robespierre, was released from prison on his orders. But the most extraordinary story was that which claimed that Robespierre was not only a secret royalist, but that he intended to marry the daughter of Louis XVI and that, with the help of the English (with whom he was in secret agreement), his ambition was to become King of France.[47] This story is manifestly absurd and has been dismissed, and frequently ignored, by the biographers of Robespierre.

But more recently it has been suggested that this dismissal has been somewhat rapid. The very fact that a rumour exists at all is, we are told, significant, and all the more significant because we know that this particular calumny was invented by those politicians who wished to get rid of Robespierre and who calculated that such a story would be accepted by the population in Paris. Such a manoeuvre, which was successful, has to be placed in the context of all the rumours, panics and legends which have been such an integral part of the Revolution. On 14 July there were those who believed that the army was about to massacre the people of Paris

[47] The story is told by G. Duval, *Souvenirs thermidoriens*, 2 vols. (Paris, 1844), and by Célestin Guittard de Floriban, *Journal*, edited by Raymond Aubert (Paris, 1974).

(and this rumour was to be repeated); there were all the stories about brigands, foreign armies, nobles, roaming the countryside in the summer of 1789, stories which led to 'The Great Fear' and to the insurrectionary counter-response of the peasantry; there were rumours about foreign agents who would massacre the women and children in Paris once the men went off to the war, who would release those who were imprisoned, who would assassinate patriots whilst the king was being tried; every time there was a defeat it was attributed to traitors and to a conspiracy; constantly it was claimed that food was short because corn was being hoarded by speculators or destroyed by enemies; constantly the news circulated that the *assignats*, which had becomc a sort of paper-money, were to be withdrawn from circulation or declared valueless. Thus the Revolution becomes a series of conspiracies, real or imagined, a struggle against hidden enemies, a convulsive reaction to rumour, a turbulent response to apparent danger.[48]

This picture confirms the idea that the Revolutionaries cannot be fitted into any pattern, or into any system of thought or principle. As they swayed before the threat of events, and sought to protect their own immediate interests, this view of their history makes it all the more preposterous that there were those amongst them who believed they were starting such a new era in history that it was necessary to alter the calendar and to claim for a particular moment the title of Year One. Jacques Le Goff has recalled how, as a pupil at school, he was deeply shocked when he learned of this measure, although he was taught that it was a necessary step in the anti-religious campaign of the Revolution. As he remembers, it affected him more than did the execution of Louis XVI or the September massacres, and it was a stage in his perception that the Revolution could not be accepted as a whole.[49] Those historians, and they are many, who stress the continuity of French history and who see centralization, anti-clericalism, the independence of the peasantry and problems of governmental revenue, all existing well before

[48] See the article by Bronislaw Baczko, 'Robespierre-roi ou comment sortir de la Terreur', *Le Debat*, 39 (March–May 1986), 104–22.

[49] Jacques Le Goff, 'L'appétit de l'histoire', *Essais d'ego-histoire*, edited and presented by Pierre Nora (Paris, 1987), 175.

1789, find it difficult to understand the mentality of those who believed that they had begun a new era.

Closely allied to the effect of the work of historians must be the fact that the Revolution has had difficulty in acquiring a place in popular mentality. Everyone knows that there were many examples of injustice and tyranny under the *ancien régime*, that the Saint Bartholemew massacre did take place, that people starved, were tortured, imprisoned, impressed, expelled from their smallholdings or dismissed from their positions: but it is as if violence, oppression and injustice are only too associated with the Revolution. Doubtless there is a connection with tourism, all the more so as it has become increasingly cultural. The monarchy and the aristocracy are presented as the creators of palaces, chateaux, art collections and beautiful gardens. Tourists can usually buy postcards or effigies which commemorate their persons or their creations. In contrast, the Revolution is inevitably presented as destructive. The saints have been removed from the church or battered out of recognition; the inscriptions have been defiled; we are told that the treasures and the libraries have been looted. The guide, or the owner, apologizes to the tourist as he shows them ruins, 'What can I say? The French Revolution has passed this way.' Add the guillotine and one can see why the French Revolution is normally seen as an era of violence and destruction, eminently unappealing.

Nor does any personage emerge who will compensate for this unacceptable face of the Revolution. Robespierre never knew, and has never known, any popularity. Danton, for all that he may once have appeared as an audacious, national hero, with attractive personal qualities, has not maintained this popularity, as the recent film on him, and reactions to it, has demonstrated.[50] One might have expected that Marat could have been different. David's portrait of the assassinated Marat, which has all the characteristics of a traditional *pietà*, is probably the finest portrait of the revolutionary period, and one feels that it might provide the figure-piece for the cult of this saint-like revolutionary. He has also been the subject of a highly controversial play, Peter Weiss's *Marat Sade*,

[50] See the article by Robert Darnton, *New York Review of Books*, 16 February 1984.

which was performed in Paris, and which created a scandal, in 1966.[51] The Marquis de Sade, who was interned in the asylum of Charenton in the first years of the nineteenth century, supposedly produces plays with his fellow inmates as actors. One of these plays depicted the death of Marat, and showed Marat as being the essential voice of the Revolution. But whilst the hysterical reaction to the play and its alleged moral degeneracy was caused by a whole variety of features, the idea of Marat as a fanatic, mad and dangerous, is an old notion. It was as such that he had been depicted some forty years earlier by Abel Gance in his film *Napoléon*. If Marat does not so often appear as the evil personification of the Revolution as he used (and it must be remembered that in the 1930s and 1940s there were many right-wing political groups who used to name themselves after Marat's assassin, Charlotte Corday), this is because he has shared in the general forgetfulness of the Revolution which has characterized recent years.[52] Renoir's film, *La Marseillaise*, was a typical product of the Popular Front era, and showed the Revolution as a series of crowd movements without great heroes (Marat himself does not appear in this film although his newspaper is frequently seen).

However, if no figure of the Revolution has assumed a favourite position in the popular imagination, the episode of the counter-revolution has become unexpectedly popular. It is difficult to remember that there was a time when historians found it necessary to justify the study of the counter-revolution, and when an American historian was, little more than twenty years ago, complimented on his work on the Vendée which was only then being opened up to historical investigation.[53] Now, after Pope Jean-Paul II beatified

[51] Attempts at depicting the French Revolution on the stage have been rare. Romain Rolland endeavoured to do this with his Théâtre du Peuple, and with his play *Le 14 juillet* which was shown in 1902. But he realized only a small part of his projects. As part of the bicentenary celebrations a contemporary drama of the Revolution, *Mirabeau aux Champs Elysées*, by Olympe de Gouges (who was guillotined in 1793) has been performed in Clermont-Ferrand.

[52] The mythology of Marat is the subject of a collection of essays, presented by Jean-Claude Bonnet, *La Mort de Marat* (Paris, 1986). I am grateful to my pupil David Shafer for drawing my attention to this book.

[53] Charles Tilly, *The Vendée* (Cambridge, Massachusetts, 1964). The review by Alfred Cobban is included in his *Aspects of the French Revolution* (1968), 131–5.

ninety-nine martyrs from Angers, who had, in his words, accepted death rather than renounce their religion, the subject of the civil war in the Vendée and in other parts of Brittany has become a preoccupation of all the media. Just as after 1945 the Communist Party spoke incessantly of those members of their party who had died heroically in the resistance movements against the Germans, just as after the realities of the Holocaust reached a wide audience, French Jews began to speak about a quarter of the Jewish population of France having perished during the occupation, so there are historians who suggest that some 600,000 Bretons were killed during the counter-revolution and this figure has been put forward so many times that it has taken on a quasi-official aspect, in spite of the fact that it can be effectively contested. Thus the Vendée has become one of the items in French civil wars, 'les guerres franco-françaises', and rivals the defeat of 1940 and the unceasing disputes concerning collaboration and resistance, as part of a national introspection.[54] So widespread is this preoccupation that one finds it expressed even in theatre programmes, when Jean Anouilh was quoted in the programme which accompanied his play *L'Hurluberlu*, shortly before his death in 1987, 'You talk about Nazism. You forget that the Vendée was an everyday Oradour.'[55] The word 'genocide', first applied to the war in the Vendée by the historian Pierre Chaunu, was used in the title of a thesis by Reynald Secher which received an unusual amount of public attention.[56]

It is relatively easy to explain why this interest in the Vendée should have grown. It is certain that great progress has been made in historical knowledge about western France in general, particularly by scholars outside France, and it is only recently that many of the persistent myths which associated the counter-revolution

[54] Amongst the many books and articles which deal with this subject see, for a useful survey, Claude Langlois, 'La Révolution malade de la Vendée', *Vingtième Siècle*, 14 (April–June 1987), 63–78.

[55] The programme accompanied the performance at the Théâtre du Palais-Royal. Oradour was the scene of a terrible massacre carried out by German troops.

[56] The article by Chaunu is in *La Croix*, 29–30 June 1986. The title of the original thesis by Reynald Secher was *Contribution a l'étude du génocide franco-français: la Vendée*, and the published version was *Le Génocide franco-français: la Vendée-Vengée* (Paris, 1986).

with aristocrats, British agents and refractory priests have been exploded.[57] It is now evident that the counter-revolution has to be seen in terms of peasant society and popular movements, and historians are no longer convinced that what counted in history was urban insurrection or working-class strikes. There is a revaluation of spiritual values and an attempt to assess, rather than to dismiss, the role of the church. There is a preoccupation with human rights, so that when there are discussions about the Armenian massacres, Stalin's Terror, the Nazi Holocaust, or the killing fields of Kampuchea, when there is praise for minorities who resist oppression, then it is natural that this resistance should be seen as particularly relevant. Whilst regionalism is popular, there is a line of thought which emphasizes all the resistances to the Revolution.[58]

One important aspect of these thoughts is the current hostility to the organization of the state of France. It is not necessary to point out in detail how in France, as in other countries, it has become common to criticize the overpowerful, overbureaucratized state, and to blame it for inflation and for a stagnant economy. The socialist government elected in 1981 proceeded to decentralize. The more conservative government elected in 1986 had used the slogan 'less the state, then the better the state' and adopted a programme of privatization and liberation, whilst setting out to reduce the number of state officials. What distinguishes France from other countries which have adopted similar policies is that centralization, and the overpowerful state, with its dictatorial, privileged and costly bureaucrats, is associated with the French Revolution and with the phenomenon which is still called 'Jacobinism'.

Another concept which has come under criticism and which is popularly associated with the Revolution is that of equality. It is not so much that the ideal of social equality has fallen from favour because it does not seem to be realizable, it is rather that the idea of equality does not seem desirable. Sometimes the emphasis is

[57] Perhaps I can mention the work of two former pupils, T. J. A. Le Goff, *Vannes and its Region* (Oxford, 1981); D. M. G. Sutherland, *The Chouans: the Social Origins of Popular Counter-revolution in Upper Brittany* (Oxford, 1982).
[58] François Lebrun and Roger Dupuy, *Les Résistances et la révolution* (Paris, 1987).

placed essentially upon the innate diversity of men and women, as has been mantained by those who have been called 'La Nouvelle Droite'.[59] Sometimes it is suggested that the bureaucratic system produces a form of elitism which is furtive and shameful, and that what is required is an open and honest elitism which will be capable of modernization and adaptation.[60] At times the argument is based upon a change in the social and historical situation. There was a time when, in the name of equality, a textile worker or a school-teacher would go on strike and would run enormous risks to themselves and to the institutions for which they worked. But now, an air-controller or a technician working in the Electricité de France can inflict the most enormous damage on a vast public with virtually no risk to themselves. The concept of equality is no longer a matter of supporting the poor, the weak and the disadvantaged.[61] Hence once again, a principle for which the French Revolution has stood, appears to be discredited.

Finally, it must be said that the idea of revolution in itself has been devalued. It is not merely that there has been disillusionment over the revolutions which supposedly looked to the French Revolution as their harbinger, the revolutions in Russia and in Eastern Europe, or the revolutions in Cuba, Africa or parts of Asia and South America. It is rather that the long revolutionary tradition in France has recently been accompanied by a certain prudence. Thus in 1920, when the Communist Party was formed, it saw itself as a bourgeois party as well as a revolutionary party, and it envisaged political power as being achieved by means of electoral victory. In 1936, the socialists, governing with communist support, denied that they were revolutionary (Léon Blum's famous words about the revolutionaries of 1848 apply to him in 1936, 'They feared to cause fear'). In 1944 and 1945, those who had lived a revolutionary life,

[59] La Nouvelle Droite usually expresses its ideas in two periodicals, *Nouvelle École* and *Éléments*. See in particular, 'Les 18 printemps de la Nouvelle Droite', *Éléments*, 56 (Winter 1985), 12–44. See also Guillaume Faye, *Les Nouveaux Enjeux Idéologiques* (Paris, 1985).

[60] Michel Crozier, *État modeste, état moderne* (Paris, 1979), 180–4. See also, expressed in more general terms, Alain Minc, *La Machine égalitaire* (Paris, 1987), and Edouard Balladur, *Je crois en l'homme plus qu'en l'État* (Paris, 1987).

[61] Alfred Grosser, *Le Monde*, 6 August 1987.

fighting the Germans and those whom they considered to be traitors, with rifle, bomb and pamphlet, accepted de Gaulle and the authority of the legitimate state. But it was in 1968, when the barricades were up in the rue Gay-Lussac, and when the great days of revolution, of 1789, 1792, 1793, 1830, 1848, 1871, were on everyone's lips, that one saw the renunciation of revolution. There was a confusion in terms of social classes.[62] There was a dispute as to where the authority lay in terms of directing a revolution.[63] There was the sentiment that if Lenin had been in command, there would have been thousands of deaths, and whilst there was a nostalgia for Lenin, and for the idea of revolution, there was the plain acceptance of the apparent fact that in contemporary European society, one does not organize revolutions. However much one opposes and detests capitalist society, one can also participate in it and even enjoy it.[64] In such circumstances the idea, the example and the myth of the French Revolution can only suffer.

Naturally there are those who are not influenced by these considerations. They can answer hostility to the Revolution at a detailed level. The Terror, they would argue, was an incident which would be recognized and accepted by every state which had known what it was to be threatened both from without and from within (by what we now call the Fifth Column). Equality, they would contend, meant equality before the law, something which is everywhere recognized as an essential part of a just state. Social equality and the end of elitism remains a worthy aim, and the *lycéens* and students of December 1986 showed their attachment to this ideal.[65] Centralization was never the work of the French Revolution, it can be argued, but rather that of the monarchy and

[62] Roger Garaudy, 'La Révolte et la révolution', *Democratie nouvelle* (April–May 1968).

[63] Jean Rony, *Trente ans du parti: un communiste s'interroge* (Paris, 1978), 113–14.

[64] See a collection of these arguments in Jeannine Verdes-Leroux, *Le Réveil des somnambules* (Paris, 1987), 190ff.

[65] 'La France est le pays le plus élitiste du monde' was an assertion put out by the student leaders in December 1986, at a time when they claimed to have no political party affiliations. For a plea for the old ideas of equality see Arnaud Spire, *L'Humanité*, 26 November 1987.

of Bonapartism. But in essence, the idea that what is right and legal in one part of France should be right and legal everywhere in France, is only logical. In any case, the Revolution, far from meaning tyranny, meant the triumph of individualism.[66]

The overthrow of aristocratic and clerical privilege; the affirmation of individual rights; the establishment of the rights to property and of transmitting property to one's descendants; the need to have a goverment which is based upon a rational organization of power. These are the principles of the French Revolution which are universally accepted whilst not always being discussed. But above all, in the 1980s there remain two inescapable truths, both of which are linked to the history of the French Revolution. The one is that of the French nation, and the belief in its unity and greatness. The other is the myth of revolution in France. Even after the inevitable discovery of the hollowness of the movements of 1968, they remain the subject of endless discussion. 'May 1968', it has been said, 'will never be brought to an end, never in France, never elsewhere, never.'[67] When the socialists won power in 1981, for Pierre Mauroy it was as if 'those in the château had gone, and now the people had their word to say'.[68]

[66] Alain Jouffrey, *De l'individualisme révolutionnaire* (Paris, 1972).

[67] Pierre Sollers, 'Printemps rouge', in Jean Thibonneau, ed., *Mai 1968 en France* (Paris, 1970).

[68] Quoted in Catherine Nay, *Les Sept Mitterrand* (Paris, 1988), 45.

[69] (See page 193 *supra*.) Edgar Faure died in March 1988 and his duties were temporarily taken over by Jean-Pierre Cabouat. At the Conseil des Ministres of 25 May 1988, presided over by the President of the Republic, Professor Jean-Noël Jeanneney was put in charge of the bicentenary celebrations.

The French Revolution and its Historians

NORMAN HAMPSON

If we are all, up to a point, the products of our past, it is no less true that what men understand that past to have been owes a good deal to their present. The profound disruption of French society caused by the Revolution of 1789 and its Napoleonic sequel made the country very difficult to govern for the next hundred and fifty years. The particular conflicts of their times directed the attention of historians to specific aspects of the Revolution and inclined them to interpret what they found in ways that corresponded to the preoccupations of their own day. Any historian is someone with a foot in two different worlds, but he is only one person and his perception of each is affected by his consciousness of the other. What he writes is, or ought to be, of relevance to a public that relies on him for its knowledge of its past, and the more unstable the present, the more acutely it will be aware of that past: history is more urgent in Northern Ireland than in England. All of these factors combined to give the history of the French Revolution a special resonance and to ensure its exceptional importance within French society.

All historians are individuals, and important ones, though they may speak for a generation, do so in a personal way. History, for them, is more than a matter of intellectual curiosity; it is a statement about life. This can take many forms. It may be a question of reassurance – that *leitmotiv* that runs through all the work of Richard Cobb – and reassurance itself can mean different things: the survival of humane values in the teeth of a hostile environment, as for Cobb; the ability of a nation to pull through against the odds, which gave comfort to many British people during the worst days of the Second World War; the demonstration of the Divine purpose (in the case of the French Revolution that was usually invoked by its enemies) or evidence that the Cause – whatever it might be – had triumphed in the past and could presumably do so again.

Historians are also practitioners of an evolving craft, which influences the way that they go about their business. The nineteenth century saw the emergence of a kind of historical writing that rejected the elegant classical narrative for more academic exposition, with its siege-train of references, footnotes and bibliographies. This tended to create an illusion of scientific precision and objectivity without making historians any less susceptible to their own temperaments and convictions. In his survey of the historiography of the Revolution, *A Jury for the Revolution* (1974), Jacques Godechot defined history, somewhat evasively, as 'an art that has recourse to more and more scientific methods'. He had to admit that its practitioners were still as far as ever from that unanimity that he seemed to believe to be their goal. The trouble about treating history as a science is that it makes people impatient with those who get their sums wrong. From the point of view of the general public, the growing professionalism of history was a mixed blessing. It possibly discouraged the wilder flights of prejudice but it encouraged the microscopic view, although French historians have never been afraid of the broad synthesis and the French reading public is more ready than the British to struggle with the detailed exposition of a complicated argument.

Historians are also carried along by the general cultural movements of their own times, such as Romanticism, Positivism or Marxism. They are as much affected as anyone else by the evolution of ways of thinking about the behaviour of men in society. They absorb, or react against, sociology; they read Freud, or at least are influenced by others who have done so. Some of them, such as Lefebvre or Cobban, attract followers and become leaders of schools. Original ways of looking at the past direct the search towards new kinds of evidence. Eventually these seams become exhausted and the venerated leaders are challenged by iconoclasts who become in time the patrons of new orthodoxies.

In the meantime the societies to which they belong are using history for their own purposes – and generally finding historians whom they honour for responding to their needs. When he published *The Coming of the French Revolution* in 1939, Georges Lefebvre was deliberately appealing to history to encourage Frenchmen to unite in defence of what he believed to have been the values of the revolution, against the threat from National Socialist Germany. Others had tried to support particular political options in the present by providing them with a historical pedigree: during the revolution of 1848 and the Paris Commune of 1871 this almost amounted to an attempt to relive the great days of 1789 or 1793–4. One form of acknowledging the past is to repudiate it, as the Vichy Government did in 1940, when it substituted for *Liberté, Egalité, Fraternité* the somewhat less inspiring *Travail, Famille, Patrie.* Vichy, at least, had no illusions about the enduring relevance of the French Revolution.

In other words, the relationship between a nation's present and its history is infinitely complex and the influence of either on the other is a two-way process. Marx began as a heretical Hegelian philosopher. His thinking was influenced by his experience of the 1848 revolutions, as a participant in Germany and a spectator in France. Driven into exile in the British Museum, he devoted the rest of his life to developing ideas that were both personal to him and suggested by his experience. These were eventually invoked as the guiding principles of a revolution, not in Germany, France or England, but in Russia, the country to which they seemed to have least relevance.

For all these reasons the history of the revolution was very much of a battleground in France for something like a century and a half. It had an urgency and a contemporary relevance in France that it could not have anywhere else. Foreigners such as Carlyle, von Sybel or Acton might write about the French Revolution, but only from perspectives that did not derive directly from it. For Frenchmen it was different. To quote Thiers, one of its earliest historians: 'Our duty is to support the same cause.' Jules Michelet more or less apologized for criticizing Louis Blanc since he was 'one of ours'. Only a Frenchman could have this sense that the Revolution *had* to be defended, that it was, in a sense, still going on. That is why, in this brief essay, I have confined myself exclusively to French historians until the end of the Second World War.

Things are different now. The collapse of Vichy brought the end of the counter-revolution. Even Poujade wanted an Estates General, though he does not seem to have known what that meant. François Furet understood very well what he was doing when he called the first section of his *Interpreting the French Revolution* (1978) 'The French Revolution is over'. For the first time, Frenchmen are free to treat their Revolution as history rather than as politics. At the same time, the proliferation of professional history throughout the world has brought foreign historians – especially those whom the French like to describe as 'Anglo-Saxons' – to participate fully in the debate on a revolution that is no longer 'ours' or 'yours'. This does not mean that its history has become any less complicated or controversial but at least certain kinds of myth seem to have been exorcised.

The first serious historians of the Revolution were François Mignet and Adolphe Thiers, who began to publish their accounts in 1823. Thiers claimed that the debate on the Revolution could not begin until the end of Napoleon's military despotism. He is one of those historians whom people advise each other to read without doing much about it themselves. Although restricted to printed sources, his knowledge of these was comprehensive and one can still learn from him. Thiers and Mignet began what was to become a Great Tradition, developed by most of their successors over the next century. They saw the Revolution as both political and social: Mignet contrasted it with the revolution in England that had merely changed the government. Thiers claimed that 1789 had put an end to a 'feudal constitution' and a society in which the nobility had clung on to their privileges when the crown had stripped them of their political role and turned them into court pensioners. This 'feudal' society had already been undermined by 'an increasingly commercial and manufacturing people', frustrated by the privileges of 'individuals, classes, towns, provinces, and trade corporations themselves'. 'All was impediments, for both industry and human ability.' On the intellectual plane, this society was challenged by the writers of the Enlightenment who dogmatized all the more boldly since they were denied any access to practical politics.

Both historians saw the Revolution as the inevitable product of circumstances. As Mignet put it, rather naïvely, 'When a reform becomes necessary and its moment has arrived, nothing can stop it.' Thiers thought it utopian to imagine that the transition from a 'feudal' to a liberal society could be accomplished peacefully. The constitution of 1791 created a virtual republic that no Bourbon could have accepted, but if the constitution had offered the king more power it would have been swept away by popular revolt. The use of force set those impatient to acquire everything against those who refused to surrender anything. This brought Thiers face to face with the problem of the Terror. He had no use for Robespierre – 'one of the most odious beings who ever dominated men' – but from his determinist viewpoint the Terror was inevitable, necessary and therefore, in some sense, excusable. When the Girondins fell they carried with them 'all that was most generous and enlightened in France' but they had to go since they compromised 'the revolution, freedom and France'. Already the Revolution had become personalized. Instead of being a sequence of policies and events, in continuous evolution, that meant different things to different men, it was a kind of metaphysical entity. Both Thiers and Mignet had no doubt that it was a beneficent one. For Mignet it involved, 'transient excesses alongside lasting benefits'. Moreover the excesses were not attributable to the Revolution itself but were produced by the obstacles that 'it' had to overcome: the resistance of the privileged and the hostility of foreign powers. It was these reactionary forces that were responsible for the sovereignty of the multitude and the eventual military dictatorship. Thiers would not have disagreed with this, although he thought there was an inner dynamic within modern revolutions that produced a 'class struggle . . . the simple bourgeois ends by being denounced as an aristocrat by the workman.' The Terror and the revolutionary dictatorship were the only means of preserving national unity at a time of extreme danger. They were therefore 'sublime and atrocious at the same time'. Thiers blamed Danton for trying to end them too soon and the revolutionary government for continuing them when military victory had made them unnecessary. Even so, the overthrow of the 'odious' Robespierre marked the end of the 'ascending march' of the Revolution. This was an interpretation rich in equivocations and ambiguities that were to enable a good many of Thiers's successors to make the best of both worlds. Whatever one made of the Terror, there could be no doubt about the beneficent influence of the Revolution as a whole. For Mignet it 'replaced arbitrariness with law, privilege with equality, it freed men from class distinctions [in the sense of distinctions founded on birth], liberated the soil from provincial barriers, industry from the impediments of the trade guilds, agriculture from feudal burdens and the oppression of tithe, property from the restrictions of entail, and restored everything to a single state, a single law and a single people.' If one had no reservations about the end and one believed the means to have been imposed by those who were trying to frustrate it, one was already half way towards justifying all that had happened.

Thiers completed his history in 1827. Twenty years later, with France on the edge of another revolution, Alphonse de Lamartine produced his *History of the Girondins* and Michelet and Louis Blanc brought out the first volumes of their monumental histories. Since the 1848 revolution was something of an unforeseen accident, these historians must be considered as having helped to contribute to events rather than as responding to a pre-revolutionary situation. From our perspective, Lamartine's contribution to the revolutionary tradition may be disregarded. Despite his title, he saw the overthrow of the Girondins by the 'people' as necessary for the preservation of the revolution, which allowed him to vilify Robespierre while implicitly justifying the revolutionary government. His book was something of a pot-boiler and he had neither the erudition nor the influence of his two contemporaries.

With Michelet the Great Tradition found its most eloquent and extreme spokeman. To present the bare outline of his argument is like paraphrasing one of Shakespeare's tragedies: one can convey a general impression of what it was all about but the real meaning is inseparable from the hypnotic language that is an essential part of it. Michelet identified himself so completely with the events he was describing that he referred to his father's death, soon after he had begun his book, like this: 'I was at the foot of the Bastille, I was taking the fortress . . . that blow took me by surprise, like a bullet from the Bastille.' This is probably why he exercised so profound an influence on most subsequent French writing about the Revolution and why his passion was transmitted to historians who disagreed with many of his conclusions. His approach was essentially that of the revivalist preacher. Ironically enough, since he believed that the Revolution had liberated men from Christianity as well as from feudalism, his conception of it curiously paralleled Christianity itself. The Revolution consisted of 'the belated arrival of universal justice', 'the triumph of right, the resurrection of justice, the belated reaction of the idea against brute force'. If this is somewhat less than explicit, it is at least clear that we are talking about the Word made flesh. The Revolution was implicit in the whole course of French history, to which it gave its meaning, just as the birth of Christ was the decisive turning-point in the Christian calendar. The spirit of the Revolution 'contains the secret of all previous time. Only in it did France become conscious of herself.' Its message, like that of Christ, was one of love and redemption to all nations. 'The Revolution, one must admit, began by loving everything. It went so far as to love its enemy, England.' Wholly pure and irreproachable, its tragedy was to be destroyed by those it came to save, but it left behind its message of redemption and hope that constituted a sacred gospel for all succeeding generations.

For Michelet the Revolution, at least during its 'humane and benevolent period', was the work, not of individuals or social classes but of 'the people itself, the whole people, everybody'. Conversely, the violence and bloody actions of 1792–4, although they were an inevitable response to France's enemies, were produced by 'the actions of a tiny few, an infinitely small fraction of the population'. It was probably not their fault anyway, since they had been brutalized by their upbringing under the *ancien régime*. The Revolution posed no moral problems. If one defence seemed inappropriate one could always use its opposite. France offered love and peace to all nations. Michelet knew well enough that it was the French who had actually declared war on Austria, Spain, England and the Netherlands, but 'they only drew the sword to bring peace by liberating the nations from foreign tyrants.' This was 'the sacred war for peace, for the deliverance of the world'. If the occupied Belgians resented the ruthlessness of French exploitation, it was only reasonable that they should pay for their 'liberation' which had cost France so much blood. If anything associated with the Revolution appeared to be cruel or unjust the fault lay – as it did for Thiers – with the king, or the church or with foreigners, who forced it to adopt measures that were alien to its true nature, as the price of its self-preservation. As with most forms of nationalism, the argument forms an unbroken circle that reinforces itself and there is no way of breaking through at any point.

Although individuals played a largely symbolic role in the great national epic, Michelet had not much use for Robespierre. He reproached Louis Blanc for his partiality towards the 'new Jesus'. Insofar as he had a hero, it was Danton, although his attitude was not entirely consistent. In one place he said that Danton's affiliation to Diderot was merely a matter of surface appearances; elsewhere he called him Diderot's 'true son'. By the time he wrote his preface to the 1868 edition of his history, this question of spiritual allegiances had assumed a somewhat bizarre importance. Although he apologized for breaking the 'unity of the great Church', since Louis Blanc was 'one of ours', this did not deter Michelet from pitching into him for dividing the Revolutionaries into ideological teams and exposing them to anachronistic judgements in terms of social class. He accused Blanc of condemning Danton and the Girondins as bourgeois and presenting Robespierre as a proto-socialist. He even went so far as to call Blanc a 'demi-Christian of the stamp of Rousseau and Robespierre'.

There was some truth in Michelet's charges. Louis Blanc shared Michelet's conviction that the Revolution was 'the most sublime event in history', 'an uninterrupted succession of prodigies. Nothing like it had ever been seen before or will ever be seen again.' He claimed in a letter written in 1866 to have written his history from the viewpoint that 'the force possessed by individuals is only to a very small extent personal to them; they derive it in the main from their surroundings; their lives are merely a concentration of the collective life in which they are immersed.' Michelet would have approved of all that, but it was not what Blanc had put in his book. Starting his history of the revolution with Huss, in the fourteenth century, Blanc had declared it to be 'essentially an idea, a principle'. The course of all human history moved from a period of authority through one of individualism to one of fraternity or, putting it in other words, from Catholicism through Protestantism to the Montagnards, which meant from oppression through rationalism to harmony. Like Mignet, Blanc saw the Revolution, and the Enlightenment before it, as dual. The rationalism of Voltaire and Montesquieu had been taken up by the Girondins as the inspiration for an individualist attack that had destroyed the corporate society of the *ancien régime*. This was necessary but not sufficient and the torch had then been taken up by the Montagnards (and more especially by Robespierre) who were the heirs of Rousseau, Mably and – rather oddly – of Necker. Not surprisingly, given this formidable pedigree, the Revolution itself was 'a struggle of Titans'. It was 'to dare and to accomplish what had been beyond the genius of the Roman Senate'. During the Terror 'human nature took on gigantic proportions'. Robespierre and Saint-Just were demi-gods whose death 'postponed the liberation of the world'. It was never very clear in what this liberation consisted and, in practice, Blanc tended to confuse it with the successes of the Revolutionary armies. Despite his canonization of Robespierre, he thought that the revolution had been destroyed by the Terror, 'an active source of ruin that it carried within itself'. The Terror was, of course, the inevitable product of circumstances but it provided a vehicle for base motives: fraud, personal ambition and the pursuit of vengeance. As with Michelet, somehow or other this did not affect the character of 'the revolution' itself.

With Michelet and Louis Blanc the Great Tradition was well launched. The Revolution was *the* event, which gave meaning to historical time. It could only have happened in France but its message was one of redemption to all nations. Revolutionary conflicts were Manichean battles between the representatives of total good and absolute evil, that transcended history itself; the history of the Revolution became a kind of *Paradise Lost*. Foreigners being what they unfortunately were, even after the French had shown them what to do, the only way to emancipate them was to subject them to military occupation. It was, in a sense, the doctrine of the red, white and blue man's burden and it underlay the attitudes of French politicians and historians in ways of which they were not always conscious.

The next phase in the improbable story of French revolutionary historiography was provided by the philosopher Auguste Comte. When Comte gave his lectures on positivist philosophy in 1839–42 he barely mentioned Danton. It was perhaps M. N. Villiaumé's *History of the French Revolution* (1850) that showed him the light. By the time Comte came to write his *System of Positive Politics* in 1851–4, Danton had been promoted to the position that Robespierre held for Louis Blanc, not so much that of revolutionary statesman as of standard-bearer for an ideology. Comte shared Blanc's weakness for ideological triads and like Blanc he identified the Girondins with a negative rationalism that stemmed from Voltaire. At this point he parted company from Blanc, condemning Robespierre as the purveyer of an outmoded religiosity derived from Rousseau. The final term of Comte's triad, a kind of proto-positivism that derived from Diderot, was personified by Danton. Comte was very influential as a philosopher, and positivism gave historians a new conception of their craft as a science and a new professionalism in their search for documentary evidence and in the way in which they presented their conclusions. He also sent the positivists away on a search for new material that could be quoted to the greater glory of Danton. A. Bougeart led the pack, with his *Danton, authentic documents contributing to the history of the French Revolution* in 1861, but Danton's most prolific champion was Dr Robinet, who published four books on his hero between 1879 and 1889. In the last of these he claimed that Danton had had 'a feeling for the elevated goal to which the evolution of human civilization was tending, and wanted to assure, by spiritual liberty and public order, the transitional regime and temporary shelter that would enable science to complete the elaboration and propagation of the theoretical basis for the regeneration of the west'. From the positivist point of view, Robinet's heart was in the right place but his style left something to be desired.

By this time – helped by the centenary celebrations of 1889 when a fair amount of hyperbole was only to be expected – the history of the Revolution had become thoroughly bound up with the defence of the Third Republic. To cast doubt on the one was seen as disloyal to the other and the more shaky the Republic appeared, in its early years, the greater the need to rally round the defence of the Revolution. In 1891 Alphonse Aulard became the first holder of the Chair in French Revolutionary History that had been created at the Sorbonne in celebration of the centenary. The tenure of the Chair has ever since been a symbol of historical orthodoxy and – especially in view of the hierarchical nature of the French educational system – a powerful means of defending it. The unfortunate Aulard, who did so much to further the publication of documentary evidence about the Revolution, was a man of such moderate views that he offended everyone. When he described Danton as 'the most modern statesman of the revolution, with a mind turned towards the future, a practical politician, an eloquent orator, but a man of weak character and lazy', such slander was more than Robinet could be expected to stand and he denounced Aulard in an anonymous pamphlet that everyone identified. In his *Political History of the Revolution* (1901) Aulard carried the demystification process a stage further by denying that the Revolutionaries were 'a generation of giants'. This must have been anathema to almost everyone. Seven years later his admiring pupil, Albert Mathiez, suddenly turned on both Aulard and Danton, heaping abuse on both for the rest of his life.

Mathiez inherited the positivists' respect for erudition and also their conviction that all the evidence must point in one direction. After his early studies of the religious history of the Revolution, most of what he wrote was a testament to the infallibility of Robespierre. He acquired a knowledge of the political history of the Revolution that has probably never been equalled; everything that he wrote is worth reading and his *Vie Chère*, on social and economic conflicts in Paris, is one of the best books ever written on the Revolution. Nevertheless, he approached the period with the pitiless partiality of the revolutionary tribunal itself. Contemporary events merely sharpened his historical animosities. Originally a pacifist, the outbreak of war in 1914 turned him into something of a jingo. When there was talk of a negotiated peace he denounced the defeatism of the arch-enemy in *Danton and the Peace* (1917). *Victory in the Year II*, in the same year, was a response to demands for total mobilization. He celebrated Clemenceau's attack on foreign agents and French spies, in 1918, with *The Revolution and the Foreigners*; a fair number of them, of course, turned out to have been Dantonists or could more or less plausibly be accused of having had links with Danton. The Russian Revolution, which Mathiez welcomed, served to justify the Terror. As always, the history of the Revolution was inseparable from contemporary politics. Mathiez belonged to the Great Tradition by reason of his fierce French nationalism, his belief that the Revolution had been a period of unique importance in French history, his Manichean approach to revolutionary politics and his conviction that the Revolution had been a movement for the regeneration of humanity that had been thwarted by the forces of evil in France and, more especially, abroad. His personal contribution to the tradition was to identify it, for the rest of its existence, with the uncritical glorification of Robespierre.

A contemporary of Mathiez, but a man of a very different temperament, was Jean Jaurès, the leader of the French socialist party who was assassinated in July 1914 when he was trying to organize international resistance to the impending war. As a logical Marxist, Jaurès saw that what had happened in France amounted to a wholly admirable bourgeois revolution, at a time when it was utopian to think in terms of socialism. He was far from being unsympathetic to the fate of the poor but his *Socialist History of the French Revolution* was actually more social than socialist. Unlike his predecessors, he devoted a good deal of time to events outside Paris and it is with him that the social history of the Revolution really began. But the heroes of a bourgeois revolution had to come from the bourgeoisie and Jaurès had the breadth of vision and generosity of spirit to applaud in 1789–94 the achievements of a class which a century later he opposed as a politician. He claimed that he had taken as his guides Marx, Michelet and Plutarch, but he did not quite belong to the Great Tradition, even if he was largely responsible for endowing it with a Marxist content. He was a consistent anti-militarist and he was even critical of the process of revolution itself. 'Revolutions are the barbaric aspect of progress. However noble, fertile and necessary a revolution may be, it still belongs to the inferior and semi-bestial stage of human development.' The emphasis here is very different from that of historians who lightly dismissed the inevitable 'excesses' of the Terror as the product of circumstances and the necessary price of progress – and even further removed from the glee of Mathiez at the smiting of the unrighteous. Despite the title of his book and his position in French politics, the man who wrote that the legacy of the Revolution was democracy looks very much like a liberal.

Mathiez was succeeded in the Sorbonne Chair by Lefebvre, another historian of immense erudition and a somewhat inquisitorial temperament, whose views tended to harden with age. More dispassionate than Mathiez – he even published an admirably impartial assessment of Danton – he nevertheless shared his predecessor's total dedication to the Revolution and to Robespierre. Lefebvre began, and to some extent remained, a historian of the peasantry. He was well aware that the Revolution benefited only a minority of the rural population and that it was violently opposed by a great many who saw it as inimical to their interests and offensive to their beliefs. Nevertheless, as a believer in its essential virtue (despite its bourgeois character) the most he could offer its opponents was a rather chilly sympathy for the ignorance and fanaticism that had led them astray. In *The Coming of the French Revolution* (1939) he integrated into the tradition what purported to be Marxism. The Enlightenment was the ideology of a bourgeoisie that had conquered economic power but was chafing at its social, economic and political frustration. France tipped decisively from feudalism to capitalism in 1789. Although every other European state was to achieve the same transition, and some had already done so, it was the French alone who proclaimed a universal gospel of emancipation whose promises transcended the potential of a purely bourgeois movement. The Great Tradition, with its heady compound of chauvinism, millenarianism and a genuine, if vague, dedication to the emancipation of humanity from what were seen as the shackles of the past, had gained in complexity over the years, but when Lefebvre celebrated its hundred and fiftieth anniversary with what was to remain his best-known book, it was still as vigorous as ever. The Revolution, more than ever, as the events of 1940 were to show, was still a matter of contemporary politics. Its battles still had to be won and its historians could hope for no demobilization.

The Great Tradition did not comprehend all French writing on the Revolution – not quite. Two books in particular challenged its basic assumptions and their reception in France suffered in consequence. In 1856 Alexis de Tocqueville published the first part of his *Ancien Régime and the French Revolution*. He died before he had time to deal with the Revolution itself, leaving us with only his account of its origins. Tocqueville's perspective was that of the liberal aristocrat. He was not disposed to romanticize pre-revolutionary society and he described 1789 as 'a time of inexperience no doubt, but also of generosity, enthusiasm and virility, a time of immortal memory'. He nevertheless regretted the loss of 'independence, the taste for greatness, confidence in one's self and in causes' that he associated with aristocratic society and he was pessimistic about a future that seemed to him to be heading for mediocrity and despotism. He followed previous historians in arguing that the monarchy had deprived the nobility of a political role while leaving it with its privileges, and in criticizing the Enlightenment as inclined to utopian speculation because of its remoteness from actual politics. He differed from them in insisting that the Revolution was born of rising hopes and expectations, rather than of despair, and in believing that it had been precipitated by the monarchy's attempts at reform. Tocqueville worked mainly on administrative history, which led him to stress something that was denied by everyone else: instead of presenting the Revolution as a clean break and a new start, he saw it as accelerating a process of bureaucratic centralization that was already well under way in 1789. What he had in mind was brought home forcibly to me one autumn day in 1944 when a rowing boat put out from the French coast towards the Free French warship in which I was serving. It carried a policeman who tried – admittedly without much conviction – to arrest one of the ship's officers on the ground that he had 'deserted' (i.e. escaped to join the Free French forces) two or three years before. Occupations and Liberations might come and go but the files apparently went on for ever. Tocqueville would not have been amused, but he would not have been surprised either. It was perhaps his emphasis on continuity that led Englishmen to regard him as the most penetrating of French nineteenth-century historians of the Revolution. In his own country he was treated with cautious respect but his message was not to be taken up for over a century. It did not tell Frenchmen what most of them wanted to believe.

The second of the heterodox historians was Hippolyte Taine, whose *Origins of Contemporary France* appeared between 1875 and 1884. Taine abandoned his initial liberalism as a result of the Paris Commune, which left him with a permanent hatred and fear of the mob. Much of his work consisted of an intemperate diatribe against what happened during the Revolution but it would be a mistake to think of him as merely a counter-revolutionary. He joined the historians of the left in condemning the worldliness of the church, the unearned privileges of the nobility and the arbitrary rule of the monarchy, and he was sympathetically disposed towards the Enlightenment. His point of view was very close to that of Burke, who also held strong views about the 'swinish multitude'. All the necessary reforms could have been effected gradually and by consensus. The monarchy was already moving in the right direction and the nobility, the main contributors to the Enlightenment, were never more liberal than in 1789. The Constituent Assembly meant well but its perspectives were utopian. It invented a virtually non-existent counter-revolutionary threat from a nobility too feeble to do more than grumble. The result was to dismantle the power of government and to open the way to anarchy, which meant not so much lack of government as rule by robber bands whose 'leaders' were the mere mouthpieces of 'followers' whom they could not control. The fall of the Girondins marked the end of a period of feeble good intentions on the part of the government and ushered in a period of rule by fanatics, butchers and those intent on feathering their own nests. Taine devoted a whole book to an analysis of the ideology of the Terror. For him, Rousseau was not the Christian of Michelet and Comte, but a fanatical devotee of Sparta whose followers were determined to deprive Frenchmen of their individual liberty and turn them into anonymous units in a patriotic herd. For Taine, this preaching of classical virtues was thoroughly retrograde; the modern individual, the heir of feudalism and Christianity, was the sole custodian of his conscience and his honour. Taine went on to celebrate the revolutionary army as the only institution where confidence and a sense of hierarchy still survived. His history was well documented although his examples were often untypical, his tone was monotonously strident and his judgement unbalanced. His history was, however, no more implausible than that of Michelet or Robinet and his claim that the Revolution was a disaster for the country as a whole, that culminated in the dictatorship of a fanatical minority, had more truth to it than many people liked to admit. He wrote, however, at a time when the Third Republic, struggling to assert its legitimacy, was calling on all Frenchmen to unite in defence of its own particular version of the meaning of the Revolution, and he suffered the common fate of those who rock boats. He was denounced by Aulard and there was enough unreasonableness in his work to allow anyone to dismiss it all with an easy conscience.

By 1939, therefore, the Great Tradition had things very much its own way. The few discordant voices – not merely Tocqueville and Taine, but a number of more or less popular, more or less royalist historians – could be safely disregarded. Since the tradition had come to be identified with what was regarded as Marxism, to challenge it was to confess oneself both reactionary and unpatriotic. The debate on the French Revolution seemed to have reached a conclusion and there was something so splendidly definitive about Lefebvre's *Coming of the French Revolution* that few were disposed to express any doubts about the quality of the emperor's tailoring.

When the writing of the history of the Revolution picked up

again after the war it had become an international busines, with British and American writers well to the fore. This in itself was bound to lead to a change of perspective since they could not be expected to respond to a tradition that had been created to satisfy exclusively French needs. In France itself, the collapse of the old right and growing disillusionment with the Soviet Union as an object lesson to the rest of the world were also to prompt new ways of thinking about the present that affected people's views of the past.

One of the first off the mark was the Israeli historian, Jacob Talmon, with his *Origins of Totalitarian Democracy* in 1952. Talmon took up Taine's attack on Rousseau as the originator of a messianic doctrine for the regeneration of individuals by society, whose grisly practical consequences had been demonstrated by Robespierre and Saint-Just in particular. Talmon's approach was open to criticism: he shared Taine's stridency and his abuse of the individual example, and he concentrated too much on one or two Montagnards when he could have found the same principles at work in others. He had nonetheless produced a serious and disturbing book, or at least, one that should have been disturbing. In fact it was swept under the carpet by friends and opponents of the Great Tradition alike and its author paid the penalty for being wise before his time.

The American historian, R. R. Palmer, broadened the issues by situating the French Revolution within the context of what he saw as an Atlantic world. This was always something of a misnomer since it excluded the South Atlantic and stretched as far as the Netherlands and Geneva. For Palmer, in *The Age of the Democratic Revolution* (1959–64), the late eighteenth century produced an international democratic movement whose leaders often knew each other, or at least knew of each other, read the same books and held similar views about politics and society. The Americans began a series of revolutions, of which that in France was the most important. This was unlikely to commend itself to the custodians of the Great Tradition, since it denied the uniqueness of the French Revolution, but Jacques Godechot for a time associated himself with Palmer.

The 'Marxist' orientation of the tradition exposed it to the sort of criticism from which the Michelet version had preserved itself by its hermetical self-sufficiency. The chief protagonist here was Alfred Cobban, notably in his *Social Interpretation of the French Revolution* (1964). In a splendid knockabout introduction, Cobban disposed briskly of both sociological and empirical history. The former was designed always to prove what it began by assuming and the latter was unable to prove anything at all. One is inclined to sympathize, but having made the lady vanish, Cobban had some understandable difficulty in getting her to reappear. His intention was to attack Albert Soboul (the spiritual heir of Mathiez and Lefebvre and the current holder of the Sorbonne Chair) and, more cautiously, Lefebvre, as Marxists of a Leninist persuasion. What he actually achieved was rather different. He had no great difficulty in showing that the 'Marxists' had been inclined to distort the evidence when it failed to support their preconceived theories. What he failed to notice was that he was really condemning them for being *bad* Marxists. His own position rested on a fairly rigorous economic determinism, even if his red flag had a Union Jack in one corner that made it look suspiciously like a Red Ensign. Throughout his book he used 'social' to mean 'economic' and he offered an economic explanation for everything: 'the strategic questions to ask about the Vendée are not doctrinal but sociological.' He really let the cat out of the bag in a revealing sentence: 'There is nothing surprising in the fact that, the economic development of English society being so far in advance of that of France, its political evolution should also have shown much greater maturity.' That put the *sans-culottes* in their place, for one of the things that Cobban seemed to resent was the extent of the fuss made about a *French* revolution. This is not to deny that many of his shots hit their targets. With mischievous glee he circled round the laager of the Great Tradition, picking off its defenders one by one. Above all, he demonstrated that its 'Marxist' version rested on an account of what actually happened that would not stand up to verification. He had, however, nothing much to put in its place. He called for a new vocabulary to replace such meaningless terms as 'bourgeois', but he made no attempt to supply one himself.

Where Cobban skirmished, the heavy artillery was brought up by an American historian, G. V. Taylor. In two monumental articles in particular, 'Types of Capitalism in Eighteenth-century France' (*English Historical Review*, 1964) and 'Non-capitalist Wealth and the Origins of the French Revolution' (*American Historical Review*, 1967), Taylor demonstrated that in the late eighteenth century the French nobility and the upper ranks of the professional middle class had belonged to the same economic class, sharing the same relationship to the ownership of the means of production and the same economic aspirations. This demolished at one blow the confusion between social order and economic class on which much of the 'Marxist' interpretation of the Revolution had rested, and put paid to the idea that the Revolution marked any kind of transition 'from feudalism to capitalism'.

While these luminaries described their more or less predictable orbits, the revolutionary skies were illuminated for a time by a wandering comet in the shape of Richard Cobb. Cobb's hatred of synthesis confined him to one major book, the *Revolutionary Armies* (1961–3). This dealt, not with the front-line troops, but with a kind of SS that had been created to intimidate counter-revolutionaries and extract food from the peasantry. Cobb's other works, even the admirable *Police and the People* (1970), are really collections of essays. Cobb, as he would be the first to agree, conforms to no pattern and follows his own course. The enemy of all authority, especially centralized authority dedicated to improving people who would have preferred to have been left alone, he confessed to 'an almost constant urge to make fun of the revolutionary apostle, the solemn propagandist of Virtue and Unanimity. This is because I am afraid of him.' 'Perhaps the main subject of my book on the *Armées révolutionnaires* might be described as the ineffectiveness of government, even of the much-vaunted revolutionary government, in the face of well-organized local pressure groups.' What Cobb saw in the French Revolution was the reassurance that, even amongst the most deprived of people, in the most violent and tyrannical periods of history, there could survive 'a world of neighbourliness, of watchfulness, of enforced "living together" which, however crude and brutal, noisy and filthy, quarrelsome and envious, was not devoid of compassion, tenderness, kindliness and disinterestedness.' He recreated the revolutionary world in a way that reminds one of Michelet. Although their attitudes to its politics could scarcely have been more unlike, they both give the impression of inhabiting it and they shared a common devotion to 'The Archives Nationales, one of the most beautiful buildings in Europe; a secure refuge from fear'. For Cobb, the Revolution was not so much a subject in itself as a theatre for the study of the eternal problems of human existence. He enriched its history in unique and personal ways, but after *Death in Paris* (1978) he left it to its own devices and departed for outer space and the contemplation of life, death and time.

Many of the cross-currents in the post-war history of the Revolution came together in the colloquium that Eberhard Schmitt organized in the University of Bamberg in 1979. G. V. Taylor demonstrated with his usual precision that the famous 'industrial and commercial bourgeoisie' had been very suspicious of all eighteenth-century governments, especially revolutionary ones, but Soboul did not appear to be listening. R. R. Palmer put the case for his Atlantic revolution, which Soboul dismissed as a product of the cold war, designed to attach the French Revolution to democracy and to America, and to deny its connection with socialism and the Russian Revolution. Soboul himself produced what was perhaps the final version of the Great Tradition, which he subsequently incorporated into his *Civilization and the French Revolution* (1982). The first bourgeois revolutionaries had been the English Levellers but they were defeated and 1688 was merely a watered-down version of their principles which allowed the upper middle class to dominate eighteenth-century England (sic). The American Revolution was 'free from any popular colouring' and Jefferson merely the spokesman of the ruling class. The *French* bourgeois revolution, in contrast, 'left far behind the empirical character of English liberties and the contradictions of the American Declarations'. This was because of the universal principles embodied in the French Declaration of the Rights of Man. Nevertheless the French Revolution, despite its evident superiority over its predecessors, remained incorrigibly bourgeois, which produced a 'contradiction' between the principles it affirmed and the most that the

Constituent Assembly was prepared to enact. This left Soboul with the awkward problem of building a bridge between a revolution that, although French, was still bourgeois, and its Soviet successor. This was the cue for the Man of Destiny. 'Robespierre was no doubt the only man, in the whole course of the revolution, to tackle this problem with resolution . . . in the end by a class analysis *implicitly* [my italics] opposed to the abstract theory of the rights of man.' All that was needed now was Marx and the Russians would know what to do. All the theoretical problems had been solved, though Soboul was a little hard on Saint-Just who had, in fact, gone further than Robespierre. It was magnificent but it scarcely fitted the facts and Cobban and Taylor had already shown that it was a complete travesty of the actual situation. Still, the veteran Dreadnought went down with all guns firing and its colours nailed firmly to the mast. Even the Marxists had deserted Soboul. Claude Mazauric argued that the Revolution saw the triumph of bourgeois *attitudes* and that there was no necessary correlation between a man's class and his political opinions. In the course of discussion he went so far as to say, 'I call a man bourgeois if he thinks in a certain way, even if he is a noble or a peasant.' This brought an indignant cry of 'But that's Idealism!' and it did look as though Mazauric had stood Marx on his head and rediscovered Hegel. He maintained that the pre-revolutionary bourgeois had been a conservative and backward-looking lot. Jacobinism – an ideological and cultural movement – transformed the nature of a revolution that had been dominated by both members of the bourgeoisie and liberal nobles. In the reaction that occurred after 1794 what emerged was a new class of notables, consisting of capitalist proprietors of mixed social origin. The Revolution, in other words, was not made by the kind of bourgeoisie that Marx described; it made them. How far Marx himself would have been happy with this, it is perhaps impossible to say, but it certainly rescued the history of the Revolution from the impasse into which earlier 'Marxists' had penned it.

Since the death of the Great Tradition and the liberation of the Marxists the picture has become more confused. Both French and American writing has been penetrated by the historical sociologists with their penchant for the *longe durée*, for the study of social groups rather than economic classes and their impatience with *l'histoire événementielle*. This is perhaps no bad thing, although it does tend to play down the fact that some *événements* were more important than others. Sociological explanations raise two major problems. As Cobban showed, they tend to be self-verifying, in the sense that 'by taking one factor in history as basic, all the others can be reduced to conditions in which it operates.' In the second place, sociological theories leave no room for contingency. Things had to happen that way if the theory is to be valid and what contemporaries saw as choices were in fact nothing of the kind. It may have been so but it is hard to prove that that is how it actually was. Lynn Hunt's interesting *Politics, Culture and Class in the French Revolution* (1984) suffers from this defect. Most historians of the Revolution have believed its character to have been transformed by the war and that the war was a product, not of necessity, but of political choice. If Lynn Hunt's view is correct, everything that happened was implicit from the beginning.

The pragmatists have gone on marshalling the evidence that fragments the Revolution into a multitude of individual, local or sectional conflicts and aspirations. W. Doyle in *Origins of the French Revolution* (1980) surveyed the controversy between Cobban and the last defenders of the Great Tradition. Without coming down on Cobban's side, which would have been difficult in view of the negative nature of the *Social Interpretation*, he mobilized all the evidence that cut the ground from beneath the feet of Lefebvre and Soboul. In *France, 1789–1815* (1985) Donald Sutherland took the pragmatic approach to its logical conclusion. For millions of Frenchmen, especially those living in the country, the French Revolution was an unwelcome intrusion that offended their habits and convictions without conferring on them any net benefit. To label their opposition to it 'counter-revolutionary' in a pejorative sense is to subscribe to the old myth that there was *a* French Revolution that was by definition a boon to humanity in general, to which all right-thinking people were rationally and morally bound to subscribe. This belief is so deeply entrenched that it will not easily be shaken but it is on the decline and the pendulum is likely to swing too far in the opposite direction. Even Taine had been prepared to admit that it *was* bliss in that dawn to be alive, at least when the sun was just rising, and history that neglects the enthusiasm, the idealism and the disinterestedness that were also part of the Revolution is not telling the whole story.

Moreover, as François Furet pointed out in his *Interpreting the French Revolution* (1978), 'erudition, while it may be stimulated by preoccupations drawn from the present, is never sufficient to modify the conceptualization of a problem or an event.' Furet set out to do precisely that. He began by rejecting the 'Marxist' version of the Great Tradition on the ground that it amounted to an endless refighting of revolutionary battles that had become unnecessary since the demise of Vichy and the virtually universal acceptance of the revolutionary legacy in France. He went on to accept Tocqueville's view that the Revolution was essentially a question of continuity, but he saw that this entirely failed to explain the exceptional nature of the revolutionary crisis with its millenarian hopes and extremes of violence. His explanation was that the period was unique in French history in the sense that it was a time when the normal agencies of political authority failed to function and the country was dominated by the practitioners of an ideology. In the first part of his book he associated this ideology with Rousseau but he went on to make the curious claim that 'most of the men of 89 had not read Rousseau.' This is much more than a matter of academic nit-picking. For Furet the Revolutionaries were the unconscious agents of an ideology that they did not understand. In that sense he joins the sociologists in their global explanation of causal sequences that the actors themselves were not free to modify since they did not appreciate what was going on. In fact, from 1789 onwards, they quite consciously aligned themselves for and against particular interpretations of Rousseau. The implementation of what were thought to be his ideas therefore turned on the political fortunes of particular groups or individuals, which restores to the Revolution that element of contingency and tactical manoeuvre without which it dissolves into an abstraction. Furet also claimed, rather provocatively, that the French had invented democracy, which sounds rather like an echo of the Great Tradition. The

Terror certainly invented something and its belief in the forcible regeneration of the rest by those who know better has had a long and infamous posterity, but to label this as 'democracy' seems rather unnecessary.

In the nature of things, any survey of the historiography of the French Revolution must always be an interim report until historians cease to think about it at all. Nevertheless, Furet is probably right: it *is* over and its bicentenary is as good an occasion as any to celebrate its demise as theology and its reincarnation as history.

INDEX

Index

FONTANA HISTORY OF WAR AND EUROPEAN SOCIETY

General Editor: Geoffrey Best

'The Fontana History of War and European Society offers more than a new view of Europe's military history, it suggests a new vantage point for analysing the modern world system. It implies that interstate dynamics, expressed in military competition between territorial nation-states, have contributed more to the emergence and the development of the modern world system than analysts have hitherto assumed. Instead of focusing on the means of production to explain the advent of the modern world, we ought to consider the impact of means of destruction as well.'
Journal of Peace Research

J. R. Hale
War and Society in Renaissance Europe, 1450–1620

M. S. Anderson
War and Society in Europe of the Old Regime, 1618–1789

Geoffrey Best
War and Society in Revolutionary Europe, 1770–1870

V. G. Kiernan
European Empires from Conquest to Collapse, 1815–1980

Brian Bond
War and Society in Europe, 1870–1970

EARLY VICTORIAN BRITAIN, 1832–51

J. F. C. Harrison

For people in all walks of life, the period between the passing of the Great Reform Bill and the Great Exhibition was one of turbulence and change, where massive events such as the new Poor Law, the coming of railways, Chartism, the repeal of the Corn Laws and the Great Irish Famine were set against a background of political manouevring and violent economic fluctuations. Professor Harrison offers a thorough and entertaining survey of this crucial phase of British history.

'I read . . . with uninterrupted delight, entranced that English historians could combine so dazzlingly scholarship and art.'
A. J. P. Taylor, *Observer*

Also by J. F. C. Harrison

The Common People: a History from the Norman Conquest to the Present

T. C. Smout

A History of the Scottish People 1560–1830

'By far the most stimulating, the most instructive and the most readable account of Scotch history that I have read . . . this splendid work carries us from Knox to Neilson, from the hot gospel of Calvin to the hot-blast smelting process – and incidentally seeks to explain the change. For always, in following this lucid narrative, we see an original mind at work, questioning and explaining as well as illustrating.

The illustrations, incidentally, are original and delightful too. The whole book has delighted me. I cannot praise it too highly.' Hugh Trevor-Roper, *Sunday Times*

'This is a fine history of Scotland. It combines rich and deep scholarship with an elegant and lucid style . . . No one who professes an interest in Scotland can afford to miss reading it.' *Times Literary Supplement*

'This remarkable book leaves the reviewer with little to say except that all Scots, and even Englishmen who are interested in Britain's development, should read it. It is admirably proportioned, based on vast reading, and brings all the main topics together.' *Economist*

FONTANA PRESS